Farmer, ex-businessman and a Queen's Messenger for the last ten years, George Courtauld divides his time between his farm in Essex and the rest of the world. A keen amateur, whether in botany, ornithology, history or the arts, he takes an interest in everything around him – particularly *homo sapiens*. Previous books by George Courtauld include *An Axe, A Spade and Ten Acres* and *Odd Noises from the Barn*.

THE TRAVELS
OF A FAT BULLDOG

George Courtauld

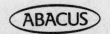

An *Abacus* Book

First published in Great Britain by Constable 1995
This edition published by Abacus 1997
Reprinted 1997

A CIP catalogue record for this book
is available from the British Library.

ISBN 0 349 10843 9

Printed and bound in Great Britain
by Clays Ltd, St Ives plc

Abacus
A Division of
Little, Brown and Company (UK)
Brettenham House
Lancaster Place
London WC2E 7EN

PREFACE

I would like to thank all those who, having read the manuscript, have allowed me to allude to them, either by name or insinuation. I have given most of them aliases, for privacy. In some cases it would be pointless to change names, such as those of my family, or Colonel Stephen Cave of Barbados, or the Archdeacon Seraphim. When I may seem startlingly frank, such as the description of my hairy great-aunt, those mentioned are now dead.

I must thank Ruth Thackeray for her painstaking and good-humoured editing, particularly over my haphazard and sometimes outdated nomenclature. As an undergraduate reading anthropology I became accustomed to the terminology Mongoloid (for 'yellow'), Negroid/Negro (for 'black'), Caucasian (for 'white'), Bushmen (for the unique San people of the Kalahari). Nowadays some people take offence at such terms, but as the alternatives also seem sometimes to annoy, I use the words I was taught, with no insult meant. I use the new term 'Amerindian' in place of the clumsier 'Indigenous American Indian'. Similarly, perhaps I am a bit archaic with place names, but I think of the capital of China as Peking, not as Beijing, so will call it that. On the other hand, to call Thailand 'Siam' or Zambia 'Northern Rhodesia' is now completely inaccurate, so in such cases I must use the modern names.

I also thank Major Iain Bamber, Superintendent, the Corps of Queen's Messengers, for 'vetting' the manuscript, and for correcting any inaccuracies about our history or routine; also Queen's Messengers

J. O. Hollis, Lt. Col. P. S. Kerr-Smiley and Lt. Col. H. M. L. Smith – they will know why.

As a civil servant I must be apolitical; thus all opinions I express are not in any way those of a Queen's Messenger, they are those of my other 'civilian' life.

The Corps of Queen's Messengers has changed much since the article I quote on page 61 was written: we are now 17 men, not 34; we no longer travel first class everywhere; Mongolia is reached by aeroplane, not that lovely train journey; we visit countries which only existed, as far as I knew, in my ancient atlas – such as Estonia, Bosnia, the Ukraine; things have speeded up, no longer do we have three or four days' relaxation during journeys, to go on safari, or collect plants, or meditate on mountain tops. Nevertheless we carry on as best we can, as we have been doing for over 800 years, and this book is dedicated to all present and future Queen's (or King's) Messengers with the normal greeting and farewell:

SAFE JOURNEYS

1 April 1989, Buenos Aires. It could be Toytown, except that everyone here is dead. It is a city in miniature: the narrow, stone-flagged streets, the 'houses' that line them, the little courtyards with potted trees, the churches and the campanile. Housing ranges from the Standard, a man and a half high and a coffin wide, to the Magnifico, with the size – and ostentation – of a fairground roundabout. Every architectural style and material is here from the Stone Age to the present day: caveman grottoes in cemented-together boulders, Egyptian pylons in plaster, Corinthian temples in marble, Byzantine basilicas in brick, the Aztec and the Inca in granite, Gothic chapels in sandstone, Nazi pillboxes in cement, and in glass and steel the high-street bank, and the Japanese hotel (or filing-cabinet).

They are all tombs. Their doors are glazed, so you can look through the glass into the little cells. You will see an altar in front of you: on it will be a couple of vases of flowers and a pair of candlesticks, perhaps a framed photograph of an occupant; over it will be a crucifix; under it will be one or two coffins, covered with lacework linens, like the best table-cloths. A flight of steps will descend to a crypt where other coffins are discernible in the gloom.

The coffins do not have the sinister, angular Hammer Film shapes of British coffins, they are more like pods or cocoons; smooth oval forms in mahogany and brass containing larvae waiting to burst out like butterflies at the last trump.

Above it all is a busyness of roofs: domes, spires, pinnacles and turrets; crosses, urns and vanes; saints and angels. Jesus and the Virgin Mary are in abundance but there is more kudos in having angels, wings being more expensive. There are two postures: looking up, both hands open to the heavens, in the 'I think it is going to rain'; looking downcast, one hand stretched out, in the 'there are moles on the lawn again'. Unlike our north European angels, who often have the vapid goggling of the Pre-Raphaelites or the wiry, bisexual limbs of gym mistresses, all these angels have attractive, smiling faces and voluptuous figures. The most alluring is the angel sitting upon the tomb of the 'Familia de Tomas Devoto'. She lounges by a large limestone bier, under a triumphal arch, gazing down at you along her cleavage: so pretty you could almost climb up and kiss her, one and a half tons though she be. Below her, to either side, are two nude children: podgy and peevish.

Sometimes my footsteps ring hollow, resounding upon the crypts beneath: from them all seeps an old, stale, musty smell.

The denizens you meet in this place of death are silent and still, fossilised in stone or bronze. Many of them are life-size so you stroll amongst them like the only person walking in a time-frozen dream: here is General Juan Lavalle, at ease outside the doors of his tomb, smartly uniformed with shako and sabre; there is Luis Angel Firpo, attired, oddly, in boots and a dressing-gown; Manuel Quintana, 'Presidente de la Republica 1904–06', lies on a bench, half covered in a rug, with the resignation of someone whose sleeping-cabin has been usurped so must pass the night on a couchette; the patriarch of the Carril family sits in a stone suit on a stone chair; a bronze widow mourns on the colossal mausoleum of her husband, the rain of decades has run down her face and left rust-marked tear runnels from her eyes to her mouth and down her chin:

> 'A la memoria de mi inolvidable esposo y a ti.
> ¡Oh! Dios mio . . . Dios mio . . .'

The terrible grief is infectious even if you don't know the language. There is a bronze girl who is willowy and beautiful and pats a bronze mongrel, the poetic inscription on the brass plate below her is 'A Mia Figla' and signed 'Il tuo Papa':

'Perché? Solo il destino sa il perché mi domando perché?'

Is it a lament written by a father grieving that his daughter will no longer go fishing with him?

The most forlorn tombs are not those which show a lively regret, they are those which show neglect, because there are no mourners left, for they have died out, or moved away, or become poor or indifferent. The flowers in their vases are brittle brown sticks; flakes of ceiling plaster besprinkle the altars, the linens are yellow and stained and the photographs by the crucifixes are foxed and faded.

Most of the photographs are of people to whom death was an acceptable event, they are old and white-haired and venerable and look content. But the one I am looking at through the dusty glazing of a small tomb, designed like a gothic telephone box, is of an elegant, attractive woman in her thirties. Her wavy black hair, styled in the fashion of 50 years ago, hangs down her face, half obscuring one of her large dark eyes; her hands have long, long fingers and long, long fingernails; one hand cups her pointed chin, beneath a becoming, wry smile, the other hand holds a cigarette.

Perhaps it is the one that killed her.

I leave the Cemetery of Recoleta for a morale-boosting lunch of steak and chips. Take off from the Argentine in the evening, back home in my Essex farmhouse next day.

2 April. All well at home. Dominie bustling about as busy as ever, the kitchen her base for family and farm, six dogs about her feet and two cats snoozing in baskets by the stove. She told me that yesterday, when trying to drive the Land Rover up the ride in Bridget's Wood to feed some ponies in Park Field, she was obstructed by an estate car parked in the ride entrance. The windows were entirely misted over but she could discern some pink blobs squirming slowly in the back. Nothing urgent seemed to be happening so after a minute or so she gave an impatient 'toot'. One of the pink blobs heaved up and a hand wiped the rear window clear and a peeved, bearded face stared out. Dominie, sitting high up in the Land Rover, could look down and see that the owner of the beard was as naked as a worm and that one of the larger of the pink blobs was a nude, female bottom.

'What do you want?' shouted Beard testily.

'I want to get past you so that I can drive into my field,' Dominie shouted back. Beard looked frightfully grumpy, nevertheless he started to get dressed. What surprised Dominie most was that he put his socks on first. 'That's really phlegmatic,' she thought.

I mentioned it to the gamekeepers at our morning meeting.

'You often get courting couples blocking that entrance,' Peter and Anton agreed.

'What do you do about it?' I asked.

'I wait until the bouncing on the car-springs begins to speed up, then I bang on the roof,' Anton replied with a cruel grin.

8 April, Washington. I enter the hotel lift at the 4th floor. A middle-aged man on crutches comes in after me. By the time we have reached the ground floor we have communicated thus:

Me: 'Grunt.'

He: 'Hi – bad weather – specially at 3 o'clock this morning – my bowels suddenly disturbed me – I've just had five operations – one on on my hip and four on my bowels – I cannot control them . . . Well, at 3, maybe 3.30, suddenly – whoosh – my bowels . . . I could do nothing to stop 'em – and the rain! – lightning too . . . Well, see ya' then – nice to have made your acquaintance . . .'

Me: 'Grunt-grunt.'

He hobbles away; I plod up Wisconsin Avenue to Pearsons Drug Store. I almost always have breakfast there: I liked it well enough on my first visit and have not bothered to try any alternatives. I became a Queen's Messenger to see the wide world and experience its great variety, but I seem persistently to revert to a creature of habit and I succumb to routines. At Pearsons I eat breakfast sitting on a stool by the counter. I have toast, fried bacon and eggs 'sunny side up' served by the caustic old waitress who waddles up and down behind the bar, frying things, pouring out coffees and exchanging insults with her regulars. A sweet-faced, scruffy old woman, stinking of stale cigarettes, laden with parcels and paper bags, comes and sits beside me. She starts to mope about the Metroline.

'You British?' she asks.

I say 'Yes.'

'What do you call the Metro in London?'

'We call it "The Underground Railway",' I tell her.

She nearly falls off her stool, so amused is she by the quaintness of it. She repeats it to her neighbours: 'Say Johnny, guess what they call the Metro in Britain. They call it "The Underground Railway".'

'D'y hear that Kelly? Did you hear what the British call the Metro? They call it "The Underground Railway".'

'Chloe. Dexter. You folks hear what the British call the Metro. . . ?'

Her neighbours merely look quizzical and read their newspapers.

In front of me, propped up on a cracked ashtray, is *The History of the Countryside* by Dr Oliver Rackham. Many of his illustrations are aerial photographs of Britain taken by Nazi Germany at the beginning of the war. He states that four and a half million of these were captured by the Americans at the end of the war and are now in the National Archive Library in Washington. It dawns on me that as I am in Washington with nothing to do all day it would be interesting to see if I can find any photographs taken over our house and farm.

Eddy, the Embassy driver, has dropped me at the Library of the National Archives and Records. I have to enrol myself as a 'researcher'. For identification I show my Queen's Messenger passport. The woman who issues the researcher permits is fascinated by it and calls her friends round, two other women and a stocky policeman who has a massive arsenal of arms, ammunition, clubs, pouches, handcuffs, chains and what-nots hanging from his belt.

'What is the Queen like?'

'Is she a bit hard to make friends with? You know, kinda stand-offish?'

'We've heard she has such a lovely complexion.'

'And isn't Di so pretty?'

'So British.' 'Those eyes.' 'That hair.' 'And tall.'

'Poor Prince Charles's ears are kinda large.'

'Yea, but he must have feelings, same as anyone else.'

'They say that the crown weighs nearly five pounds and cost twenny million bucks.'

'She's got more than one crown, Connie.'

'Well, I'm talking about the one she has for everyday use . . .'

I declare that the intention of my research is an investigation into Nazi air-photography of the British Isles.

I have had to take a shuttle-bus to Alexandria, an adjacent suburb-city, where is situated the library of cartography. There, Mr Butler, an attendant, becomes interested in my search and he and I pore over maps, grid references and diagrams which help pinpoint the right index for the right photographs. Many of them are over London or coastal defences, but after about three hours we narrow the search down to three boxes, each holding about 200 pictures. The easiest identification is Bullock Wood whose kidney shape, bisected by a wide ride, is very noticeable from the air. It has not changed shape since the war – it has not changed shape much for 2000 years.

I shuffle through the first box of 200 photographs. I recognise nothing. The second box: nothing. The last box: 50 photographs – nothing – nothing – nothing – BINGO! – There it is, Bullock Wood!

The photograph shows an area of about two and a half miles square. From Bullock Wood I can orient to my village: Colne Engaine is a quarter the size it is nowadays. The buildings to the far left of the picture must be the eastern outskirts of Halstead, those to the right are the western fringe of Earls Colne. There is my house almost slap in the middle. There, behind the house, is the old stack yard where once I used to play amid the little hamlet of thatched straw stacks and hayricks, and where we now have Tony Crisp's cottage and the combine shed. The Big Orchard is there, all the trees were grubbed out twenty years ago and it is now 120 drab acres of arable; there are the little fields I remember so well, once filled with poppies and corncockle which nodded above my head and sheaves of corn and the flittering of butterflies along the hedges; now cannibalised into prairies more suitable for combine harvesters. It is early in the morning and the shadows of the hedgerow trees spread long on the young corn and the pastures. There is a tiny dot on our lawn. I wonder if it is me in my pram. A thin white streak, slightly curved, lies across the picture.

'A fault in the film?' I ask.

'More likely the smoke from a bonfire,' says Mr Butler.

We look more carefully. Yes, it is smoke, but from the little saddle-tanked steam-engine of the Colne Valley Express as it chugs across north Essex from Earls Colne to Halstead at half past seven in the morning on the 10th of May 1940, being secretly photographed from an enemy aeroplane at 32,000 feet. (The Germans failed to destroy the little railway; Dr Beeching did that later.)

Having identified an area, I can track back and follow the course of the German enemy who spied on us that sunny spring morning. He turned on his camera over the Colne estuary at about 7.20. He flew north-west by west, up the Colne Valley, over Colchester, Fordstreet, Wakes Colne, White Colne, Earls Colne to Halstead; thence on, navigating either by the river or the adjacent railway line, past Sible Hedingham and Castle Hedingham (the Norman castle keep shows up as a solid, square block), Tilbury juxta Clare, Great Yeldham, Ridgewell, Wixoe, over Steeple Bumstead and up to Haverhill; there he turned about and flew back towards Germany, via Belchamp St Paul, Belchamp Otten, Belchamp Walter and thence to Borley and Sudbury, where finally his horrible little camera stopped.

I buy a negative of the map, it costs only $6. Mr Butler also sells me a 2' × 3' enlargement, which he rolls up and puts in a cardboard tube. Bearing these, I take the shuttle back to the Mall and from there I plod for one and a half hours along Pennsylvania Avenue, through the brick-paved pavements of Georgetown and up Wisconsin Avenue to my hotel. There I delightedly scrutinise the result of my day's investigations. The dot on the lawn isn't me in my pram, it's the old magnolia which died last year.

13 April. A macabre day: I went to view the skeleton of my great-great-great-great-grandmother.

The Church of England has emptied the crypt of Christ Church, Spitalfields, of its thousand coffins, having negotiated with the British Museum that they would do the excavating and in repayment could keep the corpses for investigation. The museum wrote to me, saying that because of the coffin plates they knew who most of the bodies were. One such was Louisa Perina Courtauld: what did I know about her: her social class, occupation, eating habits, diseases during life, age at and cause of death. I wrote back, a bit huffily, saying I did not like my ancestor's bones being disturbed; nevertheless, to help with their researches, I would tell them all I knew. Louisa Perina Courtauld was my great-great-great-great-grandmother. She was born in France in 1729 and died aged 78. She had had eight children, four of whom died young. She was widowed when aged 36, but carried on her husband's business as a silversmith for about another 40 years.

Later, I was contacted by Clare Patteson of the 'Chronicle' series of BBC television who said that they were making a programme on the investigation; she asked if I could tell them anything about my ancestor which would interest their viewers. She was particularly pleased that I had some silver stamped with her hallmark, and that there is a portrait of her – the Zoffany. She decided to make gt-gt-gt-gt-grandmamma the 'star' of the programme.

She came to interview me. We were filmed in the Oak Room which, with its panelling, cosy fireplace and ticking clocks, was thought picturesque.

'What did you think when you heard that your great-great-great-great-grandmother had been exhumed?' asked Clare (a tall, cool blonde).

'Well, I was partly indignant and partly curious,' I replied.

'Brilliant,' she said.

'We'll shoot that again, with you looking at the camera rather than at me.'

So: 'I was partly curious and partly indignant,' I repeated, trying to sound spontaneous.

'No. Not quite right. It sounded better when you were indignant first, then curious,' said Clare, 'do you mind saying it again?'

Thus the day went by. After the interview we went to the churchyard at Gosfield, five miles away, where we will eventually rebury gt-gt-gt-gt-grandmamma, and Parson Thomas and I quested around the other 32 Courtauld graves, trying to find a space. They made us walk towards the church through the adjacent field of flowering oil-seed rape. We kept being sent back as they said some people could lipread our remarks such as 'they want us to walk faster', 'don't we turn left after the fifth grave?' 'd'y hear there's been another murder in Coggeshall?', 'Yes, I'm told it was *** who did it this time.'

So, today, I have been aboard a Thames barge as guest of the BBC, to see a preview of the programme. The Lady Daphne was moored near the Tower of London. Clare greeted me when I went below and introduced me to the anthropologists who had supervised the investigation. They said the excavations were nauseat-

ing: some of the bodies had semi-liquefied, they slopped about in their lead-lined coffins when they were moved, looked appalling when they were opened, stank, and possibly fumed off the germs of diseases such as smallpox and perhaps even the Plague. Several people got the horrors and had to leave before they had nervous breakdowns.

I had mixed feelings about the film. I thought it a bit unseemly to be inspecting the pelvic bones of my maternal forebear. When a dentist picked up her skull and tweaked out a tooth I felt a sympathetic twinge of ancestral indignation. They showed the Zoffany: there she was in all her finery, her yellow silk dress with fur edging, her pearl necklace, her hair piled up: exactly as she wanted to be remembered. Then they showed her poor old bones all a-spillikins in a cardboard box. However, facts discovered during their investigations are interesting, particularly that skeletons are often not as young as they look: most of the pathologists deduced that she had died when about 45; only the dentist analysing her teeth verified her correct age.

After the film and lunch a photographer from the Radio Times took me to Christ Church. It was once beautiful, designed by Nicholas Hawksmoor in a Baroquish-Wrenish style, but now there are scabs, scars and raw patches where ornaments, monuments and panelling have been ripped out or rotted. The crypts are a subterranean maze of interlinked, barrel-vaulted, brick-built cysts and passages. They are dank and cool. The floor is covered with a white layer of mould, growing on the seepage from the coffins of my ancestors – the discotheque and tramps' watering-hole that they are going to install there will be uncommonly cheerless. I was photographed, standing in various positions, looking pensive, and then took the train home.

16 April. My escort is Wilfred. Having been a prison warder, he likes everything to be orderly and efficient, so he is peevish when we meet at breakfast. 'I detest Cairo,' he says, 'it's scruffy and chaotic, the people are completely unreliable and the food very peculiar and full of germs.' I say that generally I prefer untidiness and chaos to neatness and order, and that the Egyptians are particularly charming. As it is Sunday, we both have the day free and I persuade him to leave the hotel and come with me to 'Old Cairo' and inspect the Coptic Quarter.

We walk upriver, along the east embankment of the Nile. The sun is shining but there is a pleasantly cool wind which sends the dhows on their way over the waters. Jammed traffic roars and revs and ceaselessly toot-toots to our left, and the trees overhead are smothered in sand-dust. But to our right, between the embankment and the river, there are small market gardens with rows of terracotta pots full of plants. As it is early spring there is not much in flower except for geraniums, marigolds and some roses.

Wilf grumbles and complains as he plods along the ill-fitting flag-stones: 'If that bloke were selling flies, rather than dates, he'd make a fortune,' he says. 'But look at that beautiful woman in the bus queue, she's got extraordinary designs painted on her hands and ankles,' I reply. Wilf, who is not terriby interested in women, snorts and points out a horse 'so thin that it looks like the bastard cross-breed of a toastrack with a metal bedstead.' I point out a dhow gliding upstream, its sail curved like an angel's wing; there is the corpse of a dog in the gutter, but there is also a black cat sitting on the embankment wall so sleekly snooty that she might be Bastet the cat goddess herself. Several people are rummaging through the stinking contents of a dustbin van, but there is a trio of ox-eyed maidens mincing up the pavement and screaming with laughter about something silly. A man sits slumped on the pavement, nit-picking through his rags, 'but he's got a proud moustache,' I say. As we pass he hawks and spits a huge gobbet at our feet.

'Charmed, I'm sure,' Wilf sniffs.

We lean over the embankment beside the Saiyalet el Roda, the strip of the Nile between the island of Geziret el Roda and the mainland. I tell Wilf to look at the gulls and kites wheeling overhead, the dinghy-load of Sunday-school children being ferried over to the island, and a row of four old men on a bench, three puffing and blowing on a hubble-bubble as if it was a strange musical instrument and watching the fourth who is hopefully staring at the motionless tip of his fishing-rod. Wilf points silently down: beneath us, rocking in the depths of the green waters, is the bulging shape of a thing that had once been alive.

We enter the Old Quarter, a maze of tiny alleyways: some cobbled with ancient squared stones, most carpeted with litter; chickens peck about, hammers tap in workshops, smoke wafts from braziers, a goat and two old men sit on the same step and stare as we pass. 'Welcome,' says one of them, seemingly the goat. Outside a café more old men sit at small tables and sip something brown from little glasses and slam and clatter domino chips together.

We descend a flight of steps leading off a small passage and find ourselves in the little church of Abu Sarga (St Sergious), a martyred soldier who, together with St Baccas, was dressed in women's clothes and beaten to death. 'Typical!' Wilf snorts, but does not say typical of what. The building dates from around AD 400 and is meant to be where the Holy Family lived during their flight into Egypt. There is a nave flanked by two aisles; at the east end there are three sanctuaries, set side by side and with domed ceilings, the central one containing the altar. The roof timbers look a bit rickety and there is much plaster missing from the walls: builder's scaffolding seems to be holding much of it up, though there are twelve stout pillars helping. They represent the twelve disciples. The stoutest is the only one without a Corinthian capital and is made from granite rather than marble. It represents Judas. The informal muddle is cosily attractive, the more so because of the musky scent of incense.

A priest suddenly appears, squeezing through a small, high opening in the wall. He wears a magnificent crown: a large balloon of purple velvet encrusted with gold embroidery; also of purple velvet is his robe, and his beard is of such extreme luxuriance and fluffiness that it almost smothers his spectacles. Having fussily tidied his raiment, which has become rumpled during his emergence through the aperture, he opens a book, adjusts his spectacles and emits a buzzing, like a contented bumble-bee. The choir, a small group of youths in handsome but grimy albs of off-white beneath blue and golden chasubles, buzzes back. Now and then this comfortable humming is startlingly punctuated by the clash of a cymbal. Puffs of incense waft about.

After a bit I suddenly realise that all the women are standing on the right, and all the men on the left, and that Wilf and I are among the women. So we quit, embarrassed.

We then tour a Coptic museum. Wilf, because of his previous calling, is interested in the collection of huge monastery keys; I, because of my previous calling, am interested in the textiles which are very fine. There is an example of terry towelling from the 3rd century; we did not have it in Britain until old man Christy brought it from Turkey for the Great

Exhibition of 1851, causing me to hawk it around Commercial Road 120 years later. I am also intrigued by an icon of Sts Ahrakaad and Oghaany: they have dogs' heads.

Wilf and I then go to a nearby restaurant. By now, has he a more appreciative feeling for Egypt and the Egyptians? Perhaps not, he is grumbling over the menu: '"*Poached goat's knuckles in a hot sauce*"! Who'd a' thought a goat had knuckles.'

17 April. What a contrast everything in the Cairo Museum is in comparison to those in Central or South America! The Amerindians seemed to have had a hatred for each other, a horror of their gods, and an obsession with imaginary monsters; the Egyptians seemed to have had mutual affection, a respect for their gods and rapport with nature. How pleasant it is to see the cosy family groups, the couples holding hands for eternity, the children sucking their fingers and hanging on to their parents' legs; how noble and wise the gods and pharaohs look, and how pretty the goddesses and queens. Some of the prettiest look very like Dominie, who was nicknamed 'Cleopatra' when she was a deb.

Against a dusty wall in an obscure corner I see a life-size statue of the Pharoe Mycerinus. He is seated by a table upon which there is a telephone and for an amazed second it seems to me as if he is waiting for a call from a friend.

I am always intrigued by the macabre difference of the outer shells of Tutankhamen's burial – the beautiful golden shrines protected by the lovely Isis with her embracing wings, the serene, effeminate beauty of his golden face masks – and the horrible shrivelled blackened little toothy corpse at the heart of it all.

I hover timidly at the edge of the road. Traffic swirls past in a cyclone of sandy dust. Clapped-out cars jostle with limousines as long as motor boats, the tumbrels of dustmen creak alongside sports cars, buses career round corners barnacled with hitchhikers hanging on to every knob and fitment; they may even be on the roof.

A small man in spectacles gets hold of me by the elbow: 'Come, this way,' he says and darts in front of a bus, dragging me with him, 'you

English?' We squeeze between three bicyclists. 'Very fine, I have a brother in Oxford.' We duck under the overhanging load of a lorry carrying scaffolding. 'I am Ahmed Abdul.' We shake hands, a taxi toots at us, an old lady hobbles past at 80 miles per hour. 'You have been here before?' The fender of a passing bus flicks my trouser turn-ups. 'You like Egypt?' We scuttle across the bows of an ambulance, its lights flashing, its sirens screaming, some poor bugger is in there, trying to die. 'Quick, run, I think we might be able to get in front of this cement lorry.' It misses us, but not through want of effort. 'Very good, very good; you soon will become a proper Egyptian.' We are now in the middle of the road, together with six other people and a dead dog. 'Run – stop – again, in front of that police car, they are half asleep.'

There is an oasis of calm, a gap between two stationary cars.

'Stop. Wait. We have five metres to go. I make the perfumes. I sell them for very little to the French . . .' We dart off again. '. . . they mix it with alcohol and put it – whoops – in tiny bottles – quick, between these two – and sell it for a million times more than they buy from me.' We reach the pavement. He takes out a business card. 'You must see my perfume factory, here is the address. You will be welcome. If you see my brother in Oxford tell him to write more often. His name is Gamel. Bye-bye.'

22 April. The three unmarrieds are here for the weekend: Charlie from work, which is unusual because the television programme which he produces, 'A Week in Politics', usually needs editing over the weekend; Candy from her Sloaney secretarial work in London; and George, who has produced yet another girl: Fiona Hadlee. She is very pretty with long blonde hair but with an alarmingly determined chin. They had met when up at Cambridge. She is now a nurse at the London Hospital.

The 'Marrieds' walk the two furlongs from Buntings Green Cottage, up the farm drive and through the garden; Henrietta and Jimmy have been gardening and are sprinkled with mud and compost. They bring Ranulf; my grandson walks quite well for an eleven-month old, but his talk is mainly babble.

I potter about the estate most of today, pretending to work, but getting in the way. I must reluctantly concede that I do not do much of my own arable farming: most of that is done by contractors, other contractors do most of the forestry, Tony Crisp and his son Kerry look after the livestock, Dominie manages her Cymbelene Stud of Welsh Mountain Ponies, Peter and Anton attend to vermin control and the game, Tom Bradawl does the estate maintenance and James Hart works in the garden one day a week.

25 April. An important lesson that I have learned in my three and a half years as a Queen's Messenger is to travel light, unencumbered. Only a toothbrush is really indispensable: starting from the top this will neaten the hair, remove scurf from the collar, clean the teeth, then the finger-nails – and then, if needs are dire, ream out between the toes and the welts of the shoes. Anything else can be drip-dryable or disposable. So for this two-day, 5000-mile journey all I have packed is my sponge-bag and two books. I have donned a tropical suit and my Queen's Messenger tie. Emblazoned with silver greyhounds running below the royal crown, it acts as the pass which will allow me entry to all the places I go to. My stable clock is striking six in the morning when I drive off on the 60-mile journey to the Foreign & Commonwealth Office (FCO). I leave there two hours later for Heathrow Airport and land at Riyadh in the late afternoon.

I like the Arabs but some of their countries are pretty boring, Saudi Arabia particularly: stiflingly hot, sandstorms, little to do but stay in my hotel. The television is as monotonous as ever: prayers – football – prayers – football – prayers – football . . . The news and the advertise-ments are the most interesting: not for what they show, but for what they do not. The picture breaks up into a lot of little flickering squares whenever something appears that the censor thinks naughty. They were interviewing some female undergraduates at an American university – someone there had run amok with a shot-gun – and the censor obvi-ously disapproved of their skimpy clothing. I was bursting with frus-trated curiosity by the end of the news, my eyes all a-goggle with the effort of distinguishing thighs and cleavages amid the cubistic camou-flage. Even some pigs on a farm were edited out. What forbidden thoughts can a Saudi have when he sees a pig: the juicy bawdiness of stewed trotters, the orgy of an egg-and-bacon breakfast; in the black market can you buy magazines full of photographs of pornographic porkers – of sows lounging on straw bales, their hams apart, or from behind, looking roguishly over their loins, or in kinky underwear, the bra with a dozen D-sized cups?

26 April. Leave Riyadh in the evening on a Saudi Air flight. Luckily we Queen's Messengers travel First Class. I glimpsed into the Economy Class cabin and the rows and rows of small, dark people, all with bent heads, reminded me of some of the less salubrious clothing factories I used to visit during the nadir of my business career, as junior salesman of the Lovable Bra Company. Before take-off prayers are broadcast: the priest has an immensely deep rumble of a voice which converts the snarling yapping Arab language into a contented purr. Then the captain speaks: 'We will be landing at 01.05 London time – God willing.' I am uneasy at his lack of complete confidence. Dates are served by gazelle-eyed houris, and coffee with cardamon seeds, and we are each presented with a silver rose-water dispenser.

27 April. Arrive London early morning very tired, for only cat-napped.

I spend a couple of hours walking down the Bourne Brook from Pear Tree Corner to Stone Bridge, inspecting cricket-bat willows. There is a small herd of fallow deer in New Wood. Further downstream I see the sinister, purple-speckled stems of a clump of hemlock; we must spot-spray it before it kills the livestock. Three years ago I discovered a toothwort growing in the cruck of a pollarded willow. This is a rare parasitic plant of an ugly corpse-white hue. I clamber up the tree to see if it is still there. There is no sign of it but a mallard unexpectedly nesting in the hollow flies off with such a rush and sudden quacking that I nearly fall off the branch in alarm. Middle-aged men weighing 15 stone should not climb trees.

In the afternoon we move twelve ponies from New Wood Field to Spitfire Field. Both Dominie and I lose our boots in the mud. I also lose my temper, about a dozen times, particularly when in order to get hold of its halter I very unobtrusively sidle towards a pony, looking in every direction except in its, and it very unobtrusively sidles away from me at a slightly faster speed. And then as I break into a brisk walk it breaks into a brisker walk, so then I trot after it and it says 'Yoo-hoo called your bluff' and starts to gallop. And I bound after it bellowing 'Come back you stupid bastard come back' and it disappears round the corner of the wood and peeks shyly at me saying 'Coo-ee! I'm here fat-face come and get me'. So I walk bloody miles after it and almost reach it and it lifts its little bushy tail and farts and scampers off again and finally Dominie says 'Come here' and it wanders up to her and snuggles its loathsome little muzzle into her hand.

4 May, Costa Rica. I am driven to San José, the capital. We travel past banana groves, date-palms, little weather-boarded houses with balconies and tin roofs and gardens full of bougainvillaea. Being early in the morning, and because we are about 3000 feet up, it is not too hot; the turquoise sky is swirled over with remarkable mare's tails like huge plumes of Pampas grass. My escort from the Embassy tells me about the country. He says that Costa Rica is the size of Scotland but with the population of Strathclyde. The 'Rica' (rich) proved to be illusory; there was little gold about and only a few Amerindians, relicts of the Mayans, so the settlers had to do the work themselves and toiled hard for their living. Thus, unlike much of Latin America, there are few big estates or over-powerful minorities dominating a penniless majority: it is more like New Zealand, with a large establishment of yeomen farmers.

I have completed my business in the Embassy, unpacked in my hotel room, bathed and breakfasted. The Embassy issued my allowance in American dollars so I have come to this bank to change $20 into Costa Rican *colones*. After I had stood in a queue for what seemed hours, a curt little bureaucrat told me I was in the wrong place. He sent me to this queue instead. It's my turn at last. I stand meekly before an impassive man with a bandit moustache. He scrutinises my $20 note, assembles three forms, one white, one pink and one yellow, puts carbon paper in between, inserts the whole sheaf into a typewriter, taps out a screed of information, removes his handiwork, inspects each form, staples them together, puts the lot into an out-tray, offers me a tiny ticket with a number on it and then pompously points like the puffed-up pillock of a prick that he is to the queue where I first proceeded with this pedantic pantomime.

Here I am again. To get here I have had to zigzag through a maze of chains suspended on posts, designed to control any potential mob into an orderly queue. As I stand at the head of the line, I fiddle with the chain and it unhooks itself and about 10 yards of it falls with an embarrassing clatter. The woman behind me, rather pretty, black hair, a bit fat and about 35, asks sympathetically if I have been waiting long. We get engrossed in a conversation about the boringness of queuing until I am called to attention by petulant hissing from the teller behind his little glass window.

The teller is another little turd. He looks at my ticket and leaves his seat. He wanders vaguely about, between the desks behind him, occasionally rootling through an in-tray or chatting to the odd passer-by. He disappears round a corner. I smile resignedly and apologetically at the pretty, plump lady. She smiles back and raises both her hands to her shoulders in a gesture of resignation. A bit fat maybe, but graceful withal. Finally the teller reappears. He sits down and I see someone has stapled my little ticket to the pink and yellow forms and the $20 note. He rummages about in a drawer and finds a little instrument. He uses it to unstaple the forms, the ticket and the note. He puts the little instrument back in the drawer. He closes the drawer. He peers at the forms. He does some sums on a calculating-machine. He tweaks off the strip of paper it produces and compares its contents with those of the forms. He looks pleased. Then he looks stern and scrutinises the $20 note suspiciously, turning it round, peering at its behind, holding it to the light and goggling through it. He lays it on the desk before him, smooths it flat with a hairy-backed hand, and reads it. He prods about in a little box and fishes out a paper-clip. He uses it to unite my money to the yellow form. He puts them, thus united, into an out-tray. He gets a key, unlocks and slides open a drawer. It is full of little compartments. Each compartment holds a different type of *colone* note or coin. He looks at the form to remind himself of the total sum to be paid out, and then he counts the money onto the counter between us, mouthing out the mounting value as he does so. He arranges the notes in a neat pack on top of the pink form, assembles the coins, graded in size, into a tapering stack on top of that, and pushes the whole erection towards me. I scoop it up and quit, pausing only to exchange fond smiles with the pretty, plump lady and to tear up my pink form, as loudly and as contemptuously as possible, and ostentatiously to sprinkle its confetti into the waste-paper bin by the door.

I wander up the Paseo Colon, the high street. It is a pleasant mixture of shops, restaurants, offices and private houses. One of the latter contains a garden which enchanted me during my last visit here. It was a smotherment of bougainvillaea, hibiscus, frangipane, palm trees, elephant ears and other exotic plants. These were all pleasant enough but what really pleased and intrigued me were the two plants growing in solitary glory in a circular bed cut in the turf of the little lawn: they were a couple of Brussels sprouts.

They're still there! The stems have grown to about seven feet and their leafy tops make them look almost tropical, but they are undoubtedly Brussels sprouts. How pleasing to renew acquaintance with such eccentric friends.

5 May.

The narrow-gauge 'Jungle Train' takes you 110 miles from San José to Siquirres. There are 26 stops and the journey takes five hours. From the comfort of your private touring carriage your bilingual guide will acquaint you with the history of the region while offering you the freshest tropical fruits, pineapple, zapotes and the succulent banana. You'll pass the Irazú Volcano and the Continental Divide, glide past rich coffee fincas and chug in and out of quaint backwater whistle stop. You might glimpse monkeys, orchids or vibrantly hued birds as the train descends from the mountains over roaring white-water rivers into the lush, all-encompassing vegetation of Costa Rica's jungle. At Siquirres you'll say goodbye to the Jungle Train and continue in the comfort of a modern bus to a banana plantation. You'll see for yourself exactly how the delicious fruit goes from cultivated fields to final packing. As the shadows of the afternoon begin to lengthen the bus takes you back to San José by early evening.

The rear carriage is reserved for the tourists, mostly Americans. It has a row of about a dozen benches on each side. They are double seaters, made of cast iron and upholstered in dirty imitation leather. There is wooden panelling throughout, even the ceiling is of wooden slats and the floor is of small parquetry blocks. The wooden-framed windows are held up by brass catches. There is an open balcony at the end of each coach; from this, to either side, a small flight of steps descends to about a foot above the track. The balcony and steps are balustraded with brass railings. The other three carriages are packed with locals; there are also two small goods waggons. The engine is disappointing, a small, insignificant diesel with no personality. Clara, our guide, is a stocky, blocky woman with blubber lips and huge square teeth. Her coarse black hair has been bleached, resulting in a fuzz of rusty ginger wires. She wears a green T-shirt and khaki shorts.

A bell jangles and with a sharp jolt we move off. Soon we are clattering between farmsteads and past plantations. I quit my seat and spend the first half hour looking over the end of the rear balcony. The jungly brush begins to thicken and press in on either side. Grass has grown over the sleepers so that the lines shine amid the growth like two long, wobbly silver snakes converging into the distance. It is rather like flying, but flying backwards, which is rather frustrating.

Sometimes the jungle thins out and we transverse an area of pasture, or of coffee plantations where lines of bushes ascend the very steepest slopes to the mountain ridges. At times there are clearings in the forest: the houses in these glades are the normal ramshackle constructions in wood and corrugated iron, but however scruffy the habitations, the children playing in the gardens and the women leaning on the banisters of their verandahs are all clean and well dressed and attractive. Most of the small children wave. If one waves back their return greetings become almost frantic. One little doddymite in a frock of white tulle has just used both hands to wave at me, and jumped up and down in her excitement.

The lowest side-step of the balcony juts out about a foot. I have found that if I stand on it I can face the engine and look along the whole length of the train, the carriages bucketing and rocking and swaying over the uneven track; when we pass over bridges, crude trestles, I can look down and see rivers perhaps a hundred feet or so below me as I glide over the empty space.

A bossy American woman with her scalp covered with a little flock of blue-rinsed curls has just said: 'You'll fall off and kill yourself if you keep hanging on there.'

'I'll fall off and kill myself if I *don't* keep hanging on here,' I reply with what I think a pleasant blend of affability and wit, but she emits a testy snort and goes back into the carriage.

People come and go onto the balcony. Most of them don't stay long, but I have three frequent visitors. Two are tall, pleasant Americans in their fifties. They are twins, distinguishable because one has a moustache and the other wears sun-glasses. The third visitor is an old Texan with Bourbon-steeped eyes. His wife is a chic little Honduran with glossy black hair, a built-in pout and young enough to be his granddaughter; she is dolled up to the nines in powder-blue flounces, dark blue stockings, and co-ordinated gloves and shoes to match a blue-grey leather handbag onto which she clings. She came out once, looked around, dilated tiny nostrils, raised a plump and slightly fuzzy upper lip, sniffed, and minced back into the coach. He comes out at every stop and ogles the girls beside the track. He tells me that his great-great-great-grandfather was a Spanish slave trader. Instead of getting his slaves from West Africa he would go to North Africa and buy the more esteemed Nilotics from the Arabs. On his way back through the Mediterranean he would stop on the lower shores of Italy and do some kidnapping. When he reached the Americas, he would set up shop and his bargain offer would be: 'For every two African slaves bought, I will throw in one Italian free.' He said that his ancestor was so successful in his trading that his competitor, a Frenchman called Le Fitt, had to leave the rat-race and turn to piracy. I suspect much of this is merely a Spanish story designed to annoy Italians.

It is about halfway through the journey when we stop at Turrialba. I am leaning over the balcony, looking at the market beside us, all a-bustle under a line of tall palms, when a tired, scruffy but bolt-upright person approaches. Very dark, almost completely negroid, he has only a few teeth so his bare gums show up a vivid pink against his dark, seamed face. He wears an off-white baseball cap, a dirty T-shirt and split jeans. He looks over 60, but he may be younger: he's had a hard life. For all his obvious poverty, he has a solemn dignity.

He speaks to me slowly and gravely, in meticulous English with just a trace of the Jamaican drawl: 'Excuse me sir, but have you seen a very beautiful young lady called Clara? She may be the guide in your railway carriage.'

'Yes,' I say, and call out for her.

She appears and leaning over the rail she hands the Dignified Man a packet of raisins. He dips into his shopping-bag and hands back a dozen bananas.

'Why do you need raisins?' asks the Blue-Rinsed Woman.

'For the buns that are baked by my wife,' says Dignified Man.

He looks at me. 'You, sir, are British?'

I nod.

'That, sir, is an excellent thing to be.'

He looks wistfully at Clara, who is at the other end of the balcony, talking to two youths. 'I have a dream, sir, but to my sadness, it will only remain a dream. And in my dream the beautiful and kind Clara and I will share a moment of passion.'

'If that happens,' Blue Rinse interrupts, 'your wife will no longer bake you buns.'

He makes no reply, but his silence suggests 'to hell with the buns'.

'It will only be a dream,' he finally says, 'for, sir, look, she likes only young men, and I am old and no longer handsome. Yet, still, she is kind to me. She exchanges a packet of raisins which cost her 120 *colones* with my few bananas which she knows I pick free from the field beside my house.

'By chance, sir, do you have a dollar to give to me?'

'No, I'm afraid not,' I reply.

He is sorry I say that, for he knows I lie.

'It is only a dollar I want, just one, not to spend, just to take out some-times and look at it and admire and then put back.'

I too am sorry I lied, but my dollars are all in $20 notes and it would be uncouth to ask for change, so I suggest he talk to the people looking out of the carriage windows: 'Most of them are American and some should have a dollar on them.'

He nods: 'Perhaps I shall succeed, for it is only one dollar I want, to look at, not a million.'

However, when the train moves off Dignified Man is standing beside the track, looking glum. I wave at him. He waves back, but with the weary dejection of one who has not fulfilled a dream, nor even scrounged a dollar.

We are now running alongside a river, on the high bank above it. Quite often my feet glide over the teeming water, and I can see the line of little carriages snaking along the curves in front. I can hear the roar of the river in spite of the clattering of the train. Some of the trees are vast, and weep with festoons of Spanish moss; there are wild bananas and huge-leaved shrubs, the whole tangle is looped and draped with the cables of great creepers. There are butterflies as big as my hand, and of beautiful iridescent blues and greens; they flounder and flitter like animated slivers of stained glass. Birds fidget amid the leaves, some of them are members of the oriole family called locally the Oro Pendulo, the Pendulo referring, I presume, to their extraordinary hanging nests shaped like huge clubs which dangle in groups from some of the highest branches.

I have become over-familiar with bananas, having just seen 128 hectares of them, having had their sex life explained (male bananas are few but huge; females are small but plentiful) and having watched them being harvested, graded, washed, labelled and packed. Once harvested from the plants, the banana bunches, shrouded in plastic sheeting, are hooked onto overhead conveyors: ranks of them glide through the plantation to the packing-shed, like files of zombies.

'I don't particularly like bananas,' I tell Mustached twin.

Blue Rinse overhears: 'They are a great source of potassium, and each one has as much protein as a large steak,' she reproves.

We get into a bus and start to drive back to San José. I am sitting at the back, beside the twins. Blue Rinse gets out of her seat and starts to lecture the driver on his jerky acceleration.

'That old dame is about as welcome as a poop in a punch bowl,' says Bespectacled Twin.

'Or a possum's eye in an apple pie,' agrees Moustached Twin.

'Or a set of teeth in a chalice,' I suggest.

'Or a fart in an elevator . . .'

Clara interrupts by ordering the bus to stop and we all pile out to look at a three-toed sloth in a tree. It sits in a fork at the very top, hunched up and motionless.

'How did you know it was there?' asks Bespectacled.

'It was here last week, and they do not move very fast.'

We scrutinise it for some time, from different angles. It remains glued to its perch.

Blue Rinse shouts, 'Hey! You there!'

It doesn't stir a whisker.

She is riled: 'Hey, you up there, I said "hey!"' she shrieks.

The sloth doesn't even look down.

'I don't believe it's alive,' Moustached stage-whispers to me, 'it's been stuffed and put up there by the tourist agency.'

Dust has percolated amongst the branches and trunks of the rain forest. Sometimes a bright spark will flash and glide amid the gloom, a firefly. Lightning flutters and pulsates in the clouds above the three volcanoes. I am already half asleep, but must rise early tomorrow.

6 May. It is Saturday, presumably that is why there were so many children on the bus, and pretty well everyone seemed to be Costa Rican, a babble of Spanish almost drowned the roar of the bus as it zigzagged the bends towards the Pacific Ocean. We have arrived by the shore at a house called 'Los José' which, I suppose, means 'The Johns'. We walk through the house, which is furnished with great clouty chunks of Spanish-style furniture, all heavy carving on baulks of timber, ornate moquettes and cast-iron lamps, through a dullish garden with two good trees shading some arid flowerbeds and down to a jetty. Our boat is not yet there; we are handed biscuits and plastic mugs of coffee.

I sip. I nibble. Well, I can't stand alone all day, talking to no-one. I'll look a fool for a start, and be an object of sympathy, or derision: 'Look at the shy Englishman, he pretends to read his book on birds.' The Canadian honeymooners I met on the bus are pleasant but exceedingly dull. I shall avoid those children of course; also their mothers who have already bunched together to nitter complaints about their husbands and the price of knitting-wool. The little Japanese with the vast video-camera seems nice enough, why on earth is he filming the coffee urn for so long? That old American with the white moustache looks an amiable sort of bloke, and the girl with him is very attractive in a hard-faced way: extraordinary colouring – pitch-black hair, dead-white face, scarlet lips and dark green eyes. She is in her early twenties: what attracts these innocent young chicks to those old American buzzards?

I wander casually towards them, composing a friendly and not too provocative remark; it is not necessary. As I get near the old boy says 'Howdy, I guess you're British.'

His name is John and he is 76 years old. He flew fighter bombers during the war from an aircraft carrier in the Pacific. He also fought in Korea. He now owns a small fleet of aircraft, mainly flying cargo and passengers in Alaska. 'I still fly quite a lot myself; when I do, my companion here attends to my instruments.'

I look suspiciously at him, his face is guileless; I look at her, her return glance could curdle a churn of milk at a furlong. I decide not to make waggish remarks about joy-sticks.

The motor boat arrives and moors against the jetty. It is about 60 feet long: the lower deck is furnished with tables and benches and has a bar; the upper deck has a small awning forward. I go up and stand under it, beside the wheel and controls, leaning on the wide wooden shelf directly above the bows. Several of the children also reckon it is the best viewing-point and have grouped around me: they are reasonably well behaved. The Old Pilot ordered two of them to bring up chairs, and he and the Green-Eyed Girl are sitting nearby.

The crewman at the wheel has shown me on his chart where we are going: we started from a town called Puntares; the creek we are now in leads to a large bay called the Golfo de Nicoya; our destination is the island of Tortuga, which is about two hours' cruising time from Puntares. We have been going for about half an hour, mostly along the creek with mangrove swamps to starboard and lines of houses, marinas, small shipyards, fish-processing plants and general bustle to port. The warm, blowsy air carries scents ranging from the acrid tang of rotting fish to the hot smell of wet mud. We passed three wrecks: two trawlers and a ferry. They lay on their sides in the strand; like all shipwrecks they had a forlorn aura of something huge and dead. A few frigate birds hover and swoop in the wind above us, sleekly menacing, and there are many brown pelicans with great cumbersome beaks. Sometimes they fold their wings and lurch out of the sky into the sea.

The sun is scorching, blinding flashes of light reflect off the wavelets, but there is a cooling wind as we chug on at twelve knots. We have passed a few islets. They are tall and rocky, most are covered in vegetation, not much of this is coconut-palm, which I have been expecting, but is deciduous tree and shrub. It is not the flowering season, there is only one noticeable tree in flower, the frangipane: its strange, almost fleshy-looking branches tufted at the tip with leaves, the large, creamy-white flowers growing in clusters amongst them.

We have arrived at the island and have anchored in a sandy bay. Green-Eyed Girl calls it 'dreamy'. There is a grove of coconut-palms by the beach. The wooden pews grouped round barbecues and the thatched bar don't please me much; nevertheless, they look reasonably in keeping. There are rather too many other boats moored here and too many people sun-bathing on the beach. Lunch is not for an hour, so I will snorkel my way round that big spur of rock to the deserted beach I noticed from the boat as we approached.

I have swum to the beach. The fish were a bit dull compared with those of the Caribbean but at least there were no sea-urchins; there was an octopus, probably only a couple of feet from tip to tip, but I did not like the look of him, nor he of me by the way he slithered under a ledge. The beach is completely deserted; it would be idyllic if Dominie were here with me. Not many shells, and the few I have found are all broken or sea-worn, but there are some very pretty stones, several brightly coloured, with thin veins of pure white marble. Unfortunately some of the jetsam includes plastic rubbish but there are also coconuts and interestingly contorted branches and tree trunks.

Most people have started lunch, sitting obediently in rows on the pews. I join the tail-end of the queue and am eventually doled out a slab of barbecued fish, drab dollops of salad made from limp lettuce and with-ered tomato, sour-tasting coleslaw, and potato salad gunged up in Heinz's 57th. Pudding is a slab of squodgy 'lemon cake, served with a delicate lemon sauce'.

I sit by Green-Eyed Girl and Old Pilot and grizzle about the meal: 'It's ridiculous, here we are on a Pacific Island, in the middle of a coconut grove, eating tinned potato salad and mass-produced stodge.'

'This fish is real dandy, though,' says Green-Eyed Girl.

Old Pilot tells us what he ate during the war: snakes and sharks and captured Japanese army rations. I tell them what I ate during the war: horse and whale and rosehip syrup. Green-Eyed Girl admires my truly alluring and probably character-forming years-of-early-maturation. She says that poor little she has had such a commonplace life that she has never even eaten a proper coconut, only ones that have been desiccated and grated and sold in packets. I pick up a coconut on the sand beside me and shake it to see if it has liquor inside. Green-Eyed Girl then asks me to shake it by her ear and Old Pilot tells us the difference between coconut water (the stuff you hear sloshing when you shake it; if you can't hear it, the nut is over-ripe) and coconut milk (which is the juice from the pressed flesh). I take the nut over to the chef and with ges-tures ask him to open it. The chef is a grotty youth with deliberately short shorts and a grease-splashed T-shirt. He shakes his head. I point meaningly at his vast knife and then at the nut. He shakes his head and spreads his hands in a gesture which could mean 'I do not understand you,' 'It's not my job' or 'You haven't paid for this so fuck off.' Ghastly little swine.

I'm bloody well going to eat a coconut when on a desert isle. I go back to my pew and, picking up the feeble little knife they issued me, I proceed to saw up the fibrous outer husk into longitudinal segments and lever-cum-rip them off. It takes ages and I begin to sweat. Green-Eyed Girl and Old Pilot encourage me on. 'Perseverance and patience, that is what you need,' says Old Pilot.

'What's the difference, which is worse?' asks Green-Eyed Girl.

'Patience is the worse,' I say, 'for that is what you need if someone else is doing something, perseverance is what you need if you are doing it yourself.'

'What a very, very profound remark,' says Green-Eyed Girl, awed, 'you must be a philosopher.'

What a charming girl, I think, and it seems that she is astute as well as pretty.

'You can't tell us about patience and perseverance,' says Old Pilot. 'Geeze, talk about patience and perseverance. That's what my companion here and I had to have. Patience and perseverance? I reckon we are the world's experts in them. But we were successful in the end; with our patience and our perseverance. But did we have to be patient? Did we have to persevere?'

I do not ask if they had to be patient and perseverant: his memoirs of his wars against the Japanese and the Koreans were interesting enough; I suspect his war against his wife will not be.

Finally the nut is stripped of its husk. By now, everyone is sitting staring at me. I feel somewhat bashful. Pretending not to notice the public scrutiny, I rise to my feet – has the sea-water made my white boxer shorts transparent? – stride over to a lump of stranded coral, and dash the nut to pieces against it.

Green-Eyed Girl is excited: 'This'll be my first real coconut.'

I hand her a bit.

The chef now decides to get into the act. Leaping to his feet he grabs his knife, hurries over, snatches up the shard I have given to Green-Eyed Girl and with one deft circular twist of his wrist simultaneously scoops the flesh from the shell and cuts a huge gash in the ball of his thumb.

'Don't bleed over my nut!' exclaims Green-Eyed Girl.

I say nothing, but exult with a profound satisfaction.

Then I dole out other shards of the nut to Old Pilot and some of the children. By the time I pick up my snorkelling equipment most of the men are sawing away at their own coconuts and the chef (sticky-plastered) and the Old Pilot are showing them what to do.

The journey back in the boat was pleasant, we saw flying fish and a pelicanry, but the two and a half hour bus journey in the dark has been a bit tedious. I kept myself cheerful by thinking about the chef's cut hand. Now I've had dinner and am sitting up in bed writing this: I must be up at 5.30 tomorrow to go to the Embassy before catching the aeroplane: there will be a few moments' work in Panama and then home, via Amsterdam.

12 May. We have been sent next week's copy of the 'Radio Times'. It has an article on the television programme 'Chronicle' which is on next Wednesday about the Huguenot skeletons in Christ Church. I am described as 'farmer, consultant to Courtaulds Ltd, Queen's Messenger and Cambridge anthropology graduate'. The article starts off: 'George Courtauld studies the photograph of his great, great, great, great grand-mother. "Nobody," he says, "looks their best as a skeleton."' Alternatively, my face looks like a pink balloon; I suspect that they used a fisheye lens to exaggerate its roundness: a meaty contrast to gt-gt-gt-gt-grandmamma's boniness.

Very cosy dinner at Cousin Julien's in Blackmore End. He has given up farming and has bought a yacht and a set of bagpipes.

16 May. 'Welcome to Barbados,' says the head steward through the intercommunication. The door is opened and a gust of warm, scented air envelops us. A crowd of people are outside, they are of two varieties: adolescent female, sombrely-suited male. The steward fusses about, shepherding a few of us to the front. As we leave the aeroplane he calls out to the assembled throng:

pray

make way

for their

Royal

Highnesses

the Duke and Duchess of Kent

for Captain George Courtauld

the Queen's Messenger

and

for
MISTER
MICHAEL
JAGGER

We file off, in order of precedence: the Kents smiling affably, me already beginning to sweat, Mick Jagger combing his hair.

17 May. Of all the things I do as a Queen's Messenger, this I consider the most luxurious: breakfasting on a Caribbean beach. The aquamarine sea is slopping wavelets upon the white sand. Coconut-palms are shading my table, their fronds rustling overhead in the warm breeze. A pair of bananaquits are perched on the back of the chair opposite me, staring longingly at the marmalade jar. The smiling waitress has just served a plate of fried eggs, bacon and sausages, some toast, a jar of marmalade and a large pot of coffee. I have a good book propped up on the toastrack in front of me. A large orange butterfly with delicate black markings snoozes on the scarlet flower of a nearby hibiscus. The beach-club cat has shown me a lizard hanging from its mouth.

It is at times like this, not in moments of danger, discomfort or boredom, that I miss Dominie most.

I'm still here, two hours after breakfast, sitting alone by the sea under a coconut-palm. I have wedged my toes apart with pieces of coral in the theory that as my foot-rot thrives in the dark and dank recesses of my socks the sunlight and fresh air will kill it. Holiday makers are around me: some swimming, others basking on the white sand, or rubbing suntan oil into each other. A woman near me has spent ages at it. Her man is absolutely enveloped in hair, he's even got it on his back; his navel looks like the nest of a tunnel spider – I expect it to be full of dead flies and beetles' wing cases. The woman had to dollop half a bottle of suntan oil on his chest before it became adequately saturated and she was able to knead it in.

I've swum for about twenty minutes and it was pleasant enough but I'm not particularly interested in swimming for swimming's sake. The waves are not big enough to be exciting, and I cannot snorkel here for there is no rock or coral and the bare sand holds few fish. There are obnoxious people on aqua-scooters who kept complaining that I was going too far out and getting in their way.

A pot-bellied little man in long shorts, short socks and crepe-soled sandals is eyeing my feet, frowning thoughtfully. Quit, Fatty.

Here I am in Paradise. I'm rather bored. If Dominie were here I would be content to lie next to her doing nothing but reading and talking, but when alone doing nothing seems to be a terrible waste of the measly allocation of three score years and ten.

It's nearly 10 o'clock. I'll walk to Bridgetown, the capital, and look around; it is only about five miles away.

The road runs parallel to the shore-line: a blaze of snow-white coral sand edged by a sea whose turquoise shallows merge into sapphire deeps; blues so intense that if I paddled, my feet would come out stained like a schoolboy's inky fingers. I can glimpse this in the gaps between hotels and rows of cottages. These dwellings are small and attractive, wooden bungalows with verandahs: in design and size comparable with the beach chalets in Frinton; but the dominant colours are pink and white, or pastel blues and greens, so that they look like rows of little iced sponge cakes. Some of them are very ornate, with fretted barge-boards, ornamental banisters round the verandahs, louvred shutters and weather-boarded canopies over the windows. They are small because the locals had to be mobile enough, after slavery, to move their whole homestead, house and all, to whichever estate employed them. Because they are portable, houses are defined as 'chattels'. As the families grow larger, the buildings expand into extensions and lean-tos at the back. Most people own their own dwellings and someone at the High Commission said that it is the Caribbeans, as much as Mrs Thatcher, who have taught the British to be a house-owning nation. But perhaps it is an English influence which has inspired the gardens, not merely sensible plantings of bananas and maize but frivolous clumps of shrubs, and flowers in beds, and bougainvillaea and other creepers up walls. The cottages and hotels have English seaside names: Ocean View, Sea View, Sandy Cove, Maitland, Buckingham, Balmoral, The Nook. I pass Flo's Shoppe, it sells gingham frocks of the same printed designs that women used to wear in the harvest fields of my childhood. Many of the larger, middle-class houses have disagreeable dogs who scowl and grumble through the garden railings. In a glade of mown grass, reminiscent of a village green, some children play cricket. Casaurinas trees edge the glade like a crowd of hippies with lank streamers of green hair. I see butterflies of a rather bilious yellow; also doves of different sorts, of which a little reddish one is particularly appealing. There are humming-birds like jet-propelled jewels and many grackles, with ridiculous tails like rudders and a starling-like way of pottering about on lawns.

In spite of the sunlight there is an occasional sinister note. Someone has written on a door: 'CAUTION, Everett Porterboy is an AIDS victim.' A cemetery wall bears the scrawl: 'BEWARE SANDI, these graves are dangerous.' And a churl has a cardboard sign on his front window: 'I shoot every third salesman. The second just left.'

Here is a prostitute. She is standing on the pavement, beneath an overhanging hibiscus whose scarlet flowers co-ordinate with her red dress. An arch black beret is set pertly askew over one eye.

'Gosh, thanks awfully, but better not,' I say, 'my wife wouldn't allow it.'

She laughs in derision.

'Actually, I feel rather lethargic, the heat you know.'

That is the most pathetic excuse she has ever heard.

She has been following me now for almost a mile, babbling about her allurements and my cravings. She keeps telling me that she is clean. I was already hot and sweaty and am now beginning to steam with embarrassed irritation. An open-backed van passes by, packed with happy locals who give her a great cheer of encouragement as they zoom past. I plod on grimly; she patters on behind, cajoling.

Suggesting that I'm either a miser or a queer she finally peels off to refuel at a shack selling Coca-Cola and coconut segments. May they choke her.

*

Bridgetown is a pleasant, bustling little town centred on the bridge and a statue of Nelson. The locals are proud that it was erected 16 years before the one in Trafalgar Square. There is nothing I want to buy; the Straw Market has some attractive things that I know Dominie would like but basketry takes up too much room in aeroplanes. I overhear two women talk by a stall. One is lithe and graceful. She leans with her elbow on a wall and her hand plays with the black curls at her nape, her other forearm rests on her hip; the position curves her into a sinuous, willowy S shape. The other woman is so fat you could lay breakfast for two on her jutting-out buttocks. The graceful one is saying: 'You went on, and on, and on. You weren't arguing with me, you were arguing with yourself.'

I am strolling down a narrow side-street and have just realised that I am being followed, being stalked. My hackles have risen and I notice that I have instinctively hunched my head down between my shoulders and bunched my fists. The pad-pad-padding behind is speeding up. If I turn casually to the right, it will seem as if I want to cross the road and I can look to my right again as if I were checking for an oncoming car.

He's very tall and glowering and has dreadlocks.

'Have you any money, man?'

He's tall, but he's weedy. He has not the muscles of someone who lugs around diplomatic bags and bales of hay.

'If I had any money, I'd be in a taxi, not walking about in this bloody heat.'

I hope I was right about his muscles – and mine. He looks distinctly peeved and dubious. We stare nastily at each other. He doesn't move. I will have to use my repelling system. I open my notebook, stare thoughtfully at him, then start to write. He shies away from me as does a horse from an adder: by the time I have written '. . . instinctively hunched my head down' he is ambling casually up the street, 50 yards away.

I plod back.

That perishing prostitute is again on patrol: 'Feeling better?' she asks hopefully.

'Not at all,' I snap.

I'm starving, I must have walked 12 miles and sweated a gallon. What exotic lunch they will be serving at the beach club: fried flying fish, stewed conch, roast parrot, humming-bird on toast, coconut and mango mousse?

I have arrived. A notice on the road proclaims:

LUNCHEON
today's speciality
CORNISH PASTIES & CHIPS

Having a raging thirst I go to the beach bar, a thatched rondavel, and gulp down a couple of Planter's Punches, one after the other. 'Are you going to have a third?' asks a plumpish, baldish, pleasant fellow, sitting on a stool. He is formally dressed in a suit and wears a tie.

'Maybe, why?'

'I'm a local coroner.'

'Oh! Perhaps too much of this stuff isn't very healthy?'

'It certainly isn't. Planter's Punch is made of rum and you can't imagine what rum-afflicted livers and kidneys look like. The locals here are very prone to diabetes because of all the sugar residues in the cheaper rums.'

I order a lime juice – unsweetened.

He is an interesting man. He tells me that the local method of getting rid of an unwanted husband is with the use of a beer bottle. It must be brown, the same colour as demerara sugar. Wifey grinds it up finely and blends it with the sugar. Hubby sprinkles it on his morning porridge. No need for Wifey to cook his lunch, she is a widow by then. 'When one opens them up it looks as if they have been shot in the intestines with a right and left from a 12-bore.'

The coroner then talks about the cannibalistic habits of the Caribs: they thought Englishmen tough, the Spaniards almost indigestible, but French flesh 'very tasty and delicate'. All that marinading in wine and garlic, the coroner and I deduce.

My lunch, on the other hand, was drab. I ignored the mundane delights of Cornish Pasties and went for something local: a seafood stew. I needn't have bothered. You can tell if you are in a British- or French-influenced island just by the food. Theoretically the stew was a mixture of snapper, conch, turtle, flying fish and prawns, accompanied with fried banana-and-breadfruit rissoles. Every item in the stew tasted the same, boiled tripe with a faint tang of urine. The basic difference lay in the textures; these ranged from the slimy, through the rubbery to the sawdusty and the cottonwoolly. The rissoles were abominable: the shape and squidgyness of well-hung sea-slugs.

I'm back in my chair under the coconut tree, on the beach. The bananaquits are also back. They are natty little birds dressed in black morning-coats and yellow waistcoats. They have thin, curved beaks which can be used for puggling through the spoon holes of jam jars. The locals call this bird Bessie Coban. There are some good bird names in the Caribbean: Chuck Will's Widow (a nightjar), Crackpot Soldier (the common stilt), Kill 'em Polly (the least tern), Palomita de la Virgen (the ground dove), Whip Tom Kelly (a virco), Flêche-en-cul (long-tailed tropicbird). To translate the latter as 'Arrow-up-the-arse' would be putting it politely; the 'cul' is similar to the one in 'cul-de-sac', the obscene meaning of which we forget. The frigate bird, through its habit of doing no work but snatching food from the beaks of others, is called the Income-Tax Inspector.

I remember how my Arab friend Sayah in Abu Dhabi was amused when I told him that the nasty-looking, mottled green, spiky-leafed plant on his desk was called Mother-in-Law's Tongue; I suppose that for him, with four mothers-in-law, the name had extra poignancy. These plants grow here in formidable palisades within the shade of trees. Also called Mother-in-Law's Tongue is an acacia tree, because of the ceaseless rattle of its dry seeds in their long pods.

The three plants which produce aphrodisiacs are named Hug-me-Close, Tim-Tom-Bush and Fingle-me-Go. They are becoming rare.

There is an island of the Grenadines called Kick 'em Jenny.

18 May. I landed in Barbados two days ago in an aeronautic hotel, 70 yards long, six storeys high, with 400 residents: a Boeing 747. Now I am taking off in something about the same size and shape as a biggish shark. It is a twin-engined Baron Beechcraft 58. Within, it is less than four feet wide, but quite comfortable, with a seat for myself, two for the diplomatic bags and one for the refrigerated box containing food and drink. My journey will last all day, island-hopping at an average of 5000 feet at 180 miles per hour. There are two pilots: tall, laconic and friendly, although one seems a bit sinister, with a small goatee beard and dark glasses: 'Hey, man, how's things, and how's the cricket-bat willows that you grow?' – he has a good memory, I was last here about a year ago – and 'Hey, man, you can't be too pleased with the score yesterday, in spite of all that Botham did.'

There it is again – apart from the Queen, gin, bagpipes and short trousers, the thing that keeps the British Commonwealth together – cricket. Unfortunately I find other people's games a pretty boring subject, and I am a rugger man, if anything, but dredging to the surface of my mind the tittle-tattle from the last few Brits I have met, I bluff my way with a few second-hand opinions.

Between the two round black heads of the pilots I can see the runway speeding towards the windscreen; there is an upward surge and Barbados is now dwindling below. Being coral rather than volcanic, the scenery from above is undramatic: flattish, undulating downland sprinkled with shacks and farmsteads and with blank green expanses of sugar-cane plantations, but the sweeping beaches are white and idyllic and fringed with coconut-palms.

A couple of vast cannon, about 100 feet long, lie beside a narrow-gauge railtrack which has been built along a deserted beach. The guns were used in an American experiment, intended to fire projectiles into outer space. The experiment failed. It must have been fun trying, though.

It is a boring sky, heavily overcast, the sea is leaden below.

We are completely in cloud now, I hope these fellows know the way . . .

It is now late afternoon. I have swooped down and taken off from nine islands: Grenada, St Vincent, St Lucia, Martinique, Dominica, Montserrat, Antigua, Anguilla and Beef Island (the British Virgins). I am now on the way back to Barbados, via St Kitts. The sky is awesome, with clouds in both basic forms of streak and billow. The sea looks as if it has been wrought from different metals: iron, steel, silver, tin, pewter, sometimes the rarer glint of gold. There is a strange island on my left: a huge mountain surrounded by a ring of smaller ones like kneeling acolytes in green robes at the feet of their grey-headed high priest.

The great sweeping skirt-like flanks and high central peak of Mount Misery on St Kitts are recognisable even eight miles away . . .

Now all the bags have been delivered and I am on the two-hour flight back to Barbados.

The wings of the aeroplane are tinted an eerie, pale lilac; a strange, alien colour I have never seen before. In the sky around us there are huge grey teddy-bears, fluffy and bulbous-headed, like statues, all facing slightly away from me and standing above the leaden sheen of the sea. They seem to brood, they are strangely sinister. To port, towards the far-off continents where the sun has already set, there is a hazy gloom, lit up by faint glowing belts of pink, mauve and purple. Dominie is somewhere over there, 4000 miles away. To starboard, the western horizon is edged with streaks of burning orange. Against these, out-lined by the setting sun, there is a battle: silhouettes of soldiers, leaning forward with bayonets fixed, the turrets of tanks, guns long-barrelled. They all face north, towards a massive war-ship: the sun burns in a fiery glow where the battle rages in the dead ground behind the great arch that is the edge of the world.

The colours are fading, the battle has re-formed into a stampede of animals: the tanks are now elephants with trunks outstretched; there is a deer, some seals, a fox, a whole pack of hounds, something lithe and horrible, a pair of dinosaurs; they are all racing north where the battle-ship, now a Noah's Ark, is sinking into the gloom.

19 May. After breakfast I take a half-hour taxi journey north to St Nicholas Abbey, house of Stephen Cave. The Abbey never has been a religious establishment, it was erected around 1650 as a private house. It is one of the three surviving Jacobean houses in the western hemisphere (the others being Drax Hall, also in Barbados, and Bacon's Castle in Virginia, USA). Though the date is Jacobean the style is more William and Mary – some early Dutch influence on the island, presumably. It is a charming building constructed from field-picked rubble: this was put together like a dry-stone wall, with no cement; it was then faced with stucco. In front, it has a balconied porch and three arched gables, each surmounted with a ball. There is a pleasant formal garden which merges into the jungly surroundings where grow tall, smooth-boled Imperial palms, fish-tailed palms, coconut-palms and some of the few mahogany trees left on the island. Much of the furniture indoors is constructed from this local mahogany. The styles are simpler and more massive than their English counterparts; he has some good Georgian pieces, and much Regency. Apparently Victoriana did not reach the Caribbean; the furniture style jumps straight from Regency to Art Nouveau. There are the remains of an old sugar-making factory beside the house. Storage barns, crushing-room, power-house, separating-shed, mill chimney: they are all built from coral blocks. Cave is trying to renovate the mill in order to interest trippers.

A bus-load of trippers arrives from a recently moored Cunarder. Cave's guide shows them round the house and they then see a film which Cave recently discovered in a drawer. It was taken by his father in the 1930s and shows the working of the estate at that date. One scene depicts the sugar plantation labourers going off to work. They are all singing cheerfully. Behind them, on a horse, wearing bush kit and a pith helmet, the overseer rides. He holds the reins of his horse in one hand, in the other, a mighty whip.

The labourers are singing like anything.

Cave shows me round his estate. Most of it is sugar cane, but prices have been very bad for a long time and he is trying to diversify with vegetables: tomatoes, cucumbers, egg-plants, peppers and so forth. The birds may be beautiful, especially the humming-birds, but they are very pestiferous. So are the monkeys. Cave asks me if I want to go monkey shooting. I don't. It will be too much like shooting my own children.

We walk back through the garden. There is a lavatory at the far end:

a four-seater built above a dry well of about 14 feet. 'How do you muck it out?' I ask. 'I don't,' he says, 'when the house was built a few tortoises were put in the bottom of the well. They're still there, I think.' What a depressing thought, to be one of those tortoises: to be kept in the dark, and shat on occasionally – not unlike a farmer.

We all go to Cobblers Cove, one of the fabulous beaches of the world. Basically, it is 'a reef-protected crescent-shaped white sandy beach'. Coconut-palms lean over the strand, just as in idealised postcards. There is a very luxurious little hotel of 38 rooms centred on a small, pink-painted, 18th-century fort (it was built to combat pirates); the gardens are superb and there is a seaside terrace decked out with tables and shaded with fringed parasols. Particularly pleasant in the gardens is the traveller's palm. This has its long-stemmed leaves set out in a flat vertical like a huge fan made from feathers. Particularly alarming are the manchineel trees which lean romantically over the snow-white beach. They have green fruit like crab apples. They also have red rings painted round their trunks to warn that the fruit is poisonous and that the sap which drips from the whole plant will blister the skin of any sun-bather beneath.

Stephen and some friends sit under a parasol with glasses of gin; I go snorkelling. The water is as clear as Cave's gin. The corals are profuse and varied: the convoluted domes of brain coral, the antlers of elk-horn; towers, spikes; branches in ascending plates like cedar trees or as huge veined fans. Amongst them anemones wave their manes and fish of every colour and iridescence swim. The water is body-warm and as I glide and float through it I feel that I too am an element of this silent, exotic world.

We sit round the table and have a superb lunch of shrimps and crayfish and conch and tropical salad. It is the only place I've eaten mangoes without worrying about getting balmed up, after slurping through one all I need do is to roll off the terrace and have a quick rinse in the sea.

After lazing we all water ski. I am bad at it, never having had a good sense of balance, but I manage to get up and stay there for a couple of minutes: my skis skitter over the water, on each side of me the wake of the motor boat spreads as two white furrows on the sky-blue sea; out of the corner of my eye I can see the snowy beaches and leaning palms flashing past, the warm wind buffets my face; a lurch, a trip, a slamming smack on my face into the sea, whirling and spinning under-water; I surface to see the motor boat turning round to pick me up.

Back to Cave's house: a cup of tea, a wander round the garden, a more powerful drink, scrub fingernails, comb hair, and tie on ties; we pile into Cave's car and go off to be entertained by Her Majesty's Navy on HMS *Scylla*. She has docked here for a couple of days, having come from the Falkland Islands.

One of the guests aboard is a beefy, brainy-looking man wearing thick spectacles. He is a geologist called Mousewinkle.

'The only Mousewinkle I ever knew was a weedy whey-faced fellow at my prep school who was always homesick.'

'That was me,' says the beefy geologist, somewhat testily.

'You've changed a bit,' I titter, abashed.

'So have you,' he replies, staring meaningly at my pink-topped head. 'What happened to all that blond hair you used to have?'

'I've passed it on to my children.'

'That sounds a well-rehearsed reply.'

'It was a well-repeated question,' I say ruefully.

We're back at St Nicholas Abbey. It is about 11 o'clock. Our numbers have snowballed during the evening and there are now about a dozen of us. A couple of women that Stephen recruited from the last party are cooking dinner. I am helping open some very good bottles of wine. Other people are laying the table. It is a large, old trestle table on a paved area beside the front lawn, under a trellis of bougainvillaea. The night sky is bright with stars overhead, the air is warm, the palms rustle gently above, the people are pleasant and their conversation amusing or interesting: I shall feel hellish bilious in the morning.

24 May. *Weavers' Company Livery dinner. For the first time ever I am entitled to wear a decoration. The Queen's Messenger badge has a rare privilege in that it hangs* *from a ribbon of Garter blue. It depicts the royal monogram surrounded by the garter, all this is in gold and enamel; the running greyhound which hangs from this by a two-linked chain is, naturally, of silver. After three years of pounding the beat I received an official note saying that I was now a fully qualified Queen's Messenger – no longer a whippet, but a greyhound – and, if I took the note to Garrard's, the crown jewellers, I could order my decoration.*

So here I am, with it hanging below my too tight stiff collar and white tie, but feeling quite pleased with myself in a childish way. Dominie took ages putting it on, for it was too loose and she had to shorten the ribbon with safety-pins: gold ones, of course. (They came from the sewing-kit of a hotel in Washington.)

30 July. Landed here in Singapore yesterday evening. As we started our downwards descent, about 80 miles before touch-down, we began to glide through a marvellous cloudscape. Above, below, beside: clouds as islands, mountains, plateaux, cliffs, valleys, fields, banks, caves, grottoes, arches, stalagmites, lakes, glaciers, bridges, flying buttresses, castles, pinnacles, spires and columns, in every shade of pearl and pink and white and grey and silver; then we flew *through* a rainbow, a perfect circle starting above my head, passing round to disappear underneath and then reappearing at the windows on the other side.

I am in the Ming Court hotel. My room is very luxurious but I am 'not permitted to entertain prostitutes or catamites after 10 p.m.'

After breakfast I wander around for a couple of hours, exploring and soaking up the feel of the place. We are only about 50 miles from the equator; it is always intriguing to see everyone's shadows directly beneath them, blobbing around their feet like squat black amoebas as they walk. From the hotel I walk down Orchard Road, then Bras Basah Road, through the Mer-Lion Park to Mer-Lion Point where, together with the statue of the fish-tailed lion, I stare at the view overlooking part of the harbour and bay. The general impression of Singapore is one of cleanliness (there is a S$500 fine for littering), airiness and modernity. The starkness of the modern buildings is almost eliminated by the profusion of parks, gardens and avenues, and the many beautiful trees and shrubs within them. The tree which interests me most has extraordinary flowers and fruit. It is tall, with shiny leaves whose conformation resembles the horse chestnut. The flowers seem to grow only from a tangled mass of crooked stems which sprout from the trunk. I thought at first that they did not belong to the tree itself but to a parasitic creeper. The flowers have large white and apricot petals; in the centre these have a strange, almost orchid-like lip, covered on the inner side with stubby bristles. The fruit is completely round, large – about eight inches in diameter – and seems, like a coconut, to be made of hard brown wood.

I continue, to Chinatown. They are pulling down the picturesque old arcaded buildings and putting soulless modern ones in their place. Instead of bustling markets spilling onto the streets, there are shopping precincts in echoing concrete halls with the ambience of tower car-parks.

I then return via the Cathedral of St Andrew. It was built in the 'English Gothic' style in the 1850s by Indian convicts. It is whitewashed without and within. There are a few bits of stained glass, in sick greens and yellows and of unattractive designs. The pews are pleasant, with cool-to-sit-on seats and backs in woven cane. As usual, where the Empire has been, there are poignant memorials, several to infants – cholera? To enter the church, I have to come in by a side entrance and thence through a canteen stinking sourly of cheap food and the people eating it.

Onward, to sit by the Long Bar in Raffles, conforming to the tradition of chucking my peanut shells onto the floor – reminiscent of the behaviour of my mother-in-law's parrot, George.

I have had lunch and am now in the botanical gardens. It has been raining. Wet leaves glisten, it smells hot and frowsty, but the sweet scent of frangipane dominates. The gardens are well laid out and spruce, the plants are attractive and efficiently labelled (the strange tree with the round, hard fruit is called the cannonball tree, *Couroupita guianensis*).

I am by the largest lake; huge fish nose amongst the vast pads of Victoria water lilies, terrapin squat motionless on rocks, swifts swoop over the water and black swans float upon it. There are many mynah birds pottering about the lawns under the palms. Amid the huge arching clumps of bamboo, there are butterflies and damsel flies, some of which are of a rich plum-cum-burgundy.

A seminar is taking place: about fifteen earnest people are sitting in a circle, upon rugs. A woman in a sari dominates, she is the one who does all the talking. She gesticulates extravagantly as she speaks. I will walk close enough to see what is written on the cover of their files and folders: 'AIDS'. I look at the woman's gesticulations, intrigued, what can all those hand and finger movements be representing?

Part of the gardens is a 'preserved jungle'. I decide to get lost in it, but having been dispirited by the heat and the intertwined jumble of fallen trunks and branches and the smell of rotting vegetation I meet an enormous spider in a web the size of a bicycle wheel. I expect the vile thing catches humming-birds. I therefore leave the jungle to go back to the dull but luxurious amenities of a shower and a large dinner and a rest in bed with the television on below my feet.

12 June. Up early: Dominie has Colonel Coker coming with a mare at the crack of dawn; I must try to catch the tramp who is sleeping in Westwood's barn.

Got him. Poor chap. He is quite young and neat. He says he comes from Halstead, perhaps he has had a row with his family; but as I saw a woman's dressing-gown amongst his bedding, likely it is a love nest. Anyway, I tell him I'm sorry, but he's been here for a week and it's time to move on, the ponies in the yard are uneasy about him and I don't like people who smoke amid my hay. He looks as if he may want to argue but Peter, Anton and Tom arrive so he bundles his bedding into a bag and shambles off looking sheepish.

Last week we removed the goose and the four white duck from the moat at World's End Farmhouse as they kept straying onto the lane. We put them in the horse pond at Westwood's, but it has not been a success, they keep entering Violet Rutland's garden and eating her flowers and teasing the Electric Slug, her pug-dog, to a frenzy.

The gamekeepers, Tom and I circle round the birds, who are snoozing on the banks of the pond; they wake up, are herded into a stable and popped into a couple of sacks. They are too old and tough to eat, anyway they are friends, so I load the sacks into the back of the Land Rover and drive down to the river. I tip them by the pool of Langley Mill. They shake themselves indignantly and waddle to the bank where they stand, entranced: never have they seen so much water, never have they heard it splash and chuckle, such a lot of delicious weed, and a lovely island right in the middle of it all. When I drive away, there is a line of ducks swimming in the mill pool; the goose stands on the island, looking around with bemused wonder, like someone who has inherited the earth.

I drive on to Halstead, to North Mill, to buy pony nuts and dog biscuits. Mr Fleame is in his little office which smells of new-ground grain; mill stones rumble on the other side of the wooden panelling, his cat snoozes in the out-tray. His mill has been a family business since about 1720. It employs half a dozen people and is an asset to the community. It is to be murdered: the loathsome socialistic authoritarian tyrannical towny alien bureaucrats of the Common Market have told him that as he has wooden rather than metal bins and vats he is not conforming to one of their nit-picking little rules, and so must quit. Louis XIV, persecutor of my family; Napoleon, flashy mafioso; Hitler, soul-damned bigot; Stalin, brutal communist: all zealots of a bureaucratically united Europe, it seems that they will all have the last laugh.

13 June, Kenya. Having completed my business in the High Commission, I rang Jack Couldrey, Henrietta's father-in-law, and by 9.15 Jack is driving his wife Betty and me to the Lake Nakuru national park.

The journey of about 100 miles is through attractive countryside: undulating meadowland; steep hillsides covered with plantations of tea or coffee; areas of wild scrub where we see a Masai giraffe and a herd of Burchell's zebra; neat market gardens of cabbage and beans and potatoes; parkland, where the flat-topped fever-trees look almost like the cedars of Lebanon by an English stately home; and the heart-stopping sudden view, from the heights of the Rift Valley, of the great, dreaming plains below, dappled with cloud shadow, hazing up to the indistinct mountainsides 40 miles on the other side.

Two Masai lope beside the road: tall men with staves – or spears – in their hands and bright robes flapping in the wind; the impressive effect is slightly ruined by one who wears a leather peaked cap of the 'cor-blimey' style, rather too small, perched on his aristocratic head and a pair of sun-glasses with mauve frames.

The fields and allotments are all abustle with labourers: weeding, harvesting, thinning, digging and cultivating with that most tiring of implements, the mattock. I remark that nearly all the workers are women.

'Field work is not really men's work,' Betty says, 'and the expensive beast of burden here is the donkey, the cheap one is the wife.'

I make a few sheepish apologies for the male sex.

'They are not necessarily unfeeling, the men here,' Betty says, 'for instance, I am involved with a small home which looks after babies who have been born with AIDS. Little can be done for these babies, but they are, literally, loved to death; quite often you will see men coming in with toys or presents and sit down and give the babies a little cuddle and a bit of love. Unlikely you'd get that from an Englishman.'

Jack is involved in another project: a home for unmarried mothers and their babies.

'Most of the mothers are schoolgirls,' he says, 'and most of the fathers are schoolmasters.'

'Or so the girls say,' Betty answers.

From afar, the flocks totalling one million flamingos look like thick crusts of pink icing-sugar around the shores of Lake Nakuru. The massed slobbering and slurping of a million beaks sieving blue-green algae and crustaceans from the water make a whooshing-murmuring roar. Other birds dabble and wade about: storks, Egyptian geese, spoonbills who slosh their odd spatulate beaks to and fro in a sideways motion, elegant stilts and avocets, ungainly pelicans and squat Hottentot teals; here and there the sinister presence of a marabou stork – a large, gawky bird dressed in a shabby dark suit, bald-headed and sword-billed, executioner and undertaker to the unwary or weak. There is a sour, acrid stink: birds and stale water.

I look at a crested crane: tall, svelte and wearing a smart Ascot hat. It is mincing about beside a huge boulder on the edge of the lake. Suddenly I realise the boulder is inspecting me: it has hostile, pop-out eyes and inappropriate ears, it is a hippopotamus.

We drive round the lake. Everything in this eerie place seems alien and perverse. The heat-haze shimmers the multitudinous flamingo legs into an ethereal dance. The mountainsides are covered with a forest of stark tree-cactuses, making a Martian landscape. They are candelabrum euphorbia, related to the petty and dwarf spurges which are small weeds in my rock-gardens. We drive up a steep hill and park at the top of a cliff. Beside us, rock hyraxes scurry. These little creatures look rather like guinea-pigs, but they have hoofs and are related to the elephant. We stare over the foul waters on the soda lake. Somewhere in this stark landscape mankind may have started his development: a short, scuttling, carnivorous ape who will evolve into a tall, teetering, vegetarian whimp.

The Couldreys and I spend the night next to each other, in semi-detached chalets. They are comfortable: indoors, a bedroom and a bathroom; outside, a verandah with a table and chairs upon which one can sit and look over the pink-speckled lake and sip a whisky or two. We had dinner and watched a cabaret of some of the locals taking turns to do acrobatics – they were rather bad but one's heart warmed at their terrific concentration and desire to please – and then we wandered back uphill through the gardens to our chalets. A servant had laid out the bed and arranged the mosquito nets so that, on entering the room, one could imagine that it was occupied by a gargantuan bride enveloped in white veiling.

15 June. I have been in this blasted aeroplane for one and a half hours, waiting to fly from Zambia to Zimbabwe. They have lost 60 passengers. Their luggage was stowed in the hold two hours ago, but they have utterly disappeared.

Panic! All the missing passengers are Muslims. Are the 60 suitcases in the hold packed with explosives, all primed to blow us to kingdom come in order to make the world sympathetic to the plight of the Palestinians or to increase our admiration of the discipline of the Ayatollah? The people outside are in a turmoil of inactivity: shrugging, gesticulating, debating, pacing about and staring up at us. We stare worriedly back through the portholes.

They have been found. They were all in the aerodrome mosque, praying. Now they are filing in, looking not the least repentant for causing a two-hour delay. A couple sit down near me: Indians, a handsome woman wearing a chuddar and her husband, a smiling little man smaller than her, in an expensive suit. They are all from Cape Town, he tells me, and are off to Mecca via Jedda. They are interested in my seats beside me which contain the diplomatic bags, all strapped in place with safety-belts round them, and they make amused, quizzy remarks: 'Her Britannic Majesty must write a lot, those bags surely hold a great number of letters.'; 'We have quite a few robberies lately, and no-one knows where the booty is. Do you think it is contained within these bags, my dear?'; 'Do not touch them, they may be brim-brim-full of gin bottles and pork sausages.'

20 June, Ascot. *My waistcoat has shrunk, the inside of my top hat is felted with ginger cat fur, that dratted Millicent has been sleeping in it. I drive the Land Rover through the most ghastly traffic on the M.11 and M.25.*

I have several guests for luncheon in the Whites' tent. My mother-in-law is one of them. As usual, she looked very elegant and glamorous, but hearing that my children call her 'Granny Smith' had not improved her temper. Dominie was being sparky and witty with another of my guests and Granny Smith suddenly snapped at me, in exasperation: 'Why are you smiling at Dominie, she is not even **looking** *at you?!'*

Nevertheless, a very pleasant day, wandering around and meeting old friends; I even end a few pounds up on the nags. Knowing little about horses I always bet on the owners. I prefer them to be Arabs. Dominie prefers names: she bets on the ones she thinks pretty, or sweet, or which have some vague connection with the children. She won more money than the rest of us.

29 June, Cape Town. I am staying in the Mount Nelson, one of the famous old hotels of Africa. Built in 1899, it is painted a bright pink, with white balconies. I have a large and very pleasant room. It is furnished and decorated in a surprisingly successful blend of luxurious and cosy, Victorian with modern: ornamental plasterwork with chintz, solid old furniture with first-class plumbing. I left most of my baggage in Pretoria; when I arrived at the hotel I merely had my sponge-bag and a book, both packed in a plastic laundry-bag from my previous hotel.

With no signs of disdain, but with courtesy and aplomb, the porter carried it to my room and laid it upon the luggage stand as if it had been a Gucci suitcase.

It is winter here, and that is perhaps why Cape Town is a city I instantly like. I have tried to analyse what makes a place pleasant or nasty. Sometimes it is the beauty, like Stockholm or Bordeaux or Washington or Florence, sometimes the bustle-with-history – Istanbul or Cairo or Kathmandu or Calcutta, sometimes personal associations – Paris and Venice and Funchal; alternatively there are the unpleasant places: squalid Lima, ugly Mexico City, drab Tel Aviv, boring Bonn, even more boring Riyadh, bureaucratic Damascus, brutal Kingstown Jamaica, hot and humid Kuwait or a combination of them all: the world's fundament – LAGOS. I feel at home in Cape Town. There is a chill in the air and mist is rolling down the mountainsides which dominate the city. Gulls wheel in the cloudy skies overhead or squawk as they squabble over bits of bread. There is a smell of damp leaves. In the Cathedral of St George the Martyr the war memorials are for people who fought for familiar causes, and who were on our side. Many monuments are British Empire: regimental colours; a pair of kettledrums with battle honours of Moirosi Mountain, Basutoland and Bechuanaland; a sad little memorial for the long-dead volunteers of the Cape Peninsula Motor Cycling Club.

I am sitting on a bench in the botanical gardens as I write this. A pigeon is rootling nearby, hoping for crumbs. It has vividly pink feet with white toenails which make it look as if it has been paddling too long.

A party of us went to Finbar McSweeney's Edwardian Fish Parlour in the evening. There were six of us: two people from the Cape Town Embassy with their wives, a visiting boffin with a beard and tattoos, and myself. Whilst we ate, we were serenaded by the Riverboat Jazz Band. The food was excellent: my first course was of garlicky mussels as plump as pin-cushions, followed by a large 'sole' on the bone which was a good substitute for a Dover sole. I danced with Mrs Kirtly and, having drunk a bit too much, I told her that I thought her pretty and that her purring Devon accent was enchanting.

'Tut! You Queen's Messengers!' she admonished.
But she was smiling.

30 June. Only one couple are having breakfast at this early hour: in their thirties; tanned, fair, fit; presumably South African, maybe Australian, sometimes I cannot distinguish the accents, particularly when women are speaking. She, for example, having peered at the contents of her newly opened boiled egg, widens her blue eyes, opens her pink lips, and says: ''ere, man, this cackle-berry's got little red vines innit.'

This is to be a busy but boring day flying to Malawi and back.

You can always tell a loser. You could tell a mile off that this chap was one of these, poor little fellow. He was in the waiting-room of the airport, waiting to board the Malawi-bound aeroplane. An Indian, he was standing in a dejected slump, wearing a rumpled brown suit and a down-turned moustache, and carrying a cardboard suitcase. He was the sort of person to whom Lady Luck gives two fingers while the Wheel of Fortune runs over his toes; he would get AIDS from kissing the Blarney Stone, shat on by a pigeon when walking round a ladder, hay fever from a bunch of white heather, myxomatosis from a rabbit's foot and splinters from touching wood.

'How many passengers are there?' I asked a churlish female official.
'Eighteen.'
'But I've just counted nineteen of us.'
'Not possible, there are only eighteen seats, and I have eighteen tickets confirmed.'

I wasn't going to argue, I was going to ensure that I would be one of the first to board. Sure enough, from my seat in the front, I heard raised voices and saw outside the window the unfortunate loser, who had been at the back of the queue, being told that there was no room. There was much shouting, pleading and arm waving. It turned out that two children had been issued with a half-ticket each: mathematically, eighteen places; physically, nineteen bottoms. At last the poor little fellow was given a seat but he had to get off it and step outside the cubicle any time anyone wanted to pee.

*

1 July. I flew back to Pretoria this afternoon to give dinner to cousin Dave Dobell here tonight. I haven't seen him for 25 years, since he was a youth staying with us at Knights Farm. He was a Rhodesian. When black rule took over the country he joined what he calls the 'chicken run' and emigrated to South Africa. Almost penniless, he hired a donkey and cart and became a rag and bone man. He now has two scrapyards employing 48 people, eight lorries, a Mercedes and a house with a swimming-pool. He is married with one child. He looks the same: built like a barrel, five and a half feet high, red face, thick fair hair, large expanse of close-clipped moustache.

By the end of the evening we are thoroughly depressed:

'How is that great friend of your parents, Lady Alex?'

'Dead, died of a heart attack two months after Mamma's death.'

'How about her children?'

'The son died in a car accident. Both girls are divorced.'

'Rupert Riley?'

'Dead.'

'Bill Bailey?'

'Dead.'

'That uncle-by-marriage who lives in Stellenbosch?'

'Lived, not lives. Got leprosy: sat in a cane chair in his garden, under a jacaranda tree, and sipped pink gins and rotted. Flies carried him away in little pieces.'

'Tuh! Upsetting for Aunt Dora.'

'Not really; she'd got a bit fed up with him, and it gave her something to talk about at bridge parties.'

'Phillip Legge?'

'Dead.'

'Your mother's best friend, Princess Mamie?'

'They had a frightful fight over that Irishman, Tim Healey, and never spoke to each other till the day Mamie died.'

'What's happened to Tim?'

'Drowned.'

'Accident?'

'I don't think so.'

'Your father never liked him.'

'No.'

'What happened to his peculiar friend who was in SOE with him and used to bury people in laundry baskets?'

'Major O'Riley died years ago.'

'Mr and Mrs Ragwort?'

'He's dead; she's gone mad.'

'Cousin Harry?'

'His first wife turned lesbian; he's now on his fourth.'

'Cousin Cyrus?'

'Lost his job in the latest City crash.'

'But still alive?'

'Yes, but reluctantly.'

I tell Dave about my father's death: gasping out his last in that horrible bleak hospital in Cannes; Mamma sitting one side of him, suddenly very stoic and brave, me sitting the other, abject and useless; how the laboured, rasping inhalation of his breath sounded like the methodic, non-stop, drawn-out, come-and-go of the Mediterranean surf, outside my window, later that night, and for months afterwards it was in my dreams. Dave doted on Papa, and by the time I have finished Dave's moustache is sodden with tears. He's already had eight bottles of beer before dinner; we are having a bottle of wine each during it. He is full of superfluous liquor and spends half the time scuttling off to the loo and the other half mopping his eyes.

After dinner, Dave comes up to my room to have a last bottle of beer (his ninth) before he goes back to his own hotel. I give him a couple of old photograph albums of the Dobell family I inherited from Grandmamma. He cries. We decide to ring Dominie and say goodnight. Candy answers. She says 'Mummy is out, having dinner with the Pryors.' Dave speaks at length to her, saying several times that he is her Godfather and apologising tearfully for being an absentee one.

2 July. Dave goes back to his scrapyard in Pietersburg. I have the whole of Sunday to kill. I think I will go to the zoo; it is meant to be one of the best in the world.

On the way I go through Burger's Park, just by the hotel. I amble past the trees, shrubs, flowerbeds and ponds and enter the cactus house. It is inhabited by prickly little Martians, long-armed Venusians, dumpy Moon-men and other space monsters. The nearby church is shedding its congregation when I enter Van der Walt Street; the pavement is full of gossiping Boers, all neat in their best suits or dresses, prayerbooks in hand. I feel nostalgic for Colne Engaine, remembering the best thing about church: standing outside the porch when all the praise and pontifications are over, catching up with the village news, or as a councillor, being councilled.

In a hardware store's window there is a bundle of sjamboks – in plastic. What is the world coming to when even the sjamboks are plastic? What ignominy to be chastised by a plastic sjambok rather than a good old-fashioned one crafted from rhinoceros hide. Perhaps they are not meant to be used; you just hang one over your fireplace as an ornament.

Church Square is a gloomy expanse: most of the heavy buildings are constructed from granites and other rocks of sombre, murky colours: burnt umber, yellow ochre, blurry pink. A granite pedestal like a hulking blockhouse dominates the centre of the square; Oom Paul Kruger stands upon it, wearing a cast-iron top hat.

The zoo wafts a familiar smell: urine and raw meat. A whiff from the zebras' compound sends a nostalgic twinge through me as I recall Dominie's pony yard. This place is efficiently labelled in both English and Afrikaans. I have learned several facts of the useless sort I like, such as: one ostrich egg is as big as 24 hen eggs, it takes two hours to hard-boil; a hippopotamus weighs as much as 20 men, an elephant as 80 and a blue whale as 1500; the flamingo is a duck, you can tell by its lice; in India, 50,000 tons of human excrement are buried daily by dung beetles; 'Gorillas yawn, cough, hiccough & scratch themselves like humans' (or, if Afrikaans, they '*gaap, hoes, hik & krap hulself*'); the great ant-eater has a highly developed sense of smell (which is hard luck on it, as it lives next to the pygmy hippo).

As usual the primates are the most interesting. An old gorilla sits brooding, wondering why the nasty, brutal humans rather than the polite, gentle gorillas are favoured as the 'chosen race'.

A chimpanzee stares at a large crowd.

It is bored.

It scratches its bottom.

It examines its finger.

It smells it.

It scratches its bottom.

It smells its finger.

It scratches.

It smells.

Scratch . . . sniff. Scratch . . . sniff. Scratch . . . sniff.

The crowd melts away, talking primly of other things.

There is a baboon. He squats close to the bars of his cage, his arms folded. He keeps twitching his eyebrows up and down at me: raised in an expression of mild surprise, lowered in a massive frown. I twitch my eyebrows back. A young Boer comes up: a great, hairy blond fellow with beefy thighs bursting out of his shorts like boiled sausages. He is surrounded by friends. In one hand he holds a half-empty beer can, in the other, a banana. He eats the banana slowly in front of the baboon, tantalising it. He has finished; he tosses the empty skin at the baboon. Within a second the baboon has snatched up a handy turd and hurled it at the Boer. Unable to dodge, because of the press of friends about him, the Boer receives it full in the chest. When I leave he is gibbering with rage and scraping at his shirt-front with a paper napkin, the baboon is sitting with its eyebrows slightly raised, staring into space with an expression of the utmost blandness.

Another monkey is called a 'hamadryad': with its long-nosed, bright pink face, beetling eyes under jutting-out ridges and hair-style of fluffy grey pom-poms each side of its head, it only needs a pearl necklace, an old tweed skirt and a Wills Woodbine cigarette in the corner of its mouth to bear an uncanny resemblance to Lady **** who was the grandmother of a deb I once knew. The old woman rather disliked me, much to my amazement. To judge from its nasty way of peering at me, the monkey doesn't much like me either.

The snakes are pretty dull, refusing to move, but I quite like a green mamba with a sardonic expression: its name is Gordon.

Many of the animals have been adopted and Christened. Most of the names are mundane and obvious: Miss Piggy is a bush pig, Mr Hoppity a kangaroo, Big-Mouth a hippo. But some are pleasingly silly: I particularly like Robin and Brian, two warthogs, Maurice the lion, Fred and Roxanne the giant lizards, Cuddles the porcupine and Agatha, a bactrian camel (the Afrikaans label calls it a 'Twee-homp Kameel'). A honey badger has been adopted by the Corpus Christi Youth Group and called 'Father Richard'. There is no sight of it, it must be asleep in its hutch, so I cannot guess if it is so named for its appearance. All I remember about honey badgers is that they have an incredible temper, a nauseating stench and an insatiable greed for honey.

I like the hippos, I spend quite a long time admiring them. They have no shame. Gluttony is their sin, and they enjoy it. The hippo is constructed for one purpose only: at one end there is a huge gaping maw, ceaselessly gobbling and munching, in the middle, the bloated result of this obsessive cramming, at the other end, the almost continuous discharge of semi-digested greens: it is a machine designed for the conversion of vegetation into blubber and excreta. With their shape, cloven hoofs and eating habits it were better they be named 'Piggypotami'. Why don't these great balloons of lard float? Are their bones heavy? Do they swallow stones?

As zoos go, this is a good one. There is plenty of room, the many trees and shrubs are attractive and, above all, most of the animals seem at home in this tropical setting. One does not see, as in England, wretched shivering baboons scratching their chilblains, or runny-nosed, sneezing warthogs or ostriches with goose-pimples on their naked thighs or lions with chattering teeth and smoking breath. Yet . . . the impala amid the concrete crags, the bears in sanitised dens, the overcrowded wildfowl afloat on polluted ponds, the snakes in centrally heated, glass-fronted boxes: they are all wretched beasts being forced by man to be like man – urbanised.

3 July. The police museum is not the place to visit just after breakfast. I've seldom felt so repelled or horrified: photographs, tableaux and specimens of everything nasty: cruelty to children, cruelty to animals;

murder, mayhem, assassination and rape; skulls with holes and dents in them, together with the weapons which thus scarred them; something like a wrinkled glove – the skin flayed off a petrol-bomb thrower whose bomb exploded prematurely; photographs of several murdered school-girls with bits hacked off the insides of their thighs and arms by a witch-doctor. Extraordinary, several people have brought their small children with them. Such sights could surely corrupt or make callous, or at the least be appalling nightmare fodder?

There are two policemen outside.

'Well, that's really cheered me up,' I say.

One rozzer smiles, pleased; the other says, 'Gud, E'm gled.'

I walk further down the street and come upon a pleasant oasis of peace, set about with cypress trees and monuments: it is Hero's Acre, a graveyard. Afrikaans is not an elegant language, but I like the chunky sound of it, so I wander amid the graves, appreciating the Boer names: Jentje Evers-Blanken, Cornelia van Niekerk, Servaas de Kock, Arabella Ueckermann, P. J. Grobler. 'Hier Rust' it says on the top of most of them. That seems to drive the point home.

Kruger is here, below an elegant tomb in black marble with a white bust. This depicts him with a burly chest covered with medals and decorations. He has a Newgate Fringe beard under his chin, like a sporran which has slipped to expose a large spuddy object: his nose. Verwoerd is also here, a macabre bronze bust on his tomb; it seems to have been sculpted immediately after he was shot in the head, his face screwed up and wincing with pain.

I find a large expanse of British military graves. They are mostly of men killed during the Boer War, but many had died through epidemics of enteric fever (typhoid). They were all so young, early twenties, most of them. KING & EMPIRE is the proud heading on each gravestone. There are lots of familiar old county regimental names but also unfamiliar ones such as Lumsden's Horse, the Imperial Yeomanry and the 1st New South Wales Bushmen. A score of graves are of Grenadier Guardsmen, a dozen are of the Essex Regiment. I whisper out the names upon them, in respect and empathy; when I come upon a memorial to all those of the Brigade of Guards who fell I look about to make sure no-one is watching and then stand at attention for a moment. (I don't salute as I am not wearing a hat and some of the old boys would not approve of such imprecise conduct.)

I quit, via the sere, abandoned, lonely little grave of

THELMA MINNIE (Tookles)
only and dearly loved child
of Robert & Ada Day,
Died Jan. 15 – 1908
aged 3 years 10 months.

So small, so long ago, but you can still feel the heart-ache when poor little Tookles died.

19 July. I am off for Outer Mongolia this evening. It will be the seventh time I have done this 22,000-mile journey. The Queen's Messengers go in pairs in the latter stage, one of us as the other's escort. I am the escort to Tom on this journey. He has sent me an article about the journey and it has just arrived in this morning's post. It is from the 'International Herald Tribune' of 13 March 1986. I read it to those in the kitchen:

> *It's a dark and stormy night in Mongolia, and as the trans-Mongolian Express lumbers its way across the Gobi Desert, two members of an elite diplomatic corps are on board, carrying on a tradition almost 500 years old. They are nearing the end of a 20-day assignment so delicate that only a handful of people know their whereabouts. Their destination is the British Embassy at Ulaan Baatar in Mongolia. Their mission is the delivery of confidential and sensitive information from Her Majesty's government — sealed in diplomatic bags. These are the Queen's Messengers who are charged with the responsibility of taking messages from Britain's rulers to their lonely outposts. Today's 34-strong corps are a select, all-male group. Typically former members of the military, they have been carefully screened on the basis of their physical fitness, reliability and discretion . . .*

Cries of derision interrupt me: 'Discretion!' exclaims Dominie; 'Physical fitness!' exclaims Mr Ryan the scrap merchant, gazing meaningfully at my waist-line; 'reliable', 'sensitive' — these well-merited adjectives are bandied about mockingly. So I stomp out of the kitchen to continue packing: tropical clothes for the equator, formal clothes for Hong Kong, a jersey and corduroys for Mongolia, maps, binoculars and reference books on birds and wild flowers.

21 July. Hong Kong is exhilarating to a man who is still basically a businessman: the pavements abustle with buyers and sellers, the street vendors calling their wares; porters hastening about delivering loads, some carried on shoulder yokes; the little alcoves where craftsmen stitch or sew or hammer or weld or carve; the hotel doormen signalling for taxis to take fat financiers from one business meal to another; the jewellery shops sparkling with diamonds, glittering with gold and glowing with pearls; other shops wall-to-wall with watches, or cameras, or expensive clothes; the vast banks of skyscrapers which loom over-head, buildings which climb up the mountainsides in precipice after precipice of cement and glass. All is strange and exotic: the intriguing Chinese characters, in dash-and-scrawl calligraphy or in the coloured convolutions of overhead neon; the sudden stinks of dried fish and the warm wafts of spice and joss-sticks; the girls with their glossy black hair and long narrow eyes and high screaming voices with the long quaver-ing wail with which the Cantonese end each sentence. Many of the men wear spectacles, hardly any of the women who probably prefer to blunder about, half blinded but looking attractive. I cannot think why the Mongoloid peoples are described as 'yellow': their colour ranges from white, through tan, to red; some of the girls, seemingly the petti-est and best dressed, are of a very pale cream, like new ivory.

22 July. It is after breakfast. I am about to take the Star Ferry from Kowloon Peninsula to Hong Kong Island. It is one of the fabulous journeys of the world, the green-hulled, white-superstructured, double-ended ferryboats shuttling stolidly to and fro amid the seething mass of craft in the strait. It only lasts five minutes, but today it will take me longer as I am stuck behind some old biddy who wants to pay out in half a hundredweight of mites and groats, each one of which must be scrutinised, counted and stacked.

On board at last: the old familiar notices – 'DO NOT SPIT', 'MIND YOUR HEAD', 'BEWARE PICKPOCKETS', 'LIFE-JACKETS'; the smell of salt spray and ricey breath; the chatter and wail of conversation, the chunter-chunter of the engines. The mass and jostle of shipping is all about: ferries, ships of war, junks, tugs, luxury launches, dredgers, floating platforms rigged with cranes or derricks or pile-driving equipment, dinghies, barges, yachts, cargo boats and little coracle-like things, some of which seem to contain whole families, others just a solitary fisherman; pennants streaming, rows of white life-belts or black rubber-tyre fenders; the approaching walls of glass and concrete; the rumble and swoosh of the screw being reversed, the thump of the gangway being lowered.

I pottered around the steep pavements and alleys and passages of the antique-cum-second-hand district centred on Cat Street and Ladder Street. I saw a woman carrying some plucked duck on a yoke, their skin was very goose-pimply. There was a beggar with a bag over his head, ashamed perhaps, poor fellow. A seller of knick-knacks had stuck little bits of paper over the rude bits of his naughty postcards. The shop which smelled the most pleasant was the coffin maker's, sandalwood, I suppose. There was a little workshop owned by a wire weaver, he wove a salad basket whilst I watched. A man tried to lure me into a shop selling watches, another into a strip club. I turned down both: I didn't need another watch; I can think of few things as charmless as sitting amid a lot of seedy men who are in a state of sexual arousal. A vegetable stall was selling radishes the size of cucumbers. A shop was selling an inflatable doll – 'I'm Selina, your teenage sweetie. I have a hungry pussy and a firm ass' – so, she comes with her own blow-up menagerie as well. A shop in Cat Street is called 'Ho's Brother's Antiques'. That is rather pathetic and self-effacing; I cannot see Charlie starting up anything called 'George's Brother's Ltd'.

A medicine shop was very interesting. Many of the ingredients for cures were in bottles or cases. They included:

Turtle Shell – *when ground to powder, dispels heat from the skeleton*

Oyster Shell – *powdered, is good for spontaneous sweating*

Pipe Fish and Sea Horse – *potent stimulant for impotency*

Pearls – *powdered, good for facial nutrition and eyesight*

Dried Frog (Rana) – *nourishes kidney, unsuitable for person with excessive phlegm or loose bowels*

Tiger's Shin – *dispels endogenous wind* (how ignominious for the noble tiger, to be killed just to stop someone farting)

Chamois Horn – *treats manic and emotional excitement*

Centipedes (horrible long ones, covered in bristles) – *cures piles* (one dreads to think how)

There were also birds' nests, bears' gall bladders, toads' secretions, scorpions, antlers, silkworm moths, the sloughed shells of cicada grubs, snakes, the sexual organs of stag and seal – cures for every ailment you can imagine.

On the way back to Kowloon I walk past an itinerant seller of toys. He has a tired, worn face; pale, lined, ascetic, he looks like a don down on his uppers. His counter is an orange-box, his wares are repulsive little models of bicycles made of twisted wire. I accelerate in case he catches my eye – too late, I receive an imploring gaze, full of woe, but with dignity. However I am speeding past and leave him standing alone, the air of dejection from him and guilt from me hanging like a cloud in the dank alley.

I am now down the flight of steps and am near the Star Ferry. I stop and brood. I could walk back casually and drop a HK $10 note onto the chap's table. Here I am, having spent hundreds on a plate; there he is, a noble old man to whom even $5 would be a fortune. I dither. I trudge back. I have reached the old man. Well, well; his models have prices on them. $30 each! Good God! What a diddle! The repulsive things aren't worth a farthing. Too late, he's already handed me one. I furtively palm the $10 note and fish for a larger sum. He scrutinises each note and nods at me that it is OK, I can go.

In the Star Ferry I give the model to an infant who is looking over the gunwale next to me. His father takes it, examines it suspiciously, gives me a nasty glance and tosses it overboard.

23 July. I spent all day with Cousins William and Caroline [Courtauld], pottering about in their motor cruiser amid the islands and bays and beaches in the furthest north-eastern part of the Territories. We landed on one island and whilst the women fossicked over the luncheon salads and meats and fruits and bottles of wine, we men explored the semi-deserted fishing village. Its stone-built cottages are ruined and snake infested, its little temple smelling of the incense of long ago and a few unloved chickens scratching about vaguely. A few old, old people sat on their doorsteps and looked at us as we passed without the slightest sign of curiosity, hostility or affability.

Two of William's friends were a married couple, one animated and Welsh, the other serene and Burmese: Professor Alaun Griffiths, who is in charge of the botanical department in Hong Kong University, and Amy, his wife. Alaun has asked me to collect any potential food-plants I may find growing wild in Mongolia, the Mongolians living almost entirely on meat and needing their diet improved, he considers.

24 July. I am Tom's escort. He is the oldest Queen's Messenger. Having started his career as a policeman in one of the colonies, Kenya I think, he became a Queen's Messenger in the mid-Sixties. This is his 36th, and last, journey to Outer Mongolia; then he retires to his garden and his hobby of photography. He is tallish and thinnish and has white hair and a benevolent expression which can turn surprisingly nasty when dealing with an incompetent bureaucrat or aggressive official.

Our first sight of China is a glimpse through the cloud of a huge meandering river; it shines greasily and is of a liverish puce.

The clouds have cleared nearer Peking; the land below us looks flat, dun-coloured and dusty; there are hardly any trees, just a few regimented lines of what, from this height, look like poplar.

The first impression of the people is of stoic uniformity; crowds of black-haired people dressed in blue. Only a very few, some of the younger women, wear bright clothes. Many of the children are fancy-dressed in military uniforms. On the journey from the aerodrome to the city there are thousands of bicyclists; they go in swarms, flocks, herds and convoys. There are few cars but plenty of vans and lorries, mainly of crude and chunky designs. There are many horse- or mule-drawn vehicles: waggons, tumbrels and floats. None of the wheels are wooden, all are of metal and rubber-tyred, but otherwise the general design and construction seems basic and primitive. Their harnessing seems rather inefficient: in most cases the shafts have been fitted too low so the beasts are pulling up as well as forward; the throttling chest strap is often used rather than the collar; if there are pairs, they are harnessed in tandem rather than side-by-side (twice I saw the rear beast step over the lax traces of the leader); if harnessed in threes, the loner is at the back, sometimes doing all the work, rather than acting as leader. There are some new plantations of trees, poplars and willows, the latter pollarded rather than coppiced, presumably because of the sheep which are allowed to graze amongst them. There are some orchards. Unlike the English, who like a hollow, bowl-shaped tree, the Chinese prune theirs to encourage a tall central stem: perhaps you can get more to the acre that way; every available space is crammed in this over-crowded country. There is bamboo all about: as scaffolding on new buildings, as bean poles, roofing, fencing, or just in heaps and bundles, waiting to be used. Everything is dry and arid and sandy and dusty. A smoggy haze hangs about, from the many coal fires, like London 40 years ago.

Some time ago I was in China as a Queen's Messenger on the *Britannia*, sailing down the Pearl River under the escort of HMS *York* and five coal-burning Chinese battleships. I was, as usual, immensely impressed with the hard work and professionalism of the Royal Family, it was a pity that one of the press overheard Prince Philip saying that Peking was 'a ghastly place'. For so it is. It looks hugely dull: line after line of modern 'shoebox' buildings, wide characterless roads, very little that is old. However, there is one place that is always fascinating. Tom and I will tour it this afternoon.

There are about 250 acres of the Forbidden City. It is bounded by a wide moat and wall and centred on a long chain of huge courtyards, linked to each other with 'palaces' – really large pavilions – which have primly quaint names such as the Hall of Supreme Harmony, the Palace of Heavenly Purity and the Hall of Imperial Peace. Many of the 9000 side pavilions and ante-rooms have equally charming names. I particularly like the Palace of Peaceful Old Age, the Halls of Mental Cultivation, of

Delight and Longevity, of Character Cultivation, and of Accumulated Elegance, the Tower of Enhanced Righteousness and its opposite number the Tower of Manifest Benevolence, and the Pavilion of Floating Greenery.

One of the more remarkable things Tom and I see is the standardised behaviour of the people within, mainly Chinese and Japanese tourists. Hardly anyone roams away from the central route which leads through the middle of each courtyard: when we wander off to inspect a side galley or peer into one of the huge cauldrons which ornament some of the walls or look through battlements, we are entirely alone and can see, far off, the file of humanity ant-walking from one central palace to another, or standing in stiff little tableaux before the palace doors, being photographed.

Having walked right through the Forbidden City, about a mile and a half from the Meridian Gate to the Gate of Divine Prowess, Tom and I climb Prospect Hill, a mound made from the earth excavated when the city moat was dug. The last Ming emperor hung himself from a tree near the top. We inspect the view, then start on our return walk to the hotel.

Few people are allowed cats or dogs as pets so they have caged birds instead. They take the cages for walks in the morning. Tom takes many photographs of them, to show to his little granddaughter Tiffany when he gets home.

26 July. We will be on this train from Peking to Ulaan Baatar for about 36 hours, travelling a thousand miles. Communistic though it may be, the railway carriage is comfortably bourgeois. Tom and I have a cabin each; they are united by a shared, wedge-shaped washing-compartment which holds a sink, above which is a shelf holding a cut-glass decanter and two tumblers. Each of the cabins is wood-panelled and has a green carpet. It has a couch bed, above which is a bunk bed that can be lowered if the cabin is to be shared; there is a table with a linen table-cloth and a lamp with an Art-Deco lampshade, a cosy armchair with a white loose-cover, a clothes cupboard, an ice locker below it and several shelves and hooks. At the end of the corridor there is a water-heater;

its coal fuel makes the whole carriage smell slightly. At regular intervals the carriage attendant fills thermos flasks from it and brings them round each cabin; we can then brew tea, coffee or instant soup.

We would be even more comfortable but for the bags – we have over a quarter of a ton of them. They crowd the spare bunks, fill every shelf and cover much of the floor. Most of them are not diplomatic bags but containers of provisions for the Embassy in Ulaan Baatar, it is very difficult to get food there except mutton, milk, bread and eggs; day-to-day needs such as loo paper, typewriter ribbon, soap and matches are unavailable. There are only five diplomatic bags, and they are not very big, so Tom and I can lock our cabin doors and take the diplomatic bags with us when we go to the restaurant.

Breakfast has been edible, much to Tom's indignant surprise. He keeps on muttering 'Just you wait until we cross the border and get Mongolian cooking. They even put sugar on the fried eggs.' The menu is written in six different languages, Russian, Mongolian, Chinese, German, Vietnamese and English. Some of the translation is unexpected: Boeuf Stroganoff is 'Cowmeat shredded by a Russian'. Most of the items have been crossed off. I cannot understand why the Chinese, who are such an intelligent, inventive race, have devised the chopstick rather than the fork and spoon. Trying to eat fried eggs in a jolting train with chopsticks involves one of the most dextrous sleights of hands that I have mastered. My first egg burst and drooled all over the plate so I had to swab it up with a tile-shaped slab of white polystyrene foam which masqueraded as a slice of bread. I perfected a technique with the other egg: I slid it up the parallel rods of my chopsticks until it came to rest against the side of my thumb; then I put the ends of the chopsticks into my mouth and tilted them so that the whole egg slid down into my gaping maw like a life-boat being launched down its chute. Tom said that of all the sights that he had seen in his 36 trips to Outer Mongolia, this was the nastiest.

As we breakfasted, Peking, its suburbs and environs, slipped past the window. We began with a cityscape of apartment blocks, most with balconies from which bedding and clothing hung like the scruffy stuffing of vandalised sparrows' nests. There are many storage yards on the outskirts: lumber yards, coal yards, steel-wire yards, brick yards, tyre yards; in the gaps in between are allotments, some roofed over in tunnel housing of plastic sheeting; further on the allotments expand into fields of cabbages, potatoes and maize or into rice paddies. Amid all this are bean poles, sometimes acres of them, sometimes only one or two in a tiny back yard or squeezed between a wall and the clinker of the railway track's bedding. The only sign of superfluous ostentation is the holly-hock; but perhaps parts of it are edible, or perhaps it is allowed its beauty, for in proportion to the small area it covers its vertical show of flowers is abundant.

The landscape has been flat and ugly to start with, but quite interesting, for China seems like an enormous kitchen garden: every single square inch is being cultivated; everywhere people are digging, raking, break-ing clods, planting, weeding, irrigating, harvesting and stacking; every lane is full of tumbrels and carts and people with barrows or carrying loads. Every village is like a medieval settlement with little enclosed yards containing chickens and geese and sheep and pigs. I have seen only four dogs this morning, and those, by the look of them, were sheep or guard dogs. There are many charming pigs, often at loose, sometimes standing alone and porcinely pondering in the middle of a field, sometimes scampering around together like a group of excited children, or walking tiptoe on prim trotters, as if in high-heeled shoes, fastidious amid the litter and mud. The black pigs seem the most cheer-ful, the whites are more solemn and stately.

The litter everywhere is horrible, the pollution of all water appalling, the evidence of soil erosion dreadful, the deliberate elimination of all wild life, both flora and fauna, disgraceful; nevertheless the bustle and diligence is pleasing and impressive.

There is an immoral pleasure to be had from gliding across the land-scape in an upholstered armchair, with a glass of wine on the table in front, a good book at hand, the bed crisply made up, and the sight of millions of people sweating and toiling outside. The Germans almost have a word for it: *Schadenfreude*. It is not exactly what I feel, for that means a malicious joy at other's misfortunes. What I feel has no malice in it and could be defined as 'the intensified appreciation of one's own circumstances having compared them to those less fortunate'.

*

After the initial flat plains we have gone through the Badaling (Green Dragon) Pass. The mountains are steep and craggy and several resemble those entrancingly painted in Chinese pictures, the exaggerated pinnacles hanging in mid-air, their feet obscured by mist. The first sight of the Great Wall is always heart-stopping: there it is, the great legend, a broad, high stone ribbon, undulating up a mountainside and then looping along mountain ridges, from where the battlements stand out against the cold blue sky like the jagged crest along a dragon's back. Square stone forts are built at intervals along the Wall. We see much of the Wall after Badaling, travelling alongside it for several miles on a few occasions, for the Wall is not one, but many. Generally, the older the Wall, the further it is from Peking, and the last segment I saw was merely a huge disintegrating mud bank, with the forts existent as misshapen earthen mounds. Many of the villages round about are also walled, the rains of centuries have eroded these mud barricades into broken and gap-toothed ridges.

Now that we are north of Chi Ning the scenery is attractive. There is much less evidence of litter and pollution. However the birds are the same, almost entirely magpies. Mao Tse Tung, not content with the murder and tyranny of millions of his countrymen, issued a decree one year that all sparrows were to be slain: they were not productive and therefore un-communistic. So for a year every small brown bird (SBB) was hunted down, stamped on and eaten. Magpies escaped this fate because they are easy to distinguish from sparrows, and it is unlucky to kill one. I thought I saw a small flock of seven shifty and worried sparrows in a tree by a railway station. Although I am a farmer, and reckon sparrows to be vermin, I was pleased to see this evidence of Mother Nature's resilience against mankind.

We have run over a cow. The train stops. People from a nearby village swarm out of their cottages, or from the copses and fields in which they are working, and stand around the cow, mourning. Then they harangue our driver. He is reinforced by various people in uniform from the train, they gather protectively about him and berate the villagers. The villagers are out-shouted. Grumpily, they haul the corpse off the track and we continue the journey, speeded on by curses and reproaches hurled at our retreating buffers.

The countryside is now vast expanses of open farmland, very flat with low foothills in the distance, and small groves of poplar amongst which horses or sometimes cattle laze and graze. The dwellings in the villages are low and cosy, their roofs mud-plastered and sometimes covered with straw – too crudely to be called 'thatched'. Tom has pointed out that all the cottages face south and that there are no windows facing north.

There is a large contingent of Europeans on the train: lumpish East Germans with crew-cuts; dark little Slavs who patter up and down the corridors arguing with each other and looking shyly at their shoes as they squeeze past; schoolmasterly Britons with beards and phrase-books; tall Scandinavians with tiny rucksacks which they never seem to take off; also some rich and rare Americans.

During the night we had four hours of tedium: scrutiny by two sets of customs and immigration control, firstly at the Chinese border post at Erlian, then about a mile further on at the Mongolian post of Dzhamine Ude. Erlian was well lit by neon slogans and a loudspeaker screamed at us from the roof of the tall central building. Mandarin Chinese sounds most aggressive to those who do not know it, and I had assumed that the harridan screeching through the tannoy was hurling abuse at our departing backs, but when she translated her speech into English her voice changed to a seductive cooing and she began by saying: 'Goodbye dear friends, we wish you a pleasant journey and hope that soon we will see you again . . .' Squads of smartly uniformed people kept knocking on my cabin door, saluting me as I stood bleary-eyed before them, asking to see some bit of paper or other, scrutinising it – in one case, upside down – saluting politely once more and marching off to inflict the same routine upon Tom next door.

The most interesting thing was the changing of the wheels of the rolling-stock. This is necessary because the Chinese have a narrow (British-built) gauge, while the Russian-influenced Mongolians have a broader gauge. They like to keep it like this, it makes invasion more difficult. The process takes place in a long, dirty shed. There is a team of four men and a long-haired girl. Each carriage is hoisted into the air on powerful jacks, then the Gang of Four fiddle about underneath it, unshackle the wheels, 'bogies' they are rather disgustingly called, then an overhead crane hitches up and hauls away the undone set of wheels and lowers down the alternative set. Looking up, one can see the crane girl lit up in her box of glass and steel, her long hair flowing from her shoulders on to her control panel. Then a lot more scratching noises occur beneath one's feet, like demented rats under floorboards, the carriage is lowered and they move on to the next one.

27 July. We are now travelling through the undulating gravel plain of the Gobi desert: the 'Great Hungry Place'. It is treeless, but at this time of year is relatively lush. Many grasses, reeds and sedges grow upon it in a remarkable range of colours: powder blues, sky blues, greens of every variety from lime to malachite, golds, yellows, beiges. There are ponds or boggy areas where one can occasionally see duck, a small type which may be teal, and the chunky orange bird which is easily recognisable as the ruddy shelduck. SBBs include larks and pipits and wheatears. There are corvids, hoopoes and many kinds of raptor: kestrels, buzzards, eagles (most of which I cannot identify, but I did recognise golden eagles and steppe eagles), kites, harriers; most entrancing of all are the crane. These long-legged, stately birds nest at this time of the year. A few have hatched and I see some families standing in their familiar position in the only shade available, that of the telegraph poles which line the railway track. The birds line up in order of seniority, the cock nearest the pole, his hen behind, then the larger of the two nestlings, then the smallest who, poor little thing, has to keep shuffling into the shadow as the sun-dial of the pole creeps across the ground; the cock bird, in the privileged position, needs only to sidle a few inches each hour.

At intervals, solemn men, often on horses or camels, hold up yellow flags or batons as we pass. They are the people whose job it is to clear the tracks of camels, sheep, cattle or wolves. Sometimes they have to ride in front of the train to do this. The yellow signal indicates that their particular allocation of track is clear. Now and then they are mistaken: a couple of years ago two Queen's Messengers had to sit on their bags, heaped up on the verge beside their overturned carriage: the train had become derailed after running into 'an obstacle'.

The camel here are the short-legged but powerful Bactrians, the two-humped species which produces up to 25 kilos of coarse hair in winter and which can carry a quarter of a ton of baggage. Assemblies of these camel roam the desert, also flocks of sheep and goats, and herds of cattle and of the stubby little horse; no yak, they do not breed below 6000 feet. There are also antelopes and sometimes wolves. Marmots sit upright next to their burrows; this animal carries the flea which, transferring to the ships' rats of Venetian and Portuguese traders, spread the Black Death throughout Europe.

The train climbs up a couple of thousand feet through mountainous country before it arrives at Ulaan Baatar. The land is still basically grazing and moorland but there are streams; willows and poplar grow alongside them, woodlands of larch survive in the sheltered, north-facing hollows on the mountainsides.

The first sight of Ulaan Baatar, the capital of Outer Mongolia, is always a disappointment. It is not the small, hamlet-sized picturesque huddle of tents I had first expected. It is a large city of about half a million people, a quarter of Mongolia's population. Architecturally, it is typically communistic, a military-style barracks where people are treated by the squad rather than the individual: in long parades there are blocks of flats, about seven storeys high and a hundred yards in length; between, there are wide, soulless streets, whose only sign of personality is a plenitude of potholes and cracks; there is a huge central square where the populace can be assembled, drilled and harangued; some of the larger buildings are ornamented with photographs, either of local political big-wigs, seedy-looking men in ill-fitting suits, or of professional murderers, such as Lenin and Stalin. About 200,000 people live in the modern housing, 300,000 more live in the suburbs of tents which encircle the city.

This tent is normally known as a 'yurt' but that is the Siberian name and the Mongolians call it a 'ger'. It is round, about five paces across, with a low, domed but flattish roof, through the centre of which a stovepipe pokes, and a wooden door. It is belted round with two or three sashes which hold together the double layers of felt from which they are made. It is of a dirty grey: from afar a settlement looks like a crop of mushrooms. A ger weighs about a quarter of a ton which is within the carrying capacity of a pack camel. It can be erected in an hour and struck and packed in half that time. Inside they can be warm and comfortable, but the central stove gives off much smoke and there can be vermin. Years ago I read a Mongolian poem of abuse. I have forgotten it all but for the last, dire curse: 'And may your wife's arm-pits be full of felt lice.' Within, a ger is divided by invisible lines which define areas such as the hearth, the male and the female quarters, and the guests'. Because life in a ger has no privacy the people have learned the essence of good manners: consideration for others. They are accustomed to isolating themselves from those around them; they do not poke or pry or stare or comment if you are abluting, or arguing, or courting, or berating the children, or begetting them.

The gers around Ulaan Baatar are divided up into groups by high wooden walls: no-one could tell me if these divisions are clans, or families, or merely for some administrative convenience. They look pleasantly chaotic, with goats, sheep, cattle, chickens, dogs and children wandering about. I have seen no pigs, perhaps such a nude animal could not survive the bitterly cold winters.

It is the intention of the Russian-influenced hierarchy to oust every Mongolian from his ger and into a block of flats, from where he will be more easily controlled, no doubt.

The basic garb is a robe called a 'del'. It has a high neck and extends down to the shin for men and lower for the women; the sleeves are long and can be turned down so that they cover the fingertips; it is fastened at the right shoulder. For the men, the material is heavy wool; the colours are usually plain, dark greens or browns or burgundy; the silken sash which belts it is usually yellow or orange. Below this they wear wellington boots, leather in the summer, often of grey felt in the winter. The whole rather impressive effect is often spoiled by a teeny-weeny porkpie hat with a narrow, up-turned brim, but some men wear the traditional circular hat with flaps, in fur or felt. The women's del is lighter as well as longer, often being tailored from jacquard-woven rayon brocade with a small silver or turquoise brooch as the shoulder fastening; there are also three small toggle-type fastenings by the left thigh. In winter, dels are usually padded with fleece or cottonwool: some are quilted.

The people look friendly, but shy; though polite, they are reticent. The dry air and extremes of temperature have shrivelled and wizened the aged, but many of the young women are pretty, in a round-faced, red-cheeked way. According to a leaflet in the museum, their criteria for female beauty are:

> soft hair, symmetrical and harmonious joints and hands; a plump roundish neck; a smooth forehead; a plump pretty face and round cheeks; black eyebrows; white even teeth; big eyes; red out-lined lips; a thin nose; long arms with round muscles and soft skin; well-shaped close-set fingers; an elegant figure and a thin waist; a deep-sunk navel; broad shoulders; high breasts – close-set, smooth, white and firm; wide fleshy thighs; clear tender skin, and pink convex finger-nails.

People are noticeably bow-legged. I presumed that this is because they spend much of their time on their horses, for their chief occupation is as nomadic herdsmen, but Alaun Griffiths in Hong Kong told me that most of it is due to rickets: they eat hardly any vegetables, perhaps a few onions and potatoes: 'weed-eaters' they call vegetarians. The shortage of edible green stuffs is so acute that they have to make their alcoholic liquor out of mare's milk. It is called 'airak' or 'koumiss'. I must try some. Last foaling season – the only time it is made – the ambassador's wife put some for me in her fridge, but by my arrival it had separated into blobs of junket floating in turpentine, so I gave it to Benson, the cat.

The children are exuberant, but well-behaved and can be charming: when I took a photograph of Soviet hero Sukh-bataar, a mounted worthy on a sway-backed nag whose statue em-pimples the huge central square, the nearby children clustered round, offering advice and insisting that they hold my map and camera case whilst I snapped away. Some of the tiniest reminded Tom of his little granddaughter, Tiffany.

The Mongolians resent the presence of 87,000 Russian 'advisers'.

These soldiers are everywhere. I was pleased to see that the examples of our potential enemy are a slovenly and dispirited collection. Many of them are lank blonds, Balts possibly, posted here to keep them out of mischief.

Our Embassy is an inoffensively designed building with a back yard. At the end of this there is a small stone bungalow: Greyhound Cottage. This is where the Queen's Messengers stay. We do our own cooking and housekeeping. Tom is the cook, I do the washing up. Tom produces huge breakfasts of bacon and eggs and baked beans on toast, all of which is sluiced down with coffee bleached with powdered milk. He uses a couple of frying-pans and half a dozen saucepans. It takes me hours to wash up.

28–29 July. Tom and I have done much walking: traipsing up and down the stark streets of Ulaan Baatar, photographing, visiting the monastery, the museum (full of stuffed animals with morose glassy stares, and bits of dinosaurs) and the dollar shop (accessible only to diplomats and local VIPs with special passes), where I bought Dominie an attractive airak bowl in silver and wood and Tom bought Tiffany a small sable hat. We also went to the post office, where we bought stamps and postcards – the few which showed views rather than the cashmere spinning & knitting factory, or the power station, or the office block. I have written 22 postcards, Tom one – to Tiffany. Having stuck the right number of stamps on the cards there is hardly any room to write addresses, hardly a message. We have been out in the country in the Embassy's Range Rover. The views are enchanting in their serene loneliness: sweeping valleys and undulating plains, covered with a thin fuzz of vegetation and dotted with grazing livestock. In the valley, below the place known as the Mountain-ridge-surmounted-by-the-rock-shaped-like-a-seated-buddha, the most noticeable flower is a small but beautiful lily, bright red; below, on the cliffs that border the River-that-flows-under-a-wooden-bridge-and-is-overlooked-by-a-cairn-with-a-horse's-skull-on-a-pole, I found a clematis with thick-petalled yellow flowers, either clematis tangutica or orientalis. On the banks of the Pool-with-the-biggest-arctic-char I found some currants, the only food-plant I could find for Professor Griffiths apart from the rose species (hips), the crataegus (haws) and the abundance of rhubarb — (tulip bulbs are edible, perhaps the local wild one could be domesticated; I shall suggest it). There were many types of butterfly, including blues, tortoiseshells and fritillaries; there were larks, buntings, wheatears, martins, a hen chaffinch and white wagtails aplenty.

30 July. The train is to be four hours late so we have time to visit the Sunday Market, held in a fenced-in compound above Ulaan Baatar. There are stalls around the perimeter of the enclosure, but most of the selling is taking place in the centre. There, mats have been laid out on the ground and the vendors have arrayed their wares upon them. The goods offered are of an immense variety: there are harnesses for ponies and camels, cooking utensils, knives and other cutting things, wicker-work, brushes and whisks and brooms all beautifully made from twigs and straw and rush, shoes (oddly, they only sell one shoe of each design, if you buy a pink plastic sandal for a four-year-old child's left foot you have to seek about until you find the matching sandal on someone else's mat), bits of wirelesses, horrible garish rugs in the worst of Russian kitsch design, the cases (but never the contents) of ballpoint pens, paper-clips, nails and screws, rope and twine. Tom bought Tiffany an embroidered object which he thought was a detachable collar and which I said, to his ire, was a covering for the seat of a mobile loo.

We are now on the train, pottering down the mountain track towards the Gobi desert. When we had drawn out of the station the Embassy staff gave Tom the full 'Flag' farewell, as it is his last journey from Mongolia. I was told to make sure that he was looking out of the window when our train reached the outskirts of the city. There we saw the Land Rovers parked, with the staff standing in a tableau upon them, holding up the Union Jack and the Ambassador's house flag; as we passed they piled into their cars and dashed along the road alongside the track, the flags streaming from the windows of the cars and every-one waving and calling and smiling. Tom couldn't see it all for he suddenly got some grit in his eyes and had to return to his cabin and mop them. Very gritty, the steppe.

6 August. *All is well at home. The garden looks a bit dishevelled, Dominie and Hart have been attending to the details, but the lawns need mowing and the hedges are straggly for I said I did not want them clipped until the birds have finished nesting. Many of these are blackbirds, including one whose nest is impudently built in the upper branches of a peach in the peach house; there are a couple of thrushes' nests, but not a missel-thrush this year (the local name for this is the 'Cold-Arsed Bird', perhaps because it sings from the tops of trees); also possibly a partridge's in the heap of brushwood I leave for the wild life (Dominie thinks it an annoying eyesore, but having pontificated on Radio Essex that every garden needs at least one pond, one patch of nettles and one heap of old twigs, I can hardly avoid having this). The house martins are busy under the long overhang in the front of the house and swallows are nesting in the Home Barn. In the Cherry Orchard's hedge I found a hedge Betty's nest, one of the most beautiful sights in the world: a mossy cup lined with pony hair and wool, holding its treasure of bright turquoise beads. Very pretty too is a collared dove's nest in the bullace by the pond, an attractive contrast of the crudely twiggy platform and the shiny smoothness of the pair of eggs, white but with a pinkish translucence like pearls.*

Tom has finished laying flagstones round the edge of the new Lily Pond so I have started to fill it from a hose-pipe. It is running very slowly; Dominie is mad with impatience.

17 August. The journey to Caracas from the aerodrome is pleasant: a steady climb from the coast up valleys, past precipices, over gorges and through mountains, via tunnels. Caracas is not particularly likeable for although the setting is attractive – tall mountain ridges with jungly slopes sandwiching the populated valley floor – it is designed entirely for vehicles. Thus it is extremely difficult to walk the couple of miles from one side to the other. I am now in my hotel bedroom, on the four-teenth floor, looking over the valley to the heights of Avila opposite. I can see, in between, three sets of dual carriageway, two main roads, and the River Guaire – its cemented banks channelling a flood of fast-flowing sewerage. There are no pavements in view.

I went for a walk before nightfall, an unpleasant experience. There seems to be no centre to this nasty city: no Piccadilly Circus or Place d'Etoile, just a long concrete conglomeration of roads and building-blocks. I became enmeshed in a maze of pavementless motorways, hopping over barricades and crash barriers, scuttling up the verges of dual carriageways, wandering in the arid zones below fly-overs, being hooted at when dashing across one road to another in the vain hope of finding anything designed for legs rather than wheels. I had to cross one wide concreted culvert by using a couple of pipes that spanned it as a bridge. I eventually took a taxi back to the hotel.

18 August. The guide should have been here at 9 o'clock, it is now 9.20, but I mustn't be irritable, the people in this country were not brought up with the attitude of my generation of being 'present and correct five minutes before parade'.

Here he is, with a friend. They are both affable-looking fellows, in their mid-twenties, tall, for Latin Americans, and with brown hair, also a bit unusual, the majority here being melanic. The guide is called Marco. He is on holiday at present, normally he works as a concierge in this hotel, which is why he knows Gladys, the receptionist – with a perversely attractive squint – who recommended him as a good guide for a bird-and-plant-watching traipse amongst the local mountains. Marco tells me he is not Venezuelan at all, his stepfather is, but his parents are Italian and he has a Canadian passport. Eduardo is completely Venezuelan. His shorts and T-shirt expose sinewy arms and legs. He is of a peculiar uniform colour: hair, eyes, skin, they are all of a similar bronzy-khaki.

Marco drove us through the city to the foothills in a clapped-out little car which could move faster than its appearance suggested. Every time we passed a pretty girl Marco tooted his horn and then he and Eduardo shouted suggestive expressions such as 'Olé!' and 'Mmmmmh!' and 'Hiyah!' From the cheery smiles in return, these remarks were not ill received. We are now on foot, climbing a very steep track up the sides of the mountain range which overlooks Caracas. Marco is lagging a bit, he keeps panting: 'I am very strong usually, but my job is making me out of practice.' Eduardo has a long, easy lope with could probably outpace a mule. I suppose that this is rain forest, mist forest otherwise: patches and veils of fog hang about the huge trees, it condenses and drips from the hanging ropes of lianas and the beards of Spanish moss; there is a damp, heavy smell of wet vegetation. Here and there are clumps of towering bamboo. There are not many flowers but we have just seen some large and magnificent purple orchids. Eduardo says that the mountainsides used to be ablaze with orchids but 'Too many people come and take them away and sell them to the Americans.' We saw a couple of tiny, dark toucans and a larger, rather cuckoo-like bird which slunk furtively about the branches, it was against the sun so we could not see its plumage; Eduardo said it was a 'guacharaka'.

We had to turn back: our track had become a narrow path cut into the side of a precipice, it suddenly vanished, scraped off the cliffside by a recent rock fall. We therefore returned to Marco's car and he drove us to a road bridge spanning a turbulent little brook. We have walked and clambered alongside this stream. There is a waterfall about every 100 yards. At the base of each fall there is usually a pool, this spills over into a cataract which swirls and splashes down to the next waterfall. We have to scramble up steep rock faces to bypass the falls. Often this necessitates all hands and feet clinging to cracks or inch-wide ledges, but sometimes there are roots or lianas. It is not particularly difficult, the rock is healthy with nothing loose or rotten to it, and the biggest tumble would only be about fifteen feet, enough to break an ankle if one was unlucky. Eduardo scampers up the sheer faces like a gecko. I am more laborious, being too fat, but at least I can recall my experience in the mountain-rescue team 30 years ago. Marco is hating every minute of this, but is too proud to admit it.

We have reached the last surmountable waterfall. It is also the highest. 'This is called "Tarzan's Climb",' says Eduardo.

'Why?' Marco and I ask, uneasily.

'You'll see,' says Eduardo with a nasty grin, and starts to lead us round the pool.

The cliff looms above us. There is a large overhang. Water drips from it and nourishes lush green blankets of moss and fern beneath, and surprising clumps of busy-lizzies. I cannot see where we can scale without the use of ropes. Eduardo leads us into a cave to the streamward side of the overhang. At the end of the cave there is an overhead shaft of light. A liana dangles down this chimney.

'The only way to get up is by climbing up this creeper, that is why it is called "Tarzan's Climb",' Eduardo says.

He shins up it.

I go next. It is not as bad as it looks at first sight; there are plenty of footholds most of the way, but in a couple of places my full weight has to hang from my arms.

I emerge into a glade. Trees lean over the torrent which collects in a still pool before plunging over the lip of the waterfall. Whilst we sit on a rock and pant and look at the view I glance at my watch and say: 'Well, the four hours are nearly up, I suppose you should take me back to the hotel.'

Marco says: 'When the four hours are over, will you then become my guest and come and have lunch with me at my apartment with my sister and my girlfriend?'

Pleased and flattered, I accept.

The flat which Marco shares with his sister is cosily and fussily furnished in the Spanish style: lots of rugs, and furniture of dark wood, heavily carved and ornamented. There are several reproductions of rather badly painted landscapes, a large bookshelf full of books in Spanish, Italian, English, French and German, a balcony crammed with pots of dried-up plants, a busily cluttered and rather greasy kitchen, a bathroom and two bedrooms. The beds are neatly made.

'If only two of you live here, why have you got eight toothbrushes in your bathroom?' I ask the smiling sister.

She screams with laughter: 'I am very attentive to my teeth. Sometimes I think they want one sort of toothbrush, sometimes another. Seven of those are mine.'

She has long, brown, rather frizzy hair and a large beaming smile. She wears jeans and a T-shirt. The girlfriend is as pretty, but more exotic, with long black hair, twinkling eyes which are so dark a brown that they are almost black, high cheekbones, one with a beauty-spot, and an almost perpetual smile which discloses large, even teeth. She wears a peculiar suit in fuchsia-coloured hopsack: the shoulders of the jacket are huge and cut-off square; the skirt is minute, and slit up the back to reveal a white froth of petticoat. She is permanently making jokes. Everyone howls with laughter except me who does not understand Spanish, but my weak smile perhaps suggests to her that I am getting the point, for every time she says anything she gives me an extra large smile and a wink and a knowing shake of the head.

We have now all had lunch – spaghetti bolognaise, cheese and salami and very good bread. We washed it down with beer that I bought on the way here. The girls have left, chattering like jays, and Marco, Eduardo and I are relaxing before a wrestling match on the television before I am driven to the hotel. I shall remember this hospitable, friendly, easy-going household.

27 August. *My old agent in Nigeria, Norman Cork, came to Sunday lunch. When George's Fiona came into the drawing-room he said with the cheekiness that is the privilege of old men: 'You are very beautiful, my dear.' Fiona replied with a sunny smile and a 'thank you', which pleased me: some girls would have simpered, blushed and bitten their fingernails.*

Now, in the evening, I am sitting in the verandah and editing my grandmother's diary. She is good at summing up people. Here she is in April, 1891 (aged 15):

. . . the curate from St. Paul's came; he has a very unreverend voice, but preaches extempore and very very ernestly; he came into afternoon tea, and drank three cups, has red hands; he is shy and plain, and twists his hands about and laughs a great deal but seems nice.

. . . Leonard really has improved in looks and would really be almost passible if he talked quite differently and held himself decently; he looks quite languishingly at you with his sleepy blue eyes and has cultivated a new way of shaking hands: instead of a pump-handle action which he used to do, which nearly dislocated your wrist and broke your fingers, he now holds your hands in a lingering pressure, which is certainly preferable; he is a funny youth.

. . . Miss Ricketts has once been pretty . . . ['Miaow' Grandmamma!]

. . . Geoffrey Plant is staying here. He is a funny little atom with a strong accent

and a deep bass voice. Says 'confound it!' and 'what the devil!' and is aged 8! He
is always talking of 'living organisms'.

3 September, Canada. Probably because of time-lag I woke in my
room in the Ottawa hotel at about 3 o'clock in the morning. There was
nothing interesting on the television so I pressed the button which said
'In-house Film'. Three woman materialised on the screen; to my surprise each was stark naked, but for a fireman's helmet and a pair of
boots. They were standing in a circle licking each other's tongues. They
then got on the floor: two were head to tail, like sardines in a tin, I could
not see what position the third one was in, she was lost amid the general
squodge. The lower-most then proceeded to lick the upper-most's
behind. At least, she pretended to, but I could see that she was keeping
her tongue well away. One could not blame her, the bottom of a woman
like that could have been anywhere. I lay gazing at this scene dispassion-
ately. Am I getting old? It was a far cry from my adolescence at
Gordonstoun when in a fit of frustration I hopefully looked up 'Nipple'
in the dictionary: 'The small prominence in which the ducts of the
breast terminate externally in mammals. A short perforated piece made
upon, or screwed into, the breech of a muzzle-loading gun.' (Oh
shucks.)

Waiting for a bus is about as thrilling as fishing, with the similar tantal-
isation that something, sometime, somehow, will turn up. I have had to
queue in Elgin Street for twenty minutes for the Number 6 to take me
to the experimental farms which are on the outskirts of Ottawa; they
are open to the public.

The bus is almost empty but for a couple of adolescents near the
back and an old woman near the front. The woman has short-cut white
hair, is wearing trousers and carries a plastic bag on which are the words
'Alimentation et Cosmetiques'. It is the alimentation which interests
her. She and the driver are talking about doctors: she about hers; he, his
brother's. I have been trying to write down what they are saying but can
only hear bits of their conversation: '. . . sad when he went . . . never on
time . . . you should have seen his face . . . no, they're never on time . . .

"nothing to see," he said, but you could tell . . . "look at his colour," I said . . . my husband was getting too heavy for me (!?) . . . wound in the war . . . he expired . . . pinched his arm . . . crippled with it . . . nerve endings . . . I get that, too! All up one side . . . nervous twitch . . . you had to laugh . . .'

A hippie has boarded the bus. I have never seen anyone so hairy: he has a huge woolly beard and long hair flowing over his shoulders.

We are on our way again.

The hippie has just said to someone behind, in a rather nasty voice, 'Haven't you seen anyone like me before, then?' I wish he'd asked me. I would have said 'Not since I last dagged the arse of one of my sheep.' Perhaps I wouldn't, though; he may not know what dagging is and get the wrong idea. Then the laugh would be on me.

The driver has begun to talk about his 'great-ant'. She does not live in a hill with a lot of other ants, but in a house where she is visited by a doctor, one as useless and unsympathetic as his brother's.

The layout of the experimental and demonstration areas is attractive and tidy. Many of the buildings are in weather-boarding, painted a Scandinavian ox-blood red. There are flowerbeds and avenues, and an interesting display of different hedges. The strangest is of blue spruce. It is odd that there is no holly, privet or hawthorn; nor have different methods of laying or cutting been tried. The labels are frequently missing or broken. I am not very impressed with some of the livestock. The pigs are cramped in small cubicles. The cattle look bored. The tails have been completely docked off the sheep; in Britain we consider that to be both cruel and unhygienic. It also makes an animal which is reasonably pleasant to look at somewhat repulsive. One can forgive this anal exhibitionism in a pug-dog, but not in a sheep, whose image is to be woolly and sweet. Having scritched the head of a Suffolk blackface ewe I nostalgically sniffed my fingers to get the familiar sheepy smell and saw a fat girl staring at me in fastidious surprise. In one pigsty there was a small tabby cat leaning against the broad back of a large sow and languorously washing its knuckles. I saw a pair of nice little woodpeckers, black and white, the cock with a red patch on his nape. I think they were the downy woodpecker. They were in one of the trees of a particularly fine line of birch, a large, open-branched type with bark snowy-white right up to the tips of the branches. Long streamers of fine twigs hung, giving the effect of being in a rainstorm. A label said 'Betula pendula gracilis' but I think them more likely to be a form of *Betula papyrifera*.

The gardens are mainly of herbaceous borders. Their roses and peonies are not as good as mine; their lilies are better. I like the Japanese tree lilac (*Syringa reticulata*). It is an open-limbed small tree with thick, cone-shaped clusters of tiny white flowers which smell of privet. The leaves also resemble privet. Are lilac and privet related? There is a lilac hawk moth and a privet hawk moth, perhaps they separated into two species when the shrubs did.

Large terrapins were lounging in the reedy pools at the far end of the arboretum, their shiny carapaces made them look as if they were moulded from plastic. In the rushes there were several beautiful blackbirds, about the same size and colour as ours but with a scarlet patch on each shoulder: red-winged blackbirds.

I am sitting by a pavement table eating a bowlful of delicious mussels in a cream and cheese sauce and reading the *Daily Globe & Mail*. There are some problems with angry Red Indians. Where are the Sitting Bulls, Geronimos and Passing Clouds of yesteryear? The High Chief of the Akimiski Cree is Mr Matthew Come, the Chief of the Teme Augama Anishnabai is Gary Potts.

*7 **September**. A letter from the management of Great-Aunt Jo's old-folks-home. Reading between the lines of mealy-mouthed waffle, I gather that she is being expelled for insubordination and persistent disobedience.*

Great-Aunt Jo is my mother's closest living English relative. Mamma always liked to be thought French, but actually her father was an officer in the 3rd Hussars and she was born in Don John's Farm in Greenstead Green, the house where my brother Sam and family now live. Her parents split up when she was three and she moved to Paris with her foreign mother, whose origins are a bit obscure: Grandmère claimed to be the morganatic child of King Carol of Romania; Papa reckoned it more likely that she was the bastard brat of a Basque barber; I must admit that I have always had a sneaky hope that my great-grandfather was a king rather than a hair-dresser. So Mamma was brought up in Paris as a girl, and as an adolescent became a dancer in the Russian Ballet-in-exile, presided over by Princess Kchessinska. She moved back here when she married Papa, shortly after her 16th birthday.

Mamma, who considered herself a Parisienne, was always rather chagrined that her nearest living relation was so English: Great-Aunt Jo is brusque and sensible, she speaks in a sort of clipped bark rather like a fox terrier, she stands ramrod straight and is always dressed in drab and never wears any make-up; recently she has grown tufts of white hair on her face and down her neck. In spite of her age and hairiness her legs are long and elegant and have no blemish: it is perhaps ironic that Mamma inherited her ballet dancer's legs from the dull English rather than exotic Foreign side of her family.

Last month Great-Aunt Jo turned up at our doorstep. She had driven the 40 miles from her guest-house in Cambridge, and her car steamed in the courtyard behind her — a 1969 Morris Minor, a small, rotund car which busies about like a dung beetle.

'I will be 95 soon, and I will need your help,' she said, stepping into the hall, peeling off her beige gloves, unwinding her beige scarf, doffing her beige hat, shrugging off her beige overcoat, unbuttoning her beige cardigan and poising with surprising elegance on the edge of the scarlet leather chair beside the fire.

'Many people in their nineties are senile and cannot look after themselves. My eyes are getting dim, a doctor says that I must no longer drive my car. I am getting deaf. People are beginning to irritate me for no reason except for having silly faces and boring voices. It is probable that I will start to get disgustingly messy when I eat. It is possible that I may become incontinent. It is therefore time that I find a suitable resting-place before the grave where I can be looked after. I do not want to be bossed around or fussed over until it is necessary. I want a decent bit of privacy, particularly my own bathroom and lavatory. I want a large garden to walk in, and shops to walk to. I am not fussy about food unless it is smothered with garlic or those greasy foreign sauces. I cannot afford much. I have a list of some places nearby which I think may be suitable. You will come with me and inspect them.'

We visited five places, all of which I found thoroughly depressing; Great-Aunt Jo finally chose one of them, but seemed pretty morose about it.

So today I have to telephone her: she is indignant, defiant and enraged. I will come to pick her up on Saturday and take her to a place in Suffolk which she has heard about and thinks tolerable. She has already booked a place in it.

*

9 September. We go with the Land Rover and trailer to move Great-Aunt Jo. She is posed on her suitcases in the hall, sitting bolt upright, looking sulky. Dominie and I load the possessions of 90 years into the trailer: three suitcases, a tea-chest of crockery, another of books, a good chest of drawers, a favourite old chair, a hideous Edwardian grandfather clock with a secret drawer, some pictures. We drive off to scowls all round.

The new place looks dank and drear to me, and I think Great-Aunt Jo thinks so too, for she falls silent and her eyes have that faraway look that children have when they are opting out of something unpleasant. However the welcoming committee seems pleasant enough; they bustle around her and show us about and help us move things into the large, airy room, and arrange them. Great-Aunt Jo stands aloof from all the to-do, and as we drive away we agree that we soon will be repacking the trailer. [She died two years later, after three more moves.]

11 **September.** As usual, when in Paris, I am staying with my old friend Eléanore, in her penthouse flat in Avenue Gabriel. Her drawing-room has four huge windows which must have one of the best views in Paris. As I lean out, I can see, directly below, the round, bushy tops of the chestnut trees which screen us from the Champs Elysées. The colour of Paris is grey: not the cold grey of flints or gunmetal or of the frigid Nordic Seas; it is a warm grey, with a touch of blue in it, like a pigeon's wing. To us English it is surprising that Paris, like London, is a northern city, so that now, in September, the skies are clouded, but amid the muted veils and billows there are still patches of blue here and there and these tints merge to be reflected as a gleam on the roofs that are slated with scales like the flanks of herring or grey mullet. From where I am standing, to either side, there are rows of lead-capped window gables, like nun's cowls and wimples; below are the stone greys of the flags and cobbles that lead under the arch of the old main entrance into the carriage yard.

It is dusk, suddenly the city lighting is turned on. Almost in front, the great curved glass roof of the Grand Palais glows with inner light, its exterior is lit in mauve (the French have flashes of appalling taste); its statues are spot-lit and typically Continental, the horses rearing, the riders either pointing imperiously at the lesser mortals beneath them or blowing trumpets. Further off, I see the spires of Notre Dame; on the other side, to the right, the fretwork fantasy of the Eiffel Tower glows against the twilit sky, its laser beams twiddle long restless fingers over the roofscape.

Eléanore has had a pig stuffed. It lies on its side and is so shaped that you can sit on it, rest your feet on it, or just meet its eyes as you look up from a book.

There are seven people staying here tonight: as well as Eléanore and her daughter Adélaide (who is looking almost as pretty as her mother did when she and I were young), there is me, a Hong Kong Chinese, a Spaniard, a Bulgarian, an Englishman and a monkey. Eléanore has given us dinner, made up a bed for me in the drawing-room and has gone to bed with the monkey.

The monkey was a waif which Eléanore found in her last journey through the Sahara to Togo. No-one liked it, so Eléanore brought it home. It is tiny, about the size of a cat, and wears a pink cardigan and a crocheted skirt which converts it into a miniature replica of Sophy, my parents' old cook. It has nerves, and chitters if you look at it; it has bitten my outstretched fingers several times, not hard enough to draw blood but hard enough to indicate it doesn't like me.

In the same way that she collects unwanted monkeys so Eléanore collects people. The Hong Kong Chinese is young and futile; pudgy, with his hair done up in a glossy black pony-tail; his natural air of Oriental melancholy is reinforced by his complete inability to learn French, the reason he came here two years ago. He told me that he is a waiter but after a bit of questioning it became obvious that he is merely a scullion so I tactfully changed the subject. The Spaniard is an out-of-work photographer; tall and thin with a tiny white sharp-featured face beneath a huge fluffy explosion of black hair. Whilst he is learning to photograph he earns his living by lugging round the equipment of other photographers; arranging the tripods, putting up the cameras, setting up reflective screens and backdrops. The pay is so measly that he will never be able to afford to become a professional, he says, but doesn't seem to mind.

The Bulgarian has a wild and woolly beard and a face, in repose, of sullen savagery and, in animation, of almost Falstaffian merriment and charm – not now, for today he is quarrelsome. He sits glowering whilst Eléanore and I chatter and he suddenly says: 'The British have had it. They are passé. They are of no consequence any more.' As we are discussing the theory that cheese becomes more tasteless the further north it is made, I am taken aback by this irrelevant and tetchy intrusion, but with irritating (I hope) blandness I say: 'True. It's someone else's turn. Every dog has its day. Perhaps it will be your turn soon, though personally I think it will be the Turks.'

'You should not belong to the Common Market, you can contribute nothing to it.'

'True again,' I say in oily agreement. 'Few Englishmen want to be in the Common Market. It's bad enough that our next Prime Minister may be a Welsh socialist, how much worse is the possibility of a dishonest Greek, an incompetent Italian, a devious Frenchman or a despotic German. The worst thing that has ever happened to us is the digging of the Channel tunnel.'

He chews his beard with irritation.

I carry on being witty and charming. The aggressive fellow gets more and more annoyed. He suddenly says: 'How true is the French saying that the women in your country have very large teeth and very small breasts?'

'About as true as the saying that the women in your country have very short legs and very long moustaches,' I reply.

He gobbles a bit, and then Eléanore says to me, in the way that women like to stir things up: 'He was being rude about Tante Claudine.'

I try to simmer things down: 'Mamma was really French at heart, although she was born in Greenstead Green.'

'Baby Jesus was born in a stable, that does not make him a cow,' persists Eléanore with complete irrelevance.

However the Bulgarian, irked either by my witty repartee or Eléanore's sudden antagonism, rises to his feet and heads for his room, muttering into his beard.

*14 **September.** John Seedwell of Parleybien Farm is giving up farming and emigrating to the coast. I went to his sale this morning. It was a sad occasion: 'When I* *moved into the house 35 years ago I thought to myself "that's a nice staircase, wide enough to carry my coffin down when the time comes." We'll miss the village too, and all our friends. Still Mersea Island's only fifteen miles off.'*

I always get rather steamed up before I bid. So to get my hand in, and because it coud be useful for the garden, I bid for a ball of old-fashioned binder twine, made of hemp rather than plastic. I got it for £5. I then managed to buy what I came for, a ten-ton grain trailer. On impulse I also bought an old canvas-topped waggon, once used by the railways but converted to a sheep trailer.

There were a lot of old boys there, farmers and yeomen, with good proper square Essex faces and proper Essex accents, all in corduroys and rubber boots and holding themselves up with ash or blackthorn sticks. I knew a few, but many I didn't. I was surprised at this, telling Dominie later that I would surely have seen them in Halstead High Street, if nowhere else, but she said that sort of old boy wouldn't be seen dead with a shopping-bag.

We went to a cocktail party in the evening.

Captain Firecrest and I were chatting up a newcomer's attractive wife. The Captain, whilst jesting and munching on a 'bijou' vol-au-vent at the same time spat a huge gobbet of it on the lapel of her blouse. She did not notice, having flung her head back prettily to laugh at his joke. It stuck there messily. To old Firecrest and me it was as big as a custard pie. Suddenly, whilst looking down for the peanuts, she saw it; she froze in horror. The Captain and I looked away: casually, guiltily. Out of the corner of my eye I saw her whip it off with her finger and as quick as a flash pop it into her mouth and swallow. I noticed old Firecrest's appalled expression and snorted a half-chewed olive clean through one nostril. It was the woman's turn to be revolted.

21 September, Vienna. This is our base for distributing bags to some of the East European communist capitals such as Budapest, Bucharest, Belgrade, Sofia and Prague.

I like Vienna, but I am getting too used to it. It is a pleasant city, with many pedestrian-only streets lined with expensive shops and orna-mented with fountains and statues and abustle with buskers, shoppers and tourists. But it seems strangely frozen in time. The Habsburgs are still everywhere: Francis Joseph's portraits are depicted on postcards, statues of Emperors pose on pedestals in magnificent Baroque surroundings, the huge royal quarters make Buckingham Palace resemble a suburban bungalow: it reminds one how small England is and how trifling to much of Europe's history. The Strausses dominate the airwaves, they can over-sweeten the senses: one lands to the strains of the *Blue Danube*, the hotel megaphone drools the waltz from *Der Rosenkavalier*, the fiddles of the buskers tweedle away with selections from *Die Frau ohne Schatten* and at departure the aeroplane intercom seeps out the *Skater's Waltz*. People strut about wearing coats or capes in heavy green wool, upon their heads are pork-pie hats adorned with feathers or tufts of bristle. In Olde Teutonic Taverns lavish helpings of excellent food and drink are served by buxom maidens with laced-up bosoms and rubicund fellows in leather shorts. The opera here is very fine, but I am not very musical so have not taken advantage of it; anyhow, it seems a bit melancholy to go alone. Nor have I seen the famous Lippizaner horses; the sight of tame animals prancing and mincing about fills me with utter boredom. On the other hand, it is very pleasant in the evenings, when the work is done, to visit one of the out-of-town villages which specialise in parish-produced wine and food.

Today I revisited the Kunsthistorisches Museum. This was established by Maria Theresa in 1781. It includes most of the Habsburg collections, much of these being artefacts gleaned from the Empire, and swag looted from the Jesuit Order after its suppression by Maria T.

I first went to inspect my favourite coffin, the great granite sarcophagus of Nes-schu-tefnut. They have up-ended the lid to reveal the carvings underneath: how magic to lie for eternity under that beautiful nude goddess outstretching her arms over one's body, surrounded by stars, and with the lovely Isis kneeling with half-opened wings at one's head.

Nearby were some pre-dynastic pots: it is poignant seeing little dents on them made by fingertips which have been dust or bones for thousands of years.

The Habsburgs were a remarkably hideous gang, if their busts and portraits are accurate: that extraordinarily protuberant lower lip; the gormless, goggling eyes; the Spanish royal family with stupidity and vanity apparently dominant as facial traits, particularly on the poor half-wit, Prince Don Carlos, whose afflictions include an uneasy, furrowed brow, hunched shoulders, a wry neck and pigeon toes. It seems as if God had designed them to be caricatures. Nevertheless, if I'd been any of the monarchs who had been thus portrayed, I'd have lopped the artists' heads off.

My hero Joseph II looks all right, but a bit feminine, rather like V**** I knew for a time at Cambridge, she with the aloof features and hooded eyes and pert lips.

There is a bust of Marie Antoinette, her neck is long and slender.

The English are barely represented: a couple of Holbeins, one of Jane Seymour, shamingly plain with her whey face and pinched mouth, another of Dr John Chambers, toothless; a balloon-faced man by Joseph Wright of Derby and a small fuzzy view of Suffolk by Gainsborough.

It is pleasant to experience the occasional shock of recognition: there is Tintoretto's *Susanna and the Elders*! There the *Tower of Babel* by Peter Bruegel the Elder! There is Caravaggio's *Madonna of the Rosary*! And here the Cellini Salt (which seemed better in photographs, in black and white, I had not realised that much of it is enamelled, rather garishly and seemingly rather carelessly, with the daubs of colour sloshed on).

Next, I went to the crypt where many of the Habsburgs are buried. One descends a flight of steps, the carpeting, walling and frosted light-shades being reminiscent of the décor of an Edwardian cinema. The crypt has a clammy mustiness which suddenly reminds me of the crypt of Christ Church, Spitalfields. The coffins are grotesque, hybrids between vast bronze baths and prehistoric tortoises, all limpeted and encrusted with Royalty and Angels, frozen to stillness as if they'd caught the eyes of Medusa. Many of the tombs depict skulls wearing the Imperial crowns, a macabre bit of silliness.

In the evening I spent most of the time sketching out the basics of a play I am thinking of writing. It is in praise of chaos, with the theme that if there was not a bit of uncertainty, if God knew what exactly was going to happen in the future, He would go mad with boredom.

23 September. In the afternoon we went over the valley for the wedding of my niece Melissa to James Jones in Greenstead Green church. She looked very sweet and happy. Sam had spruced up the garden at Don John's farm to an immaculate degree, Annette had organised beautiful flowers and buntings in the marquee. Finch-Hatton as Godfather made a very good speech. The best of all parties: a multitude of friends and relations.

24 September. *Dominie has had to rush off to her mother, who is apparently very ill, so I have to deal with our ten house guests and also the pony people who came to Sunday lunch. Eighty came, the pony club had only catered for fifty. God, what a day. It makes me realise how much Dominie does. I'm not so sure if I'm that keen on chaos any more.*

25 September. *A strange day: George and Fiona announce their engagement; the doctor has told Dominie that her mother is fatally ill. She has cancer of the liver and has less than a year to live.*

3 October. This is one of the isles of legend, the island of the dodo, Mauritius, so perhaps it is not surprising that the scenery looks unearthly, almost Martian: rising sharply out of the undulating plains are weird volcanic peaks, some of them are pinnacles, almost as fine as church spires, others are angular blocks with massive, sheer perpendicular edges, like the bows of vast ships. The peaks are sometimes arranged in groups and sometimes stand as individuals; in either case they resemble distorted chess-pieces which have been plonked casually onto a chess-board of green. The plains are covered with the tall fronds of sugar cane, there are many fruit trees including mango, banana, avocado pear and paw-paw.

The locals call the island 'Maurice', which rather squelches the exotic mystique.

My hotel is pleasant, everything thatched: the central, barn-like main building, the dining-verandah, the little chalets which stretch along the beach; even the parasols on the snowy white sand are roofed with palm fronds. I have arrived as the sun is setting in a magnificent purply, plum-coloured glow.

*

4 October. It is early spring here, so perhaps that is why the water is not as warm as I expected, about 76°F, but I'm not cold, even though I have been swimming for about three hours, for the sun has shone the whole time. This island is almost completely surrounded by coral reef; the water within the lagoon is fairly shallow, ranging from one to two fathoms at this section. Close inland there has been much destruction of the coral, human pollution I suppose; but further out, towards the reef, the coral grows freely and there are many fishes. Strangely, none of the people in the hotel have been swimming in the sea, the few that bathe do so in the hotel swimming-pool. They might as well have stayed at home to puddle about in the public pissoires of Pudsey, Putney or Pietersburg. Perhaps they know something that I don't. Anyhow, they are all out of sight now, a mild current has taken me a mile or so down the coast.

There's an odd fish, box-shaped, with its dark skin speckled with vivid turquoise spots; a lovely shell, conical, white with spirals of choco-late-brown rectangles (*Conus abraeus*, probably). I'll swim down and see if it is empty, some of the inhabitants of these shells have a lethal sting. Pity I didn't pack my flippers, it's difficult to swim down the eight feet to where it is lying, but flippers take up so much room in my bag and I try to keep to one piece of luggage. The shell's empty – got it – put it in the pocket of my bathing-trunks. The coral here is even more profuse: the stag's horn, mostly, but plenty of the round types that look like brains and the ones whose flat tops branch out into horizontal plates like cedar trees.

Strange that there is absolutely no-one else in this paradise, even if it is quite a long way from the shore.

I'm alongside the reef now, waves are breaking over it.

Christ, oh Christ, I'm being dragged towards it by the current! Swim towards the island. Swim, swim, SWIM! No good. God I'm now being swept over the reef. I'm dead if I get to the other side, the Indian Ocean is full of sharks. Just grab anything and keep the mask and tube on. God the waves are rolling me over and over – the mask and tube have slipped down round my neck – I'm choking in water – I'm going to drown – how stupid of me – the water hurts in my nose – JUST GRAB ANY-

THING. Got it, hold breath, my head's out of water, retch out water, take in huge breath, pant in more; the water is only about a foot deep over this part of the reef now the waves have ebbed back. Don't panic, think. I must quickly get on my mask and tube before the next wave sweeps over me – quick oh quick – thank God they went round my neck and weren't torn off. Done it, the waves are now coming in, hang on tight, hold breath and look to see what the surface of the reef looks like.

The waves are over me, but not budging me, I'm hanging on like a limpet. It's a large lump of brain coral. There are lots of such lumps of coral, but hundreds of very long-spined sea-urchins. The waves are trying to push me back over which is good but when they ebb back then they will try to drag me with them. They're ebbing now, the water above my head is getting shallower, shallower, the end of my tube is out, blow hard through it to clear, pant in air.

Think. Look up. No-one in sight, no swimmers, no boats; the beach is too far to see anyone, or anyone to see me. It's all up to me.

The waves are sweeping back. God, I've choked in some water. Don't panic, hold your breath and try not to be sick. Interesting, I'm almost talking to myself as if I was a friendly schoolmaster talking to a pupil. I needn't drown as long as I keep the mask and tube, so that's my main priority; the next is not to be swept completely over the reef. Think. You can't hang on here for ever, at least try to get to the island-side of the reef, further away from this terrifying ocean and where people will be more likely to see me.

Now, I must wait until the incoming waves are pushing me in the right direction, then clamber from coral to coral with their current, hand over hand. My head will be under the surface so I will be able to plot a route avoiding the sea-urchins.

The next wave is coming, take in plenty of air, don't try to go too far, there is a good solid-looking lump of coral about six feet away. The wave is over me, I'm being pushed forward, let go of the precious knob which probably saved my live. Going forward, grab that small lump with left hand, now the other with my right, now grab the big one with both hands. The waves are ebbing, hang on; good.

Next wave forward, do nothing this time, just look under and plan a route for the next bound forward. There's another good-looking bit of brain coral to the front left, but it's surrounded by sea-urchins, I'll try the one more to the right, but it is a bit further away. Got it.

Next wave forward, plan next clamber-and-grab. What about that large bit of elk's horn coral sticking up right in front? Hang on whilst the waves ebb, now they're coming back, release, clamber forward, grab the elk's horn, waves ebbing . . .

GOD, THE CORAL'S SNAPPED, I'm being dragged back towards the ocean, hang on – can't see – too much foam – bite hard on mouthpiece – GRAB – GRAB! But the sea-urchins. To hell with that – GRAB! GOT IT.

Hang on and pant. God, this is getting depressing. 'Be a British boy.' Look around. I'm hanging on to a barnacle-encrusted lump. I'm now right on the very outer edge of the reef. Look back. Oh God, a vertiginous drop beneath my feet, mile after mile of darkening blue to black to the depths of the Indian Ocean. The sun's rays like great bars dwindling down to eternity below. I must move, a shark may be looking up now, it will see my feet, they look huge and white and already dead. I was very lucky to grab this lump. Thank you God. No mistakes this time, one error and I've had it.

Plan. First that sturdy-looking lump just three feet in front, then that larger one four feet further, then I think there is a good bit of brain coral further on and then I think I can see the lump I was originally holding on to.

No problems this time, but it must have taken me about twenty minutes to plan and pick my way to the inland side of the reef. Now I am hanging on a strong ledge which is overlapping the still waters of the lagoon. There is an area of snowy white sand below me; about 30 feet away there is a pinnacle of coral rising from it. I wonder if I can make it. If I swim along the bottom there should be less current there. I'll try. Plan, think. If I fail I must turn and make for this ledge again. Fill up with oxygen. Gulp in a lot of air to bursting point. The waves are coming towards me – almost here – right – let go. Down to the bottom, kick, kick, kick, arms sweeping wide, hands cupped, the pinnacle is nearer, nearer . . . I'm running out of air, no you're not, it's just mild panic. Kick, kick kick, here it is, covered with those bloody urchins; float up, grab a bit near the top, head out of the water, pant . . . The waves are ebbing, I can't feel any current but better not take any risk, when they come next I'll do the crawl straight as an arrow towards the island. Pant, pant, pant, NOW! Legs threshing, arms windmilling, I'm another chain or so out from the reef, it should be safe now, lie in the water and pant, yes I'm not moving, I'm safe.

Thank You God, sorry Dominie, most careless and foolish.

Now to swim back to the beach.

Hello, that's a lovely fish. I wonder if I can pick up that pretty shell.

It has taken me about half an hour to swim back to the beach, then I have had to walk a couple of miles along it to get back to the hotel. Most of the women are sun-bathing round the pool, many of the men are sitting on the stools round the thatched rondavel of the bar, a few children are paddling. Heavens, that woman is fat! She has peeled down the top half of her bathing-suit so that her back gets sun-tanned; now that she wants to sit up her man is trying to pull the bathing-suit up again, he is covered with sweat and panting. He'd find it easier to put the skin back on a sausage.

'I'll have the flying-fish and chips please.'

5 October. I have been woken early by the pain of sunburn, all the way from my nape to my calves; my back in the bathroom mirrors looks like a piece of raw liver. My fault, I usually wear pyjama tops or a shirt when I am swimming in the tropics, but I didn't yesterday as I had not planned spending nearly six hours in the sun. Still, it has resulted in a very enjoyable early breakfast, with hardly anyone about. It was on the open verandah overlooking the beach; I shared my marmalade with a pair of red-vented bulbuls, clown-like birds with crests like pointed hats, red ear patches and red underpants.

It is hot and dusty on this road. The sea to my left looks cool, it is turquoise and the beach is a dazzling white, but my sunburn would sting in the salt water. I shall explore instead.

The road has small shack-like bungalows along it, often with granny and the mutt dozing together in the shade of the verandah. There is a grove of Casuarina trees. Families are sitting in groups amid the trunks talking and picnicking. Most of them look Indian. They are friendly and cheerful. Here is a little graveyard to the landward side of the road, I shall wander around it.

It is overgrown with scrub, wiry grass and bushes. Lizards sun-bathe on the gravestones which are mostly made of coral, all the names have been eroded away; how sad and forlorn; some look as if they were impressive once, family tombs of families which are no more, or have no interest in their past. Much litter about: cigarette packets, plastic bottles, a pile of burnt tins and a heap of coconut husks, mynah birds argue and scrap and peck amongst it; a stink of human ordure. Litter in a hot country is vastly fouler than in a cold one. What a pretty flower, like a small, maroon sweet pea; it is from a creeper which twines on a bush that shades a crumbled gravestone.

I follow a track which goes inland, towards the mountains. It becomes shrubby; squat palms, thorns with mimosa-like leaves and powder-puff flowers, cactuses, occasionally tallish, angular trees. There are bulbs about in the coral-grit soil from which sprout scarlet flowers.

I've come upon a small, shallow brook. It is running quite fast and the water looks clear between the flowing beards of weed and low clumps of growth. The shallows on the other side are busy with birds drinking and pecking about and arguing; flitting from the sanctuary of a thick, glossy-leaved bush to the bending stems of reed and rush. The birds do not seem worried about me, there are plenty of scarlet ones, some brilliant yellow oriole-types with thickish black beaks and black throats, a sweet little couple which sit side by side and kiss, they have a scarlet eye-patch-and-streak, there are red-vented bulbuls, some mynahs and small, elegant brown doves. The dodo was a dove, how spellbinding it would be to see its fat bolster-shaped body plod from the shade of the bushes, hooting mournfully. A very rare member of the dove species still lives here: the pink pigeon. Two nests like little baskets hang from the thin tips of palm leaves, they swing and bobble about in the breeze; it must be unpleasant to be inside. A small hawk suddenly streaks overhead. The Mauritius kestrel! It was once the rarest bird in the world: there were only four left a few years ago, but the banning of DDT has increased their numbers to about 200.

*

7 October. *I allow a few people to go metal detecting on the estate. My rules stipulate that any important find be told to me at once, so we can get proper archaeologists to do any excavations necessary, and that we share 50/50 on any sale or reward. One of the metal detectorers came round and showed me what he had discovered over the last couple of months. He has been much more successful than I have been: all I found were bits of plough, the metal ends of shot-gun cartridges and many iron crescents which turned out not to be ponies' horse-shoes, as I had thought, but the heel-plates off farm labourers' boots. But his machine is much better than mine. It had found several bullets fired from aeroplanes during the Battle of Britain, a handful of musket balls, ranging in size from the goosegog to the pea, nearly a double handful of sheep bells — round ones with a dumbbell-shaped aperture (exactly the same design as some I bought in Turkey), buttons and badges, many coins, mostly within the last two centuries but one very corroded one that may be Roman; most interesting was a horses' ornament in the shape of a shield. It is about three inches high and has a broken hanging loop at the top. Intriguingly one can just discern the faint traces of three gold leopards. Those leopards were the English arms for a very limited period, and by deduction his Metal Detectors' Club concluded that the horse must have belonged to the Earl of Oxford, Aubrey de Vere, who lived locally in Castle Hedingham in the 14th century. On the other end of the social scale he had found many thimbles, mostly small, some tiny. They had been worn by stone pickers. Our Parish History says that the casual family work on the local farms was 'The Four Pickings': Stones, Peas, Potatoes and Acorns. In Edwardian times payment for a cart-load of stones (18 bushels) was two shillings. They were used for road repairs.*

12 October, Tel Aviv. The waitress in the hotel restaurant recognises my name. 'My father worked for Courtaulds in Skelmersdale!' she exclaims.

She has lived in Israel for twelve years.

'Why did you move here?'

She gives me a slightly nasty look: 'Had to, didn't we, after you shut the mill and sacked Dad.'

'Um, yup. What do you miss most about England?'

She looks wistful. 'Oh the rain, the lovely rain!' she sighs.

I scrutinise the menu. 'What is a "Traditional Gefilte Fish"?'

'Sort of carp, mushed up into a rissole – eyeballs, bones and all; it then has sugar added. Ours has a sort of jelly with it.'

'What's it like?'

'Horrible.'

'Have you any other interesting traditional Jewish food?'

'Well, there's our "Hot Favourite", the "Cholent with Kishka".'

'What is it?'

'Dunno, never tried it, but it looks a bit funny. Bits and pieces. All over the plate.'

At heart, the waitress is still a True Brit.

13 October. My driver from Tel Aviv to Jerusalem is a Christian Arab, Zosimus. He has the angry blue eyes of his crusader ancestors and the dark, wavy hair of the girls they raped. As we drive into Jerusalem we see many strict orthodox Jews looking hot in their East European-type black suits and overcoats. Zosimus says that the angle at which their hats are tilted depends on which rabbi they follow. Some wear their trouser bottoms tucked into their socks at the ankles; they have a strong antipathy against followers of another rabbi who wear their trousers tucked in at the knee, knickerbockers rather than plus-fours. 'If they can't argue with their neighbours, they will argue with each other,' Zosimus says.

Zosimus is now moaning about the price of beef: '45 shekels a kilo,' he grizzles, 'that is because the rabbis have to go to the Argentine, to see if the cattle are all kosher killed, and we have to pay for the cost of their aeroplanes and big cars and girls.'

We reach Jerusalem and I deliver the bag and am told to report back in six hours.

Zosimus and I agree that it is not often that we take a fancy to army sergeants, particularly when they are two metres tall and pointing a light machine gun in our direction. This soldier's face, above the crumpled khaki collar, is very dark, but not dark enough to obscure the exquisitely beautiful features: huge, brown eyes that ox-eyed Juno would have envied, and lips curved like the bridge to Paradise. 'She is from Sheba,' says my companion, 'he chose well, their King Solomon.' Praise indeed from Zosimus, who rarely has a good word for anyone.

'Just because we say she is beautiful, it does not mean we wish to be unfaithful to our wives,' he adds, primly.

'In the same way that though she is a soldier, we don't want to go into the army again,' I agree.

There has been some 'trouble' recently, nothing unusual, a woman and a child killed, and the soldiers by the Jaffa gate which leads into the Old City of Jerusalem are jumpy and officious. Now, within the ramparts, all seems at peace – but not peaceful, for as I take a small manual out of my pocket I am plagued by a dozen guides, attracted to me like wasps towards a honeypot. Zosimus hates Jew, Muslim and Christians of other sects with biblical zeal, and he sends them on their ways with the curses of three faiths.

We are now walking down the Street of Chains, a narrow alley, typical of the City: about five paces wide, steep, stepped, flagged with rectangular ashlar blocks which have been polished to a slippery sheen by sandal and slipper; awnings and gables meet almost overhead, caged birds twitter above the babble of trader and tourist bargaining to either side in the little open shops. The wares of the spice merchants waft scents which percolate throughout: of saffron, cinnamon, paprika, zator (for bread, Zosimus tells me), cardamine (to put into your coffee), sommak (to cook with chicken). There are many booths selling rugs and carpets, from the Arab shops they are likely to smell of wool, from the Jewish or Christian ones, of rayon. In other booths there are bags and scarves and leather jackets; or jewellery and watches; mementoes such as terracotta 'Roman' lamps, brass Arabic coffee sets and backgammon boards inlaid with bone and mother-of-pearl. Here is a fruitier with dates, apples and bananas; there is a confectioner with nougat, Turkish delight and jelly beans. Religious souvenirs are crammed together with commercial impartiality – icons, crucifixes, rosaries, tableaux of the Last Supper or of cribs carved from olive wood, Jewish menorahs, Arab charms and worry beads, a sweetly feminine prayer printed on a tea-cloth starting 'Oh Lord, I thank you for my little kitchen . . .' Amidst hubble-bubbles and packets of cigarettes, there are kaftans, blouses, djellabas, and T-shirts with printed slogans: 'HOLY ROCK' or 'SHALOM Y'ALL' or 'REAL SUCCESS IS GETTING TO HEAVEN'.

We turn up Muristan Road towards the Temple of the Holy Sepulchre and arrive at the centre of Christendom.

In AD 326 the site was identified as the place of Golgotha by Queen Helena (a good Essex girl, born and bred in Colchester – or so we aver, we in the river valley from Steeple Bumpstead to Colne Point). Her dutiful son, the Emperor Constantine the Great, erected the first church, which was soon refined into a large rotunda. The Roman design was elaborated by the crusaders who rebuilt on the site, but over the years a lot has been destroyed, a lot added.

It is a busy place: once St Helena had identified the area as Golgotha she got the bit between her teeth. On this small plot contained by the church one can see many places associated with the final hours of the earth-bound Christ, including the last six of the fourteen Stations of the Cross: from Station IX, 'Condemnation' (where Christ was convicted by Pilate) to Station XIV, the Holy Sepulchre itself. The whole complex is run by an uneasy confederation of the Greek Orthodox, the Syrian Orthodox, Copts, Armenians, Roman Catholics and Ethiopians. The last-mentioned have been squeezed out so that they now live on the roof and tend just a small area, a rock-hewn cell which is reputed to be the tomb of Joseph of Arimathaea. The resulting effect is a fascinating disarray, but cosy rather than imposing: a scruffy shambles full of tawdry adornment.

The entrance portal has two doors, one of which was temporarily bricked up about 800 years ago and has remained thus ever since. The pillars and wall are covered with graffiti; one can understand and forgive the hundreds of tiny crosses, but not 'NED' or 'LIZA' or 'TONI' or 'FRANCESCA'. Within the porch someone has stacked half a dozen life-size crucifixes. We notice that one has drawing-pins stuck where the hands and feet would have been nailed. Zosimus is indignant at the bathos of it. We enter the dark gloom of the Place of Mourning and see the stone pillars of the Rotunda before us and a muddle of arches, shrines and side chapels all about. You would expect a building of such a history to be such a hodge-podge. But you would not expect the most important place in Christianity to be paved with cracked flagstones; to have pitted and mildewed walls; to have scaffolding everywhere, obscuring roof and walls, blocking out the light, and covered with dust;

to have pictures black with old varnish, warped, wrinkled and scabby with flaked-off paint; to have the linens of the altars protected by plastic panels in imitation wood; to have much of the building unused, side chapels lying silent and unlit and dank and empty. In one, we see a stack of pews, in another, building-blocks. I particularly like a tiny side room: small and barrel-vaulted, with pillars, and three shrines at one end. It is supposed to be the prison in which Christ was confined after his arrest in Gethsemane. Of its shrines, one has a candle burning in it, too dim to illuminate the shadowy picture within; the others have iron grates drawn across them, and are padlocked. Judging by the stink, the Tomb of Joseph of Arimathaea is dark and isolated enough for its surreptitious use as a pissoir.

For a millennium and a half the artistic geniuses of Christendom have produced works of art in praise of God: you would expect at least one Michelangelo saint, a Virgin by Leonardo, a gold and silver crucifix wrought by Cellini or a font hewn by Henry Moore. Instead, there is the artistic equivalent of Walt Disney: simplistic daubs of worthies, posed like ham actors, staring goggle-eyed at blobs of heavenly light; iconic saints whose features are either smug or vapid; clutters of gimcrack altar ornaments; festoons of lanterns reminiscent of a discotheque.

In the tiny Coptic chapel a monk sits by the offering-plate, his spectacles glittering avariciously in the gloom like the eyes of a starving spider.

The place is swarming with people as it has been for generations. And why not? But gone is the devout awe of the past. The Tower of Babel has spewed its denizens: Dutch is gabbled, Spanish lisped, Russian burbled, French minced, English sibilated, Hungarian moaned, German chuntered, Arabic hawked, American twanged, Cantonese whined, Japanese yakked. The camera has taken place of the pulpit or lectern or chalice: people pose in demure obedience, in lines, like communicants. A man in an anorak turns his back to the Altar of the Crucifixion and spreading out his arms in imitation of the figure of Christ behind him smiles shyly into his wife's camera. He'd smile even shyer if he knew what I think of him. A woman prays in the Chapel of Adam. A photographer sears her eyes with his flash; he reckons she's a bit unusual, a bit quaint, being on her knees, staring up at a God he cannot see.

The tomb of Christ is now just a stone shelf where His body once lay. More evocative, to Zosimus and me, is Station XII, the hole left by the post of the cross. But, somehow, I had pictured the place as the gaunt crest of a windswept tor, not a silver-rimmed pockmark in a murky recess below an altar.

Zosimus genuflects and crosses himself at the altar of the Sorrowful Madonna. I give a sheepishly curt English nod, and we quit for the sunlight and the traders and the soldiers.

My map shows an obscure building down a narrow valley: 'What is the Monastery of the Holy Cross like?' I ask. Zosimus shakes his head and says he's never heard of it, but when I show him the map he says that he thinks it is a 'prison for bad monks'.

We see it below us, but have to drive in ever-decreasing circles, and up obscure mule tracks, until it is nearby. From afar it looks like a great craggy block of stone; nearer, one can see it is heavily buttressed, with a few small barred windows but no discernible door. From the centre, out of place in the crude, fortress-like setting, rises a graceful belfry.

I leave the car, with Zosimus reading the sports section of the *Jerusalem Post*, and stumble across an arid patch of wasteland to the monastery wall. Having been taught that it is unlucky to walk widdershins round a religious building, I stumble clockwise round the rock-strewn path which surrounds the walls and finally, almost where I started, find a tiny door hidden by a buttress. I have to crouch low as I enter, it is only about four and a half feet high. There is a small, many-cornered courtyard within, dappled by the shade of an old tree. Everything is slightly miniature, as if it has been built by a troop of dwarfs.

A sign says:

NO ANIMALS
NO WOMEN
NO LITTER
No ShORTs
Guide books & souvenirs →

The 'No ShORTs' has been put in a different coloured paint, obviously as an afterthought.

I follow the arrow which points to a door, enter, and find myself in a stone cell. There is a trestle table, on it are some postcards and booklets, behind it is a small, smiling man who seems astonished and delighted to see me. 'Come in, my dear,' he cries.

I look at him suspiciously. 'Is he "one of them"?' I wonder.

'Are you open to the public?' I ask.

'My dear, my dear one, we have been open for three years. You are the fourth person I have seen.' He prods the heap of guidebooks with a nicotine-stained finger. 'The Blessed Patriarch says that to keep open I must sell thousands of these. I have sold two, my dear.'

'Well, here's another customer,' I say cheerfully.

He shakes his head. 'No my dear, perhaps not. Are you from an Embassy?'

'Well, temporarily, I'm with the British Embassy.'

'I knew it, my dear. All diplomats have our guidebooks free.'

In no way will he accept payment for the guidebook, so I buy too many postcards instead.

It is an enchanting place of utter peace, even the tree seems to doze in the sun and the angled walls lean against each other in lethargy; my busy shadow blobbing over the flags and cobbles seems an agitated intruder.

I climb a flight of steps and am confronted by a complex roofscape of different levels of paved yards, flights of stairs, walls, a large dome and the belfry. In one of the yards there is a washing-line; the vividly coloured clothes-pegs hold no washing. I descend and enter a side room. It must be the refectory. It is long and cool, whitewashed, with a barrel-vaulted ceiling and wide arched windows. There are three long marble tables, the tops being of inlaid sheets of diamond-shaped white marble with a framing of pink marble. This material is also used as a hanging frieze which is carved into arches. Each arch is the shape and size and position to take a man's knees as he sits to eat; if this is the intention the tables would take 62 diners.

I have now entered the main body of the church, 'a three-aisled basilica with a central dome'. The guidebook also says it was built in the

Byzantine style about the year AD 600. It is open and airy, the large dome being supported by square-sectioned pillars. Upon each side of these a saint or worthy has been painted larger-than-life. The saints have lovely names. Although several centuries old, many of them look like people I know:

St Romanus the Melodist resembles old Alf Reynolds who worked
  on the farm when I was a boy;
St Eluetherios resembles my foster-brother Gregory de Polnay
  when he grew a beard to act in *King Lear*;
St Athanasius the Athonite resembles the man with the huge white
  beard who owns the junk shop in Harare;
St Isidore the Pelousite is exactly like Lord Dundreary;
St John the Forerunner resembles the man who has a knick-knack
  stall in Halstead market (he almost sold me a stuffed albino mole
  in a glass case, but Dominie disliked it);
St Pachomius resembles Mad William who walks about the lanes,
  leaning on his bicycle. It seems appropriate that the Archangel
  Raphael, who is talking to him in the painting, is tapping his fore-
  head in a sympathetic manner, as if to say 'Bonkers, poor chap';
Sts Demetrius and Nestor, side by side in the same painting, both
  resemble Elvis Presley wearing sheets;
St Theodore the Studite is like Mr Colbourn, Quaker headmaster
  of the first school our children went to;
St James the Persian resembles the old fishmonger in Earls Colne.

As I am recording all the above, a monk approaches. He speaks in immaculate English and introduces himself as the Archdeacon Seraphim. He is tall but doesn't look it, being somewhat Pickwickian with spectacles and a jolly burliness – if one can imagine Mr Pickwick wearing a rather dirty purple dressing-gown, his hair bunched up with an elastic band into a small pony-tail. This hippie-esque touch is miti-gated by a large, woolly, white, forked beard. We talk for a long time, about everything from Turkish poetry (which he says is amongst the best in the world), through war ('a waste of good adrenalin,' he thinks) and the world being the worse for tourists, to the Celts (he is partly

Highland Scots, partly Cuban-American, partly Greek-Armenian and may have a bit of Arabic somewhere). We also discuss the difficulty of recruiting monks nowadays.

'Are you a working monastery?' I ask.

'Well, there's me. The other monk is in the pub.'

Finally we get to the knotty theological problem of Jesus being admiring of shepherds. 'I am a shepherd,' I say, 'and it sometimes worries me that the intention of all my ministrations is to fatten them for the butcher.'

'A happy mutton chop is a good mutton chop,' he says. 'Anyhow, maybe it was the sheep who domesticated the humans, to make them feed them, cure their ills, help them have lambs and protect them from wolves.'

We finally part, him bent double in his tiny doorway, waving at me with a large, friendly hand and crying 'Happy chops, happy chops.'

Back in Tel Aviv. Zosimus advised me to go and see the Christian cathedral in Jaffa: 'It is full of beautiful things.' The walk to the cathedral has been pleasant enough: an hour-long ramble up the beach in the bright afternoon sunlight, past sun-bathers and swimmers, parasols, restaurants, piers, surf-boarders and ugly hotels. The cathedral has been a disappointment: the building is quite interesting but the ornamentation inside is gimcrack and fussy, the usual Roman Catholic peasant art of gaudy plaster saints and agonised Christs with horrific wounds.

I am now outside. There is a hillock in front of me. An arrow points along a path which meanders up it and says 'Prospect View'. I won't go up the path, the flowers on the grassy sides of the slope are particularly numerous and attractive.

There is a wall here, at the top. It is low and wide. A crowd of people are on the other side, all with their backs to me. I wonder what it is that they are all looking at? I'll stand on top of this wall to look over them.

!!!ZZZAP!!!

What was that blinding flash?

Oops. Oh Lor. Deary me.

I duck down and scuttle off, down the hill. When those people's wedding photograph is developed they will see that above all their faces is another one, large and round and foolish, surmounted by a Panama hat and goggling curiously at the camera.

15 October. Meet Fiona's family, the Hadlees, at their house for Sunday lunch. They have just moved into an Old Rectory. It is a pleasant but rather run-down place and they have been making many enjoyable plans for doing it up. Roger said that the cost of the wedding is going to set back some of their schemes for a bit. As well as Roger and Gill, all three daughters were there: Georgie, Caroline and Fiona. They are a very attractive family. Roger has an art gallery in the Royal Exchange. He specialises in ships and seascapes.

Spent the late afternoon brashing the conifers in Black Bat's Wood. I've got resin ingrained into my hands and scratch marks on my arms and face. Lost a bill-hook and broke the wet-stone. Looked for fossils in the raw earth of a rabbit warren: fairy loaves, devil's toenails and thunderbolts (bellamites) are quite common here, but found none. The rabbits have ring-barked some self-sown oak saplings: bastards, the ferrets will visit the warren next week.

1 November. Gaborone is pleasant, but small and dozy: barely a one whore's town. There is the main Mall lined with shops; in the middle stretches a long gravelled yard, made attractive with little groves of shadowing trees and neatly decorated by costers with lines of fruit and piles of vegetables; there are some ugly hovels and some pleasing houses with pretty, flower-filled gardens; a few unostentatious Governmental buildings; an occasional office and the hotel and that's that. The heat muffles everyone with a drugged languor. I am an alien here with my hasty clumping footsteps and busy prying eyes. After breakfast it took twenty minutes to walk from one end to the other of this, the capital city of Botswana, and then an hour to walk round it. Now I'm sitting in a fat armchair doing nothing but sweating: the general lethargy is infectious. I must do something somewhere somehow during the next 32 hours.

*

The British High Commission has a spare Land Rover which I can have for the next two days. I'm told that its steering is a bit unreliable – it is inclined to swoop to the right without warning, and it rattles like a tinker's van but it is a sturdy old trooper.

I am now fully equipped. I bought a tank-full of petrol and the High Commission lent two full jerry cans 'just in case'. I have also borrowed a pillow and a blanket, a knife-fork-spoon set, a bowl, a mug, a box of matches and two plastic cans of drinking water. I went down the Mall shopping for four meals: a lunch, dinner, breakfast and another lunch. I bought six avocado pears and a bottle of salad dressing to go with them, three pounds of raw carrots, two pounds of peanuts, a dozen apples, two melons, a large block of mouse-trap cheese and a packet of cream crackers: all rather rabbit-foody, but meat will addle in this tropical heat. A kind man has lent me his camera; he does not know how hopeless I am with machines. This has many abilities and is studded with knobs and buttons which manipulate them. It lives in a custom-built bag which has compartments to hold different lenses and a variety of gadgets the purpose of which I do not know. Finally, I have a map: it is a photocopy of a plan I saw pinned to the wall in an office. There is not much to see. Gaborone is near the bottom of the sketch; from there the main road runs NNE for about 250 miles to Francistown. The Limpopo runs approximately along the same line as the road, veering away from it as it goes up the map. To the west of the road there is a large area of scrub which merges gradually into the Kalahari desert. It should be almost impossible to get lost as long as I know if I am to the east or west of the road for I should be able to guide myself back to it by the sun – presuming my watch hasn't stopped or the day is not overcast. I have always wanted to see 'the great grey-green, greasy Limpopo River, all set about with fever-trees' so today I'll seek it out and explore it. I'll spend the night by its banks – 'Not too close,' I was advised, 'hippopotami and crocodiles are liable to get testy if you get between them and the river.' I'll either sleep in the Land Rover or I may charm some settler into feeding me and putting me up in his ranch. Tomorrow I'll drive west and inspect the Kalahari desert; I must be back at the High Commission at 5 p.m.; my aeroplane flies at 18.15.

*

I have now driven the first 80 miles from Gaborone to 'The Tropic of Capricon' (as a sign says). The journey has been pleasant but uneventful: hardly any traffic on the road, rolling countryside thickly cluttered with scrub and the occasional tree. I have become rather excited at the sight of a tawny beast lurking in the bushes. I hop out of the car and stalk it: downwind, bush-hopping, sidling and tiptoeing.

It is a cow: surprised to see me but amiable, with huge handlebar horns. I photograph it. The machinery breaks into a cocophony of wheezing, interrupted by four clicks. I have taken four photographs: during my fiddling I had changed the controls from single to automatic. This would have been useful if the cow had been doing something interesting like speeding through the landscape pursued by a lion, but as it is merely chewing the cud and peering at me all I shall get is four different stages of its mastication.

Ten more miles, and no sign of photogenic wild life.

There! Something dark and hunched behind a bush! Determined not to let it escape, I slam on the brake, skid to a stop, grab the camera, leap over the fence and race round the bush. With dignity a fellow pulls up his trousers and with a curt, peeved glance at me melts into the scrubland.

As I have stopped, I decide to eat an elevenses: a couple of slabs of cheese with the cream crackers. I munch, sitting on the car bonnet and looking hopefully into the scrub for a savage beast. Another Land Rover draws up. The driver is a tall local in an immaculate bush jacket and a boy-scout hat.

'You all right? Car broken down?' he asks.

'Thanks, I've just stopped to rest,' I say.

Other occupants of the car climb out. Two are American. He is sober, she is not. They are middle-aged, fussily attired in Hollywood's idea of safari kit – leather, linen and canvas, with high boots and wide jodhpurs, their jackets with more pockets and pouches than there are drawers in a haberdasher's chest, their hats and waists girt about with bands of leopard skin and thongs round their necks from which dangle teeth and claws. He looks a bit like Vice-President Quayle, tall, clean-limbed, square-jawed, plastically handsome; basically unremarkable except for pale green, protuberant eyes like boiled goosegogs. She is attractive, not unlike Goldie Hawn and just as giggly. The third passenger is their guide. He is an ancient Briton. He is sober, but reluctantly so. He has a glum red face and wispy grey-ginger hair and eyes of the characteristic colonial poached-eggs-floating-in-saucers-of-blood. He tells me that he stayed on in Africa because he liked the way of life and loathed the thought of rainy Frinton but his wife has died and all his friends are gone and his money has dwindled to nothing because of inflation. 'What I always say is, "all you need is a laugh and a shout".' One meets many of these sad bits of jetsam stranded by the ebbing tide of our departing Empire. It says much for the honesty and honour of the Empire's servants that so many of them are scraping a meagre living on inadequate savings and a measly pension, rather than living a high life in some fleshpot on the stolen riches of the people they ruled.

We natter. Luther and Precious are on a 'camera safari' and are off to photograph the Kalahari. I admire the thong round Precious's neck and she tells me that the nails and teeth with which it is festooned are from 'animals culled with consent from a Conservation Programme'. They offer me a thermos of coffee, I offer them cheese and biscuits.

'Biscuits!' exclaims Precious, 'how British!'

'British?' I ask.

'Yea, British, the word "biscuits": so crisp.'

'What do you call them then?'

'Cookies, but these little brittle things are not my idea of a cookie, perhaps "biscuits" is a bit snappier for one of these.'

(Being a bit tiddly, she finds it difficult saying British and biscuits: 'Brish', 'Brissish', 'Briddish', 'Bishkitz', 'Bitskits'.)

Finally they go, waving out of their car windows, the old Brit shouting 'Don't forget, a laugh and a shout,' Precious calling 'Bye-bye, Bishkitsh, be sheeing you!'

Having turned right at the sign of 'The Capricon' (sic) I am heading towards the Limpopo which should be about 70 miles due east, near a place called Buffel's Drift. The road is a sandy track, bumpy and rutted but generally good going; I am averaging about 40 miles per hour. I can see a thick haze of billowing red sand in my driving-mirror, churned up by the rugged tyres of the Land Rover. Luckily there seem to be no sharp stones, so I am unlikely to get a puncture, but some of the dead twigs lying in my path may have spines. I *suppose* the spare wheel is OK, perhaps I should have checked it before I left.

Tracks occasionally veer off this main one. Though rutted with tyre marks, they do not seem to be used much for I have not seen a vehicle for 50 miles. No animals, except domestic cattle and goats; but there are plenty of birds including rollers with vivid Cambridge-blue wings, and yellow-billed hornbills, as big as crows and dressed in a smart livery of black and white meeting at a 'V' behind. They have inelegantly cumbersome beaks, curved and horny like a mandarin's thumbnail. They look like women at Ascot with dresses designed by Hartnell and hats by Mr Shilling. I have passed a few small settlements of two to four homesteads. The buildings look cosy: thatched rondavels with mud walls, some of which have eaves attractively pillared by circles of wooded posts. Often, beside them, there are livestock yards enclosed by hedges of thorn and brushwood.

I can't find the bloody river. Surely it is somewhere. Every time I think I am getting near it the track curves away and I have to find another track which branches to the east.

I have found a big village. The largest building is constructed nastily from breeze-block and corrugated iron; it seems to act both as post office and village store, just like the shop in my village. There are a few people within, leaning on a counter, and they eye me with about the same friendliness as one of them would find if he suddenly arrived in Colne Engaine. The man behind the counter is a self-important little sod. Having given me a brief glance, he pretends to peruse the document on the counter before him. I wait politely. In silence, the locals stare at me staring at him. Finally his eyelids are dragged upwards, like someone lifting the heavy awnings of a shop, and he condescends to look at me. I ask him where the Limpopo River is. He says he does not know. Liar. It is a mile wide and a thousand miles long and must be within spitting distance from here. His eyelids droop down to his manuscript. He is finished with me. May the devil poach his balls in the cauldrons of hell. The locals are pleased with his *savoir-faire* and gaze blandly at me as I stomp out of the shop, into the car, and drive angrily away with the setting sun at my back.

Over the last ten miles I came upon several barriers of tall, rusting wire fences. They were penetrated by gates bearing signs such as 'KEEP OUT', 'PRIVATE', 'NO ADMITTANCE'. That is all I have found of the anticipated hospitable settler whom I was going to charm into giving me dinner, bed and breakfast; perhaps, I was beginning to muse, he might even offer me his beautiful daughter, in order to get some new genes into his interbred blood-lines.

I have just come upon a particularly rusty and ramshackle iron gate and have found that one of my rear tyres is nearly flat. Oh sod it! Oh bloody hell! Oh damn, damn, damn! I bet the spare tyre is also flat, they almost always are. Why the devil didn't I check it before I moved off? Because I am a lazy, stupid fool. Damn! And it's going to get dark soon. Oh **** it! And where the hell am I? I have been trying to follow my meanderings on this futile map and I think I am near Maartin's Drift, but God knows.

I must find somewhere to spend the night. There was a sign four miles back which said 'To the Camp'. I'll try to get there; I hope the sandy track will be reasonably kind to my wheel.

Well, here's the camp. It's deserted. It must have been built for safari tourists. I am in an enclosure of beaten earth. There are five modern rondavels, thatched and built of whitewashed cement, there's also a small bungalow. Looking through its windows, I reckon it acts as living- and office-quarters for a manager. There is no telephone wire; no electrics either. The whole site is dominated by a large water-tank on stilts. Someone has coupled a hose to the tap beneath it and has been watering clumps of flowers, mainly busy-lizzies, which have been planted in rings round the trunks of the spreading trees which shelter the area. The gardener has been here recently, the soil round the flowers is still damp. The general effect is pleasant enough, but I am too worried to be cheered. If a Queen's Messenger misses his aeroplane he is likely to get the sack. If my spare tyre is also punctured I may have to walk 80 miles before I get a lift, and all the way I'll have to carry one of the full cans of water with one hand and the borrowed camera with the other. What about lions? No, cattle-herding locals would not allow those to be around. But what about hyenas? Can't they bite through a buffalo's femur in one snap?

I won't change my wheel now. Even if the spare tyre is not flat it may have a slow leak and subside during the night.

At least I have one bit of luck: a rondavel is unlocked and is furnished with three beds. They are narrow, iron, military ones and they each have a mattress. There is also an alcove with lavatory, sink and shower. It's about six o'clock, the gloom is gathering, it soon will be dark. I'll check this building for snakes and bugs and then eat and then go to bed.

The melon and avocado pears are good, but I feel a bit queasy after all those nuts I munched as I drove.

This mattress is not uncomfortable, but it smells a bit musty. I'm glad I remembered to borrow a pillow.

No-one in the world knows where I am. Not even me.

Goodnight, darling Dominie, far away at home. God bless. I miss you frightfully.

I wouldn't *really* have accepted any offer of settler's daughters.

What's that funny noise? . . . I hope to God that the spare tyre is OK . . . Is that a monkey, or a hyena? . . . If that spare is flat . . . God, it's hot . . . Horrible horrible little whingeing whining mingeing mosquito, I must get out of bed and fumble about in the dark for my sponge-bag, and then grovel through it for the Jungle Juice . . . Was that screaming something getting killed, or mating? . . . Phew, it's even hotter . . . The spare tyre . . .

2 November. Apart from the occasional alarming noise, I had one almighty fright during the night. I wanted to go to the loo at around midnight and found my way to it by the light of my box of matches. As I reached the alcove a pale face with goggling eyes suddenly swam out of the wall towards me. It took a couple of horrified seconds before I realised it was my reflection in the looking-glass above the sink. I finally went to sleep about three o'clock, and have been woken at six to see a couple of worried black faces staring at me through the window. One is of an old toothless man, the other of a young girl, perhaps his grand-daughter. It had been twilight when I inspected the rondavel last night, in the clearer light of dawn I can see that the rafters above my head are swathed in a festooning of spiders' webs. There is a spider on the window-sill next to me. It is huge. It is so large I can see its eyes. They are staring straight into mine.

After my ablutions the girl, who was obviously quick-witted and bright, led the old man and me to the Land Rover and implied with gestures that he would help change the tyre; she had noticed it was flat. All my fears crystallised as we let the weight of the car down on the spare wheel: I saw, with dread, the tyre getting flatter and flatter; finally, when it was two thirds flat, it stopped. I tipped the old boy, left some money on the window-sill for the management, turned the nose of the car away from the rising sun and headed due west, towards the road.

I have now gone about twenty miles and have checked the tyre: a bit flatter perhaps, but not much. This is a much busier time of day than yesterday afternoon; I have seen a warthog, several buck and a large snake. It was a shiny metallic green and almost long enough to extend two thirds across the track which is about ten feet wide. I ran over the poor thing before I could stop. I thought I should put it out of its misery and perhaps then skin the corpse, but it had disappeared; I saw marks in the sand where it had writhed, they were as thick as my arm. I decided not to follow.

Thank God, I reached the main road. After a dozen miles I could fill up my tyre with air at a petrol station; it should have read 32 lb., it read only 7. It is not leaking any air, I still possess a can of petrol, there are eight more hours before I report for duty, I'll never find that blasted Limpopo River but I have a few hours to look for the Kalahari desert:

I had better not be so stupid this time and keep closer to the road, then if the worst happens I can at least hitchhike. If I go back to Gaborone a road leads north-west from it towards Moca, the desert starts about there. It will be a two or three hour drive to Moca.

Off I go. I can now relax and munch at breakfast as I drive: carrots, peanuts, carrots, peanuts, carrots, peanuts, apple.

Moca is just like Celesteville, Babar the Elephant's capital: rows and rows of neat little thatched rondavels; chickens pecking about, children running, grown-ups sitting and gossiping; stacks of fire-wood, heaps of maize and yams, a circular threshing-floor, a hedged-in pound containing goats.

As I stand by my car, inspecting the town whilst the townspeople inspect me, a Land Rover drives up.

'Why! It's Biscuits!'

The Americans have 'done' the Kalahari and are off to Zambia to do the Victoria Falls. I tell them of my puncture and they tell me about some Bushmen, the men with peppercorn tufts of hair and wise, leprechaun faces, the women with steatopygous buttocks like pumpkins. Then they drive off in a cloud of dust, with a waving of arms from them and a wry grin from the driver.

I must turn back, there is no time to explore the Kalahari, for I fly from Gaborone at 18.15 hours.

The checker-in at the aerodrome had such long, curved fingernails, such high, foxy cheekbones, such white, pointed teeth and such a sharp little wedge of a chin that it was a surprise to see that she had the soft brown eyes of a herbivore rather than a carnivore's yellow glint.

9 November. *I dreamed that I was dead.*

I had thought death would be busy: a crowding of people and benign spirits and horrific things that would meet me: a multitude, all jostling and arguing and pushing; some trying to pitch-fork me down into the fires of hell, others pleading 'No, no, Your Divine Holiness, there are mitigating circumstances, though indeed they are few.' And over and away would be the old relations and friends: Papa and Mamma, immaculately dressed and with dry martinis in their hands; Miss Pearson, my governess, whom I sometimes still pray to; poor Douglas who died at school; Grandmamma, with her giggle and green umbrella; cynical, wise, Great-Aunt Ruth who loved me; Doctor Chilton the parson; Xavier, still laughing; and pretty, pretty, died-so-soon Diana whom I kissed and kissed and kissed in the conservatory on my 16th birthday; all waving and smiling and standing on tiptoe to look over other heads, like people at the barrier when you've gone through Immigration and Passports and Customs. But behind, breathing at my heels, the frightful demons of terror and pain and remorse, chanting out my sins, and most of my sins being embarrassing rather than vile.

But in my dream there was nothing. No-one. Nothing to see or to feel. I could not even hear my breath or the soughing of blood through my veins.

Death was utter isolation.

20 November. I arrived at Islamabad at 6.10 this morning and this afternoon I climbed Mount Happiness. 'Mount Happiness' is sometimes called 'Mount Prospect'. They are both bureaucrats' effete names; its real name is probably something better like Thunder Mountain or Tiger's Stoop. It is the highest local point of the Margalla Hills, a steep ridge which rises from the plain of North India. The plain is the very edge of the Indian Geological Plate and is moving towards the landmass of Asia at about three inches a century with such force that it is causing the Himalayas to buckle and rear out of the vast landmass of Euro-Asia. The ridge I climbed is the first of the wrinkles; one day it will be a multi-thousand-foot mountain.

A notice board at the entrance to the mountain path says the walk to the top is 5.5 kilometres, the climb about 1000 metres.

I started too late, around 2.30. I reached the top about two hours later. The sun was low against the mountain ridge so that the valleys below me were gloomed in twilight. I reckoned that I had at least 90 minutes to walk down and that half the time would be in the dark. I photographed Islamabad spread below me and turned back, in a hurry. The stars were out by 5.30. Luckily I had passed the dangerous bits by then, where the path zigzags back, away from precipitous drops, but the last half hour was awkward: the track littered with boulders, only just discernible, and occasional places where rocky outcrops create jagged and irregular staircases. Whenever I walked through the pine groves the long needles whispered a dolorous sighing above my head. I heard a grunting cough once and remembered Steven saying he had heard something like that, and he thought it was a tiger. Strangely, the central, worn part of the track seemed to give off a faint phosphorescence, which helped me navigate. Could it be feet-crushed quartz crystals, shining in the moonlight? I only fell once but I stubbed my toes painfully several times and the thin soles of my chukka boots did not insulate me from the pounding on the hard ground: the soles of my feet feel that they have been bastinadoed.

21 November. I am off to the Khyber Pass. My car takes me from the hotel at 5.30 in the morning and drives me through the dawn to the aerodrome. There are several people about, even at this hour. Many are shrouded in the plaid-cum-blanket that most of the men here seem to wear. They stride alongside the road in the early morning mist like loping ghosts. There are several people on bicycles; milk churns are strapped to some of them. My driver, a small, cheerful man with a large black moustache, points to one: 'That person, he is delivering milk, he is going all the way to Rawlpindi, sir.'

'With roads as bumpy as this, it will be butter when he gets there.'

The driver deems this an amazingly amusing observation and breaks out into a tintinnabulation of chuckling: 'Oh my goodness, sir, that is a most humorous idea. Oh, sir, to think of it, instead of saying to his clients "are you wanting one pint or two?" he will be saying "is it one *lump* you want, or two?" And then, sir, instead of a ladle, to measure out the milk, he must cut it up, with a knife, and weigh it upon the scales. And then they are saying to him: "What is this, you damnfool? How is it that we can pour our milk into bowls to make the lassi?"'

My next driver is in Peshawar. He is called Ashraf. He tells me that he is an old soldier, having been in the British army for eighteen years – the Frontier Rifles. I am a bit disappointed in him. Many of the old soldiers are still bolt upright and as smart as pins; he is a scruffy old man with bad teeth, a week-old beard and a shy, sly, sideways glance. However he seems to know the ropes and takes me to the four different offices we need to visit before I am issued my pass and my 'gun man'.

The first office issues me with a pass to allow me access to the next office. I recognise, with gloom, Indian officialdom at its most pernickety and tedious.

Office No. 2 is dominated by two large desks behind which sit two small bureaucrats reading newspapers and sipping tea. A row of dejected beseechers sits on chairs against the wall before them. The desks are piled with papers. The man behind the slightly larger desk is in his late middle age, with a greying moustache and wire-rimmed spectacles. He looks up as we enter, takes my letter from the Ministry of the Interior, scans it and puts it on a pile of other correspondence. He then gestures with curt flips of the back of his hand that we must join the line of applicants. He picks up his newspaper and continues to read it.

There is a girl in the chair next to me, in her early twenties. She looks British, a pleasant, plumpish face with freckles and mousy hair done up in a couple of pony-tails on either side of her head so that they flop down like spaniel's ears. She has the frowsty aspect and stale smell which characterises people who have bummed halfway round the world.

'Where are you from?' I ask.

'Bristol.'

'Where are you going? Kathmandu?'

'Yes, how d'y know?'

'Everyone like you seems to want to go there. Do you need any help, not having any problems?'

'No thanks, I'm fine.'

Just then the man in the larger desk puts down his newspaper, looks at the clock on the peeling-plastered wall beside him, picks up a bit of paper and initials it and hands it to the plump pleasant girl, saying 'It is now the right time for you to have your pass.'

She takes the paper and leaves, wishing me luck as she goes.

I sit about. I take my book out of my pocket and read for five minutes. The men behind their desks peruse their newspapers. Nothing can be heard except the sipping of tea, the rustle of newspaper, the ticking of the clock, the occasional creak as one of the supplicants shifts in his chair.

I am beginning to get riled.

'Why are we waiting?'

'Because you have not got a permit.'

'My driver has taken me here because he told me that you were the person to issue permits.'

'It is not the proper form. You will have to wait until 10 o'clock [it is now 8.30] when the man comes with the correct forms.'

'How long will all that take?'

'Perhaps you will have a permit by noon, midday.'

'But I have to go back to Islamabad at 4.'

'That is your misfortune. I cannot help it, you should have come with the right form.'

'But the High Commissioner told me that letter would do.'

'Very nice letter. Very polite. Very correct. "Beseech you will remember our esteem," I like that. But a letter from your High Commissioner to our Ministry of Foreign Affairs is not good enough.'

'It is not a letter *from* our High Commissioner, it is a letter *to* our High Commissioner.'

The man goggles and freezes, as if I had shoved an icicle up his arse. With reluctance, his eyes crawl away from me, down across his desk, up the pile of bumph, up to my letter which lies on top, and along the heading. He snarls suddenly at the chap at the other desk who jumps with alarm, puts down his newspaper and hurries out of the office. He returns a minute later and twitters to the first chap.

The first chap turns to me. He is all smiles and little bows. He says, 'My superior will be here in 30 minutes, in one half hour, at oh-nine-hundred hours. He will be seeing you.'

'But I thought you were the person to deal with.'

'Not with an introduction like yours. You will see my superior.'

This honour is apparently worth the delay. Cups of tea are produced for my driver and me. We sip, sit and wait. We are smiled at, whenever we look up. We are summoned. We are taken to a larger and more imposing office where officiates a larger and more imposing man. He is courteous and efficient. 'I presume you have had to undergo some of our superfluous bureaucracy,' he says, 'I will not even waste your time by offering you a cup of tea.' He then initials my form; the driver takes it, we shake hands, we go to two other offices and collect more initials on bits of paper. We drive somewhere else and collect my 'gun man', an armed guard; we are now on our way. It is about 30 miles to the Khyber Pass.

My gun man is an unremarkable man but for one thing. He is wearing the normal sensible and comfortable dress of 'pyjama' trousers and long-tailed shirt called a 'kurta' (is that where the English 'kirtle' originated?) and over these he wears an old army great-coat; he has an army beret and dirty boots, an impressive hawk-like profile spoiled by a vacant expression, and a tatty old rifle, a Lee Enfield .303 which he wears on a sling. His distinguishing mark is the colour of his eyes: blue. Perhaps he inherited it from the soldiers of Alexander the Great who passed through here; certainly some of the many white-bearded old men would not look out of place sitting on a cloud above Mount Olympus. Perhaps, though, he inherited his blue eyes, like his rifle, from the British Army.

The local people are generally very handsome: eagle-faced and stately. They all wear head-gear. An embroidered skull-cap, usually white, is a common hat. Turbans vary from the colossal to the neat; the smartest is the Pathan one in which one end appears as a long streamer down the back and the other as a tuft to the side. Many wear a hat like a tweed cow-pat. Ashraf says it is called a topi. I am interested in the word topi, and wonder if English 'toupee' (wig) originates from it. Urdu is an Indo-European language. I ask Ashraf to count to ten in Urdu: 'ek, doh, teen, char, paanch, che, saat, aath, naw, dus.' It certainly has an ancient, long-ago echo of English or Latin. Their 'lakh' is similar to our 'lac', though I have only ever heard one old farmer use that word for 100,000.

'What do you call father and mother?' I ask.

'Pop and Ma,' he says, 'but they are dead for many years.'

Ashraf is a wretched driver: he dithers, he crawls, he is enraged when overtaken but dare not overtake, he incessantly hoots and mutters petulantly. Our road is now zigzagging towards the hills. Sometimes one can see forts, with battlements. They are mostly British-built. The home-steads are interesting: they are walled compounds, up to an acre or so in size and built of a sand-coloured clay. The walls appear blank with no windows but sometimes there is a turret at the corners with fire slits. The entrances are huge: forbidding, unfriendly portals of metal. When they are open and one can look in, a guard is often noticeable lurking about just inside. There are houses, barns and outbuildings with their windows and doors facing onto courtyards; there are shawled women drifting gracefully about, sometimes balancing bundles on their heads; there are children playing, old men sitting about gossiping and chickens pecking. All is as cosy as a dormouse's nest but Ashraf tells me that there are many disagreements between the homesteads, sometimes out-right wars and vendettas.

The Khyber Pass is a bit disappointing; I had expected something like the gorge which leads to Petra: high and narrow and over-shadowed, but the pass is basically a valley and it only looks really dramatic in two places: from high up, looking back, where the steep mountainsides to its south-east entrance give a gate-like effect; and at the narrowest point, where you can imagine being suddenly ambushed by the mountain tribesmen. The whole effect is marred by the modernity of road, railway line and profusion of electric and telegraphic cables; however the little forts perched on the top of the steep cliffs and knolls are what one expects. The mountainsides are dark and gloomy: the rock is of rotten slates and mudstones which break up easily into scree and pebbles; I see few birds and not much vegetation. Here and there, carved into the sides of cliffs, there are the badges of British regiments. I keep a special look-out for my county one, the Essex Regiment. A whole battalion was wiped out here, all but for an ensign who wrapped himself up in the colours and because of his gaudiness was worshipped as a god, rather than being slaughtered and dismembered like the other soldiers. The Essex Regiment is very proud of it and it is one of its battle honours; it always surprises and annoys foreigners how we can turn our disasters into triumphs: Mons, the Somme, Dunkirk, Arnhem et al. I will not see the Grenadier badge of course; the Brigade of Guards never went to India, having to stay within 1000 miles of the monarch. That is why we have no Anglo-Indian slang, like mufti, char, kushi, buckshee or chota peg.

I am at Michni Point, the fort at the far end of the Khyber Pass, over-looking Afghanistan. The fort commander is a surprisingly mousy little officer, only an ensign although he looks about 40, scruffy, unshaved and with the lenses of his specs as thick as fish-bowls. However he is friendly and points out all the other forts under his command; they seem little bigger than sentry boxes and are scattered about on the mountain tops. Each fort has its number painted in huge white numerals on the cliff below it. Afghanistan disappears as a series of mountain ridges into the hazed blue horizon. My gun man is silhouetted against the battlements. He is squatting, his robes about him, his gun slung over his shoulder. He stares impassively towards the plains of Afghanistan: he looks impressive and noble. I take a photograph of him. He stands up and 'adjusts his dress'. He has been having a pee.

We have now driven out of the Khyber Pass, through Peshawar and thence on for another hour to Darra Adam Khel. I should not be here: it is out of bounds to foreigners, even the army and police avoid it. It reminds me of a Wild West setting, a real frontier town with men strutting about with guns slung across their shoulders and their chests criss-crossed with bandoliers; there are street traders selling heaps of vegetables and textiles and hardware, there are shops piled to the ceiling with white sacks, heroin or opium, above all there are the gunsmiths. Every other shop is selling or building guns: Stens, Brens, Stirlings, Lee Enfields, Remingtons, Winchesters, Berettas, Heckler & Kochs, Jawags, Mausers, Smith & Wessons, Lugers, Brownings, Colts; pistols, revolvers, automatics, shot-guns, rifles, machine guns. The craftsman-ship is excellent, not particularly refined, but accurate; this is the more surprising when one looks at the gunsmiths at work. Some gun-barrels are being made from builder's steel reinforcing rods: they are bored with the help of lathes turned by hand or foot; sires and sights are filed from chunks of metal with farriers' rasps; stocks are carved with rickety spoke shaves.

A fellow steps out of a shop. He is holding a light machine gun. He looks about, sees three black birds flying overhead (choughs?) and points his gun at them – 'rat-a-tat-tat-tat-tat'. The birds fly on. The fellow looks discontent and re-enters the shop.

There is a tooting. Zigzagging down the street, swerving to avoid the milling mass of humanity, of tumbrels and waggons, bicycles, market stalls, dogs and donkeys, packed to the gunwales with spotty adolescents, thunders an old, mighty, red London double-decker bus. Its destination board says

Bristol
Istanbul
Teheran
Islamabad
Kathmandu

Hauling at the steering-wheel is the plump, pleasant-looking girl with her mousy hair done up in a couple of spaniel's ears.

22 November, Karachi. As I am driven to the Consulate I am able to take a quick glimpse of the city. It is older, smellier, much more crowded and very much hotter than the capital. And in comparison to Islamabad's great, straight, wide, empty, modern roads, the streets here jostle with every sort of transport: dominated by ornately painted buses and Bedford lorries; delayed by ox-drawn tumbrels and push-carts powered by abject human beings in rags. At every traffic-light beggars swarm towards you and exhibit their physical problems. The more fortunate are those who are missing bits; the less fortunate have them, but they are contorted, or the wrong size or, most horrific of all, in the wrong place.

23 November. *00.45 hours, home. Dominie still up, waiting for me. She has cracked her wrist, slipping on a pony turd.*

01.00 hours, bed, and I still haven't prepared my speech for the Heritage Awards tomorrow. Oh God, it's not tomorrow, it's today.

07.30 hours, get up, shave etc, brew Dominie's tea and my coffee, dogs' walk with Monk, try to plan out speech.

09.00 hours, Kerry arrives with six of the ram lambs I sent to the knacker. They are in eighteen plastic bags. We transfer their joints and saddles and chops and collops and innards into smaller bags, label them and put them in the deep freeze.

09.30 hours, concentrate on speech.

11.00 hours, Jonathan Chaplin of Strutt & Parker arrives to ask me where I am going to find the money for the sheep fencing I have bought, to tell me that the people at Goldington's have agreed to my price on the fifth of an acre they want to buy round their cottage, to tell me that the electricity people say we have put too many heaters in Rooktree Lodge so they will now have to change the fuse box, to say that the planting on the new wood, Hill Meadow Wood, will start next week, to chat about the old calf-shed by the Knights Home Barn which has finally collapsed, to discuss the new spring which has broken out on the side of Sewell's Field (the water is superbly pure, I had wondered if we should bottle it and sell it), to regret that he cannot find a French speaker to investigate the sales of squab in Europe, to explain why the Huzzey's house needs re-painting . . . I ask him to push off so I can finish my speech.

11.30 hours, drive off to the Head Office of the Braintree District Council.

11.50 hours, arrive, same smell of damp carpet in the committee room where I used to sit for hour after hour, week after week, year after year. Some faces I recognise, nice to see them again.

They seemed to like it. Have eaten too many sausage rolls and sandwiches and drunk too much wine.

It's been quite a busy 24 hours. I'm jet-lagged. I'll go to bed early.

16 December, New York. As the smell of Communism is compounded from boiled cabbage and damp serge so the smell of Capitalism is a combination of the warm scent of popcorn and the sour stench of pizzas. It wafts over the tourist cruiser, 'a converted coast guard cutter, 165 feet long, capable of carrying 585 passengers, though at present there are only 375 of you folks'. The commentator is a nice old boy in a yachting-cap; he has a pleasant, rather venerable voice which he lubricates with an occasional bottle of beer. He is quite interesting and amusing but, like many Americans, besotted by numbers:

'On your right you will see at the intersection of 92nd and 139th Streets Number 354 Parkside, which was built in 1982 at the cost of $33,605,000. It is 72 storeys high, which equals 880 feet 10 inches. It has 4320 windows equalling 648,000 square feet of glass. Floors 35 to 48 are a 660-room hotel; the rents of the top apartments go up to $14,000 a month whilst those beneath the hotel are as low as $1200 a month. It has 776,800 square feet of office space whereto commute daily over 3500 white-collar workers.'

We are now berthing at the end of our 35-mile tour round the island of Manhattan which also involved going up to Liberty Island upon which stands the Statue of Liberty and passing under 20 bridges: 'The weight of this bridge relies on four huge strands which are themselves each composed of 27,600 individual lengths of braided wire. If you tied them all together – the bridge would fall down. Just jesting, folks.'

It has been a pleasant three hours: the Statue of Liberty looked as large and as impressive as expected; the groups of skyscrapers, when seen across the water, were science-fiction in their alien strangeness, like clusters of colossal crystals; from my high position, by the port-side gunwale, I could sometimes see two or three miles down the streets, long and narrow concrete canyons. The ramshackle wrecks of rusting piers and warehouses were eerily evocative, the wooded slopes of Washington Heights and Inwood Hill surprising and attractive.

I plodded the two-mile walk back to my hotel. During this ramble I saw some pleasingly odd people, the oddest was an ancient woman tripping lightly along Third Avenue. She was dressed entirely in white from her gym shoes, up to her tights (rather wrinkled on her pipe-stem legs), her ragged, chiffon mini-skirt, her long-sleeved satin blouse, to the bow in her long grey hair which was fanned out, Alice in Wonderlandwise, on her shoulders; her face was powdered dead-white; the crimson of her lipstick was a startling splodge of colour. She resembled Peter Pan's Tinkerbell going to her hundredth birthday party. There was also a peculiar negro on the way: old, tiny, and wearing a long blond wig and a hat like a flowerpot. We smiled at each other, he somewhat mockingly, me a bit warily.

I am having dinner in an Italian restaurant. The old cannot mature here: the ancient granny sitting by the table next to me, sucking at the spaghetti, is wearing gym shoes and a T-shirt emblazoned with Garfield the cat. I can see a television through the window. It is above the bar and is on showing some sissies in tights playing rounders: the Americans have a penchant for playing school-girls' games, except that they call rounders 'baseball' and netball 'basketball'.

Suddenly some police cars come racing past, their sirens screaming and whimpering and gibbering like the souls of the damned. It is a sound which makes my hackles rise, not because it reminds me of the supernatural, but because it is the clamour of brutish authority.

19 December. Dash off to London to buy Christmas presents. I already have some things from Halstead and abroad, but I do my usual Christmas shopping round: the bookshops of Heywood Hill and Hatchards, Liberty's kitchen shop and oriental basement, Fenwick's, Asprey's, Harrods, and Swane, Alderney & Brigg. The crowds are appalling, the prices frightful, the underground railway stinking. I make White's and the Special Forces Club my bases, and retire regularly to the bars there to recover.

My nephew Sammy is earning pocket-money by selling ties in Harrods. 'Buy yourself an initialled silk tie,' he suggests.

'Frightfully vulgar, anyhow, I can only see "H" on the ties.'

'We only have H,' he replies.

'Not everyone is called Henry, Hubert, Herbert or Horace.'

'H is for Harrods,' he explains.

'If your employers want to advertise their shop, I'm certainly not going to do it for them.'

Sammy is puzzled by my indignation, but sells me a green tie with a red pheasant on it, for Monk.

20–23 December. A 'special' short journey to Angola.

The capital, Luanda, is a nightmare. The poverty is appalling – but for the rich, rare and rotten who swan about in Range Rovers. Leprosy or landmines have maimed many people. The civilians are in a permanent state of agitation: sudden terror will assail them; looking down at the pedestrians from our window, I would see the round black heads below suddenly stampede across the road in panic, or mill round and round in blind delirium, swept by fear like the wind-blown autumn leaves about my stable yard. Much of this alarm is caused by the police who are trigger happy after 6 o'clock and spend the evenings firing indiscriminately.

The President's Memorial typifies the place. Construction began after the assassination of the founder and president a decade ago. It is a huge phallic symbol. As it is in solid cement, with no stairs up it, the light which was put on top remains unlit. It is beginning to lean, and cranes prop it up like a gang of lanky giants. It took so long to build that the President, lying in a crystal coffin in an unairconditioned basement, began to disintegrate – but for his hands, feet and head, these have done a Michael Jackson and turned white.

All round the skyline are the skeletal frames of partly built hospitals, hotels and office blocks. Building stopped a decade ago – all the cement was sacrificed to make the memorial. Now they have forgotten how to construct.

24–25 December. Terrific bustle on the day before Christmas. Dominie in the kitchen, surrounded by steam and smells. Our Christmas tree is in the well of the staircase, it is a 15-feet high spruce felled from Coppin's Wood. Dominie and Candy have done most of the decoration, festoons of tinsel and galaxies of balls and lights and twinkly things on the tree in such profusion that you can hardly see the branches, also the crib on the chest in the back hall – some of my old Noah's Ark animals are still turning up – and the holly up the stairs and behind the pictures. My job, as usual, is to tie the angel and star to the top of the tree. As usual, I loose my temper. I also hang the mistletoe from the nail on the ceiling-beam in the front hall; I remember Papa hanging mistletoe on that same nail 50 years ago. The balls keep falling off the tree. If they don't smash, Claude retrieves them and carries them out into the garden.

On Christmas Eve we had about 60 people in for drinks. They drank nearly eight gallons of my mulled wine. We went to Midnight Mass, as usual – it was nice to see the village church packed – then we all spilled out of the church and cheerfully wished each other Merry Christmas and walked or drove back to our houses to get ready for the morning.

At home everyone went to bed, having hung up their stockings over the bigger fireplace in the drawing-room and left a mince-pie and glass of madeira on the chimney piece for Father Christmas. Dominie and I bedded later, having 'supervised' him.

Next morning was a big change from a few years ago; this time it was the wrinklies who were awake and eager, the pimplies who had to be roused. We opened our stockings before breakfast. It was our turn to go over the valley for lunch: we went to Don John's, Sam eked out the drink with an eye-dropper but Annette's turkey and plum pudding were delicious. After that we returned home, collecting Hart from his cottage on the way; then Violet and Teddy arrived. We opened the presents from each other, and from uncles and aunts and godparents and friends, all of which Dominie had put under the Christmas tree. I roasted chestnuts on the hall fire. The floor became strewn with wrapping-paper and string and crumbs; we had tea of mince-pies and brandy butter. As the afternoon changed into the early evening it seemed to me that between Hart and Nanny, as they sat side by side on a sofa, there was a very ancient and slow and shy flirtation taking place. Finally we had dinner and the wrinklies went to bed and the pimplies stayed up.

28 December. Dakar is the capital of Senegal, previously a French colony. It looked very un-French when I arrived last night, even as early as 8.30 the streets were deserted, no sign of nocturnal crowds or open bistros, but now in the bright sunshine it is busy and cheerful. It is attractive, light and airy with many trees and flowering shrubs, dominated by oleander and bougainvillaea. The buildings are human sized, rather than corporation sized, even the President's Palace looks inhabitable, rather than being an ostentatious hulk large enough to house several battalions of secret police and tithe gatherers. A charming pantomime doll stands sentry outside the palace gate. He has a scarlet tunic and a scarlet hat. This is shaped exactly like a paper bag, but has a Grenadier badge in the middle and a scarlet ribbon under the chin. The trousers are short, more like plus-fours, and black with a complicated clocking in gold braid down the side. A pair of leather wellington boots, an old rifle and a fine moustache complete the effect.

I walk from the hotel to the far point of the town, along the sea cliffs: sloping mud banks covered with the spiny growth of salt-wreaked wattle and barricading an ugly shore of black and rust-coloured boulders. On the banks to landward are many creepers, dominantly one with clusters of small pink flowers; millions of little pale butterflies flitter among all these, thousands of dragonflies dart and hover above them, and hundreds of kite wheel and glide above it all. Part of my walk is along the back of the Presidential Gardens: suddenly, over the wall with its line of rusting spikes, a black face surmounted by a scarlet bag pops up and stares at me.

The people here generally look cheerful, but many of them are on crutches, and there are many beggars, some with leprosy. The hawkers are particularly pestiferous. One fellow came up to me immediately I had walked out of the hotel. He was nattily attired in a sky-blue robe (fatara), but the horny great toenails peeping from his plastic flip-flops could have disembowelled an alligator.

'Mon ami!' he exclaimed, 'Ce n'est pas toi? Mais oui! Tu es ici encore!' I found myself shaking hands vigorously with him.

'Et comment vas-tu, mon vieux? Je suis desolé que je ne t'avoir vois pas le dernier . . .'

'We have never met before,' I said firmly, removing my hand and sidling off.

'But that is my great misfortune,' he replied, no whit abashed. 'This is your first time in Senegal? I give it to you. It is your country. You are at home here. I have here a present for your wife . . .'

The trouble is that one never knows when a man is being genuinely friendly, and when he is trying to scrounge. The answer is usually both, I suppose, so one should be polite but determined.

The women here have very complicated hair-styles. The basis is long thin plaits; these are then made up into an immense variety of shapes. I have rarely seen any duplications. From behind, many of the heads resemble sea creatures: the carapaces of crabs and lobsters, sea anemones, long-streamered jellyfish, gulper eels, conches and cowries. I was told that a woman will spend up to £30 to have her hair done thus; the average monthly salary is £12. Perhaps because of this, one sees fewer women carrying things on their heads than in other parts of Africa. (I wonder why we Europeans don't do this? Are our neck muscles weaker or our sense of balance inferior? Apart from

Billingsgate fish porters, and a picture of Simple Simon's pieman in a Victorian nursery book, I do not remember any example of this in England.)

29 December. I have been a Queen's Messenger for four years and as such have travelled a million miles, but this is the first time by river ferry.

The useless aeroplane from Senegal to the Gambia was 'cancelled' – i.e. broke down – so I had to get up at 3 o'clock this morning to be driven the 300 kilometres to Banjul. My driver from the Embassy was Jahan, a small, wry Gambian with a face like a crumpled leather bag. Unfortunately the whole of the drive was in the dark: through the deserted streets of Dakar, then along a road which skirts the very edge of the Sahara desert. The moon lit up the sparse bushes and the extraordinary upside-down silhouettes of the baobab trees. Our headlights occasionally flickered on a bird, startled from the centre of the road. Once we saw a hare, once a low slinking creature with a huge shaggy tail – a honey badger? – and we ran over a damn-fool rabbit who decided to charge us in panic rather than escape into the 3.5 million square miles of the desert. There was almost no traffic. What there was, was commercial: a couple of oil tankers and half a dozen lorries, packed up to 20 feet in height with sacks – cocoa? We turned off the 'main' road after Kaolac. 'Not a nice place,' said Jahan, a pee stain in the sand, from what I could discern, and the road became appalling, so many potholes in places that it was more like a cart track. It was a relief to drive over the softer places which were carpeted by sand drifts.

Most of the passengers on the ferry were women going to market. They wore the brightly patterned robe called, somehow appropriately, the 'gran-buba', accompanied by a – usually matching – headscarf tied with the ends fanned out into wings. They looked much more impressive than the men, who were mainly a dispirited, scruffy lot, in dirty clothes, some wearing little knitted tea-cosy hats. The women assembled in groups and nattered throughout the half-hour journey: they ignored the men; the men ignored each other. There were 32 head of cattle, zebu type with long, graceful horns and humps on their whithers. Poor things, they kept slipping on the steel plates of the decking and then getting whacked by the drovers; one at least got its revenge with an almighty kick with a rear leg. The many chickens were not much happier: tied together by the legs they lay in heaps, stoically silent but for the occasional despairing squawk. There was an old beggar into whose plastic bowl I emptied my few Senegalese coins: he smiled and babbled at me and pointed to the livestock and laughed. There was a half-wit boy who squatted down beside my car and, pressing his lips to its rear bumper, remained thus for the whole journey, like some peculiar limpet. He had a chicken between his knees; I did not look too closely, lest I be revolted.

When they got ready to disembark, the women put their bundles on their heads. I inspected the nearest one who was balancing a large bowl and saw that she was keeping it steady the whole time with little movements of her head and neck, unconscious adjustments similar to the steering-wheel movements of a driver.

I took off at noon on a flight to Ghana. Our approach to Accra is like flying over a great slab of flesh: the bare soil is pink, it turns red where it has been disturbed so that the marks of tracks resemble livid weals over the surface of the land; on them one can see – from up here smaller than lice – lines of cattle. The bushes which grow upon it are spaced sparsely apart like the peppercorn tufts of hair on a Bushman's head.

5 January 1990. Dominie has been to her mother's for the last two days, now she is back. The doctor told her that her mother will probably be dead within six months. Dominie says she probably will have to go and stay a lot with her mother when she gets worse.

Mr Dewbit the farrier came to pare the foals' feet. I had to help hold them. The nervy bay colt kicked me in the mouth. As I drove down the lane from Westwoods I bared my teeth into the driving-mirror to see if my gums were still bleeding. Old Mrs Bullace who was taking Brandy for a walk saw me thundering towards her with my face stretched into a bloodied snarl and nearly threw herself into the ditch.

*

10 January, Zimbabwe. After a restless night I arise at 6 o'clock and have time for one cup of coffee in the hotel lobby before I join the bus queue just outside; the 6.30 coach arrives on time and I board it to find myself sitting next to an Australian biddy. She is wearing gloves and a hat as if she was off to tea at the vicar's. She's never been out of Australia before. She natters at me in a nasal cackle, mainly about Brisbane; it sounds a boring sort of place. As we proceed, she seems increasingly fretful. Finally she looks about furtively and then whispers: 'I'm surprised to see so many of these ... um ... *darkish* people about.'

'Darkish?'

'Er. You know. Tinted.'

'Oh, I see what you mean. Yes, there are a lot of them about, here in Africa,' I say.

She falls into a pensive silence. She starts, amazed, and points at a 'darkish' person wearing a natty suit and overtaking us in an expensive car; I think she'd prefer him to have a bone through his nose and be astride a donkey. She tells me about her grandchildren, all of whom have names that sound like synthetic fibres: Charlene, Neolene, Vincel, Sarille.

We disembus at the airport. I show the tickets I had bought at the tourist agency last night and am soon in the air heading towards the Victoria Falls. We can see the spume from it on the horizon, as we land. From the landing-strip we take a tripper's bus on the 15-mile journey to the falls. Australian Biddy has come all the way. I rather avoid her and seem to have teamed up with two pleasant fellows who are both in their late fifties, tall and gnarled and grizzled and slow-smiling: though very similar they are friends, not relations: one is an ex-Rhodesian settler, now a Zimbabwean, the other is a Briton from Wessex. Their names are Pinkston and Maiden. As we are driven to the Victoria Falls National Park, we are lectured to by a guide. She is a willowy, young tinted person with the even white teeth and lustrous brown eyes of an impala. She is called Scholastica (it sounds pretty, but reads ugly). She tells us that the falls are about a mile wide, have a 100-yard drop and the spray goes up about 800 yards; because of this the local name is 'Mosi-o-tunya', 'the Smoke that Thunders'. She speaks of the falls with a certain bored resignation; her real interest is in public buildings and she becomes animated at the sight of a library or police station, and quite effusive over a hospital or a school.

When we reach the gates which mark the entrance of the small National Park we are pestered by hawkers trying to rent or sell mackintoshes. I refuse, in spite of a persistent hawker who gets more and more angry with me, insisting that I will get soaked. I do not believe him; besides, no matter if I am wrong, I am wearing only a shirt and trousers, and it is warm. Scholastica leads us to the banks of the Zambezi, just above the falls. The noise is a steady booming roar, the spray towers above as a billowing white cloud. We walk towards it. There is a fine mizzling fog, which sometimes turns into a drizzle if the wind gusts our way. Drops patter on the leaves overhead; Scholastica tells us that this continuous drenching has created a unique pocket of rain 'forest', a mixture of deciduous trees, ferns, sedges, reeds, mosses and lichens. We descend below the lip of the falls. The water spurts out above us so we can see the sheer, glistening wet cliff behind; the roar is intense, the mass of water a mixture of creamy amber where the curtain is smooth, and snowy billows of spume and foam and veils of mist. We climb up again and walk along the edge of the canyon, opposite the falls. They do not sweep down in one continuous curtain; the flow is separated by rocky islands which have saved the lives of many animals, human or otherwise, which have been caught in the current. Scholastica says she knew a person who had a friend who met someone who had seen a hippopotamus being swept over: 'It landed on that sticking-out rock and burst apart like a rotten watermelon.' Australian Biddy, swathed in a plastic mackintosh, clutches at her throat to stop a scream of horror at the very idea. By now I am soaked. That maddening hawker was right, how annoying. We walk further on, the drizzle becomes a downpour; several of the party peel off and wander back through the woodland to the bus. Hoops of rainbow arch out of the grass, some as small as semi-cartwheels, some as big as a footbridge. Diamonds twinkle in rows along the arching stems of reeds. It is a crystal wonderland. The downpour, in a sudden gust, becomes so intense that I can hardly breathe, I seem to be inhaling more water than air, the iron smell of wetness catches at my nose; I have to shut my eyes against the pain of the pelting.

I am standing on the edge of Zimbabwe looking at the edge of Zambia for I have finally reached the end of the path and am on a jutting-out rocky platform overhanging the canyon. A double-arched rainbow gleams far below, the yellowish waters hurl down before me, the mountain of spray towers above, the whole environment is thundering and booming and shaking; I feel like some Wagnerian god about to do something dramatic.

In fear that I shall have an irresistible impulse to spread open my arms and swoop like a swallow down into the canyon I turn and start on the return journey to the bus.

I'm thirsty. A local brew is for sale in a stall of poles and canvas. It is called 'Mosi, the Beer that Thunders'. It should have an interesting effect. Maiden and Pinkston have already had a couple of pints each, I shan't sit next to them in the bus.

I dried out rapidly in the hot sun during my walk back to the bus; now we have been driven in it to a crocodile farm. It is full of concrete tanks, each one contains a batch of crocodiles of the same age – if they were of different ages the big ones would eat the little ones. The sizes range from little doddymites not much bigger than lizards to hulking great brutes. The biggest are the breeders, several females and a colossal bull over five yards long and weighing about a ton and a half. He has his back to us, his snout pressed against the wire the other side. I walk round and squat down to inspect him; his eyes are shut, I peer closely at his teeth in his lipless mouth, they are the size of my thumbs.

His eyes are no longer closed but are staring unblinkingly into mine. Uneasily, I move off.

Scholastica calls us over to a tank and a keeper blethers in a bored monotone about crocodiles: they are even more primitive than the dinosaur; they kill their prey by drowning and tuck them under banks to rot; they lay eggs; and so forth. He holds up a baby, six months old and about a foot and a half long. It mews, like a cat. He asks if anyone wants to feel it. There are no offers. Finally, deciding it would be a bit feeble not to, I volunteer. To hold, it is about the same size and shape as a ferret, but rubbery to the touch. I also have to grip it as if holding a ferret, round the neck and shoulders so that it cannot twist round and bite. As I hold it up, it widdles down my trousers. Australian Biddy snickers into her palm, Pinkston and Maiden guffaw. Peeved, I hand it back.

The crocodiles are bred for their skins: they are made into bags and belts; the tails are sent to hotels to be eaten by trippers; the rest of the corpse is chopped up and fed to the remaining crocodiles. It seems rather immoral. Perhaps Buddhists think the same thing about my sheep.

We have finished our buffet lunch in the garden of an hotel. It was pleasant enough, but packed with trippers, and a tented stage contained a band whose chief intention was to beat the living daylights out of resounding things: drums, bongos, hollow logs, ewers, steel cans, metal pipes, wooden bells; one could hardly hear oneself shout. We have been driven to the banks of the Zambezi and have embarked on a 'boat', a sort of floating platform; square-ended fore and aft, with a bar and a bridge at the stern, railings all around and seats and tables in rows on the deck. We chunter upstream, between forested banks fringed with great patches of reeds. For a second, I see a hippopotamus: a great, shiny, macabre head rearing out of the water, gaping wide an awesome, vast mouth and subsiding. It is the only hippopotamus seen; we land on an island and see several huge footprints on the sandy beaches; once we hear a rumbling roar like a motor boat starting up; that is all the evidence that hippopotami are about. I stroll into the woodland and find some strange 'fruits' below a palm. They look like rusting cannonballs; they are very hard and about the size of a tangerine. I bring one back to the 'boat' and Scholastica tells me it is called an ivory nut and, once the husk is removed, it can be carved.

11 January. It has been raining. I have spent much time trying to get the husk off my ivory nut. It is 11 o'clock in the morning. I don't quit this morgue for another eight hours. But now it has stopped raining so I'll go out and wander about; the cathedral is the other side of the square, Cousin Stephen's art gallery is not far and there is an interesting botanical park beside it.

*

The Cathedral of St Mary and All Saints is a pleasant enough building, made simply from the local granite and with a square belfry. There are only three people here: two cheerful fellows with brooms sweeping round the font and one tragic-looking soul, sitting in a rear pew and staring sad-eyed at the past or drear-eyed at the future. There are memorials on the walls. Not only are the people they commemorate mostly forgotten, but so too are the units and the causes for which they fought: who were the Mazoe Patrol and the Mashonaland Squadron? what was the Matabele Rebellion of 1893 about? why did Captain Charles Kenelm Digby Jones die in the service of his country in Siberia on the 23rd of September 1918? Here, on a wall, hangs the most inspiring of all flags, the White Ensign. It is thin and worn and old. A plaque says it is the battle ensign of HMS *Mashona*, a destroyer sunk in action against the *Bismarck* on the 28th of May 1941. The first church built here was of wattle and daub, and thatched. All that remains of it is the altar cross, made by a Trooper Tom Purdon out of cigar boxes and brass tacks.

BLARE! I've nearly hit the ceiling. I was just peering at an icon in the gloom of the Mother Cecil chapel. All was as quiet as a mouse except for the distant sough of sweeping when the 2014 organ pipes above my head suddenly bellowed out:

> 'We plough the fields and sca-a-tter
> The good seed on the land . . .'

The National Art Gallery was endowed by Cousin [Sir] Stephen [Courtauld]. It is an ugly but well-windowed building. Downstairs, there is a show of local stone sculptures. They are well carved and there is nothing vulgar or commonplace about them, they certainly do not pander to 'pretty-prettyness'. I find them unpleasant. They are of squat, hunched-up, puggy-featured figures; nothing smiles or even looks placid, the average expression is morose, several are distinctly belligerent and a few are agonised. Even the stone looks ugly, smoothed to show leprous yellow blotches or left rough in scabby patches; one stone, lepidolite, is of a virulent mauve. They are very well presented, singly or in groups of three or four, on simple pedestals; the whole effect is of a motionless and rather sinister crowd of brooding goblins.

Last time I was here there were many pictures on show given by Cousin Stephen. His taste must not have been to my taste: to me the landscapes were gloomy and the abstracts were daubs in muddy browns and dingy greys; he did not have the touch of his brother Sam who founded the Courtauld Institute of Art. Today, upstairs, they are showing the works of local painters, and at least they are more colourful and cheerful.

I have decided to go to the junk shop I have often visited before. It is still full of rubbish, remnants of the Empire, ranging from cheap framed pictures, mostly of idealised English pastures or Scotch glens, to old books and magazines (e.g. *Sussex Countryside* 1925). There is even one shelf crammed with empty whisky and gin bottles. Amongst all this chaos there is not a single thing which catches the eye because of its antiquity, beauty or interest; it is a work of genius to have assembled such vast variety with such consistent grottiness.

The genius is sitting behind his counter. I always like to see him, his huge white beard and moustache make him look pleasingly eccentric and although his smile is hidden in the shrubbery his eyes twinkle merrily. He must be a horrible sight at mealtimes: does he use brain or brawn? Does he carefully manipulate his fork beneath that enormous overhanging woofly moustache and then puggle about until he finds his mouth; or does he ram the fork into the centre of the thicket and force it through, like a bush flail? How much of the liquor is sopped up and how much of the solids is brushed off before they reach their destination?

21 January. The organisation which records and protects badgers in Essex heard that we have a sett in Aldercarr Wood and asked if they could send their recorder round to check. I agreed, but only on condition that they keep the site secret; I do not want any badger baiters hearing about it. The man who came is a bit like a badger himself: whiskers all over his face and a busy way of fossicking about under bushes. He has been most interesting: 'Most setts will be in an area of very light soil. They are clean animals, and usually change their bedding every day, you can often see the trail of old leaves and pine needles where they have dropped it. They also bury their faeces, you sometimes find the little graves where they have done this. In spite of their cleanliness, they have lots of fleas, so the first thing they do when they get up in the evening is go outside and have a good scratch. You can often find their hairs.'

Sure enough, the sett is in a sandy patch in the corner of the wood. He confirmed it is in use: the soil outside being freshly trampled on, and with badger prints upon it. We found some hairs. Badger hairs are brindled, with dark, pointed tips; they are oval in cross-section, so you can feel them 'bumping' if you roll them between finger and thumb. I took him to a bank in the adjacent wood, a furlong off, to see what I presumed was a fox's earth but which could be another sett. He confirmed that it is a sett: there may be two families of badgers, or merely one bachelor who moves from sett to sett on alternating days.

'As you're here,' I said, 'would you like to see the place where it is rumoured that badgers used to live before the war?'

We went. As we scrambled down the steep bank off Dark Meadows I saw, with my newly learned knowledge, that the five huge burrows in the sandy soil were likely to be setts. They are. We found three more under blackthorn bushes.

'You must have at least a couple of families living here, probably more,' the badger man said. 'There are only about 400 badgers in Essex, your estate may have quite a good proportion of them.'

So this has been a most satisfactory day.

26 January, Costa Rica. There are about ten of us in the mini-bus being driven to the Carara nature reserve. Most of the passengers are Canadians and by the look of them, nonagenarians, so we won't be walking particularly briskly through the jungle. Our driver is also the guide. His name is José. He is in his mid-twenties and has a small black moustache and a Mancunian wife who is in her home-town of Manchester at the moment, about to have their first baby. As he drives he lectures us through a microphone. He says that Costa Rica has an enormous range of natural environs: Pacific, Caribbean, humid jungles, temperate uplands, cloud forests, meadowland, mangrove swamps, lagoons, rivers, volcanoes and caves, ranging from below sea level to 12,580 feet above. There are about 850 species of birds, more than the

USA and Canada combined, more butterflies than the whole of the African continent, 378 species of reptiles and amphibians, 205 species of mammals, uncounted numbers of plants including thousands of orchids: all this in an area of 19,700 square miles, two thirds the size of Scotland.

I ask him what are the huge stone balls, up to six feet across, which can be seen in people's gardens, or in church yards or parks. José says no-one knows, but they were made by the indigenous Amerindians and may be money like the 'millstone coins' of Polynesia.

It is election week. There are two parties of consequence: the supporters of one bear green and white flags, of the other, blue and red. They also hoot their car horns according to the syllables of the party leaders. As each leader has three syllables, CAL-DE-RÓN, CAST-ILL-O, they sound exactly the same to me, perhaps there is some subtle nuance to the initiated; but as everyone seems to be hooting at the top of their horns it must be pretty difficult to discern the subtlety amid the bedlam. The coloured flags of the political parties are everywhere. There seems very little hostility between parties. A taxi has just driven past with a huge red and blue flag tied to its fender, presumably the driver's. The passengers have stuck about four green and white flags out of the windows; driver and passengers are all wreathed in smiles. Sometimes one will see both flags fluttering from the same roof, or tied to different trees in the same garden. Groups of children stand by the roadside waving flags, sometimes of both colours. If the children won't fight or argue, who will? There seems no particular characteristic which indicates what party a man will support. Hovels and rich villas can fly one flag or the other; old Fords or new Range Rovers the same. The few Negroes or Amerindians seem equally impartial, perhaps there is a bit more green/white in the country and red/blue in the towns, but not much. Overall there does seem to be slightly more red/blue. That is the present opposition. I ask José what is the main difference between the political parties. 'The colour of their flags,' he says briefly.

An iguana runs across the road. For a moment I think it is some sort of mongoose: it is the same size and conformation, but then I see it is a sickly green and has a row of frill-like flaps down its back; it looks like a little frightened dragon. José says that a scientific survey deduced that you can get 500 times as much meat from breeding them in almost natural conditions in the jungle as you would get from conventional grazing animals on cleared pasture. It tastes of chicken.

We have stopped by a bend in a river. On the far side we can see six long shapes lying in the shallows, they are crocodiles. It is intriguing to see such an animal out of a zoo, one feels that someone will come along and say bossily 'They shouldn't be allowed, they are nasty and dangerous and neither tame nor useful. Cage them up.'

We have arrived at the beach where we will swim until lunch. Round the headland there is a small bay, attractive with its coconut-palms and deserted but for a little man in ragged shorts who is lurking amid the trees. There are many brown pelicans floating in the water and frigate birds flying above them. There are rocks, but not many fish; I have been in the water for about an hour and have hardly seen anything. Some of the pelicans let me swim within ten feet of them until they laboriously flap off.

As I leave the little cove the Canadian professor arrives. He is one of our party: tall, thin, with tiny hands and feet, a grey goatee and tightly pursed lips; likeable, although fussily anxious.

'I am going to lie in the sun and go to sleep,' he says.

It is ten minutes later. I am inspecting a heap of shingle on the main beach when the professor hastens past.

'You didn't sleep for very long,' I say.

He looks fretful: 'That man in short pants drove me away.'

'Did he throw coconuts at you?'

'No. He just kept staring. From behind trees. A different tree each time. Every time I looked up, there he was, peeking at me. I couldn't catch him on the move. He must'a kind'a flitted. It made me real nervous.'

'Was he looking at you in a hostile way, or affectionately?'

'Neither. Just curiously.'

'Were you doing anything peculiar?'

'No, certainly I was not,' he says somewhat icily, 'unless by "peculiar" you mean lying on the beach minding my own business.'

'Perhaps he was interested in your beard.'

'Perhaps,' he says dourly, and moves off to the beach bar.

The jungle is warm but dry and smells of leaves. The undergrowth is not too thick so one can see quite far between the great tree trunks. Lianas loop and dangle overhead. There are many clumps of bird-of-paradise plant, all in full flower; also wild bananas, which have a strange almost obscene purple flower on the end of a long dangling stalk, looking, as a jovial Lancastrian with us put it, 'like a donkey's dong'. Butterflies are everywhere, there are several of different species basking in a patch of sunlight.

'What sort are those?' I ask José.

'They are blue butterflies, red butterflies, yellow butterflies, many-coloured butterflies,' says the twerp.

The mosquitoes are bad, there are also lice on the end of leaves, waiting to pounce and suck. They resemble short-legged, fat, green spiders. José brushes some off and lets them run over his hand.

We have reached an attractive lake, or perhaps it is part of a large, slow river. There are patches of water hyacinth, some with their pale blue spire of flowers. Varieties of water birds wade or meditate in the shallows. There are three boat-billed herons, droll creatures: with their outsize, cumbersome beaks, they look more like the ungainly pelican than the graceful heron. Two least grebe are flirting near a log that floats in the centre of the largest weed-free patch. The log blinks as they get close and drifts towards them. They scuttle off over the surface of the water.

There it is! A macaw! An almost unbelievable, unnatural, legendary vision painted in fiery scarlet, glowing yellow and vivid blue. It is in the top of a tall tree, fidgeting about. An extra blaze of colour, like the phoenix bursting into flame, and it has spread its wings and gone, flown further into the depths of the jungle. What a comparison to the dejected prisoners one sees in drawing-rooms, manacled to guano-encrusted perches!

*

Back in the hotel. It is getting seedy: paint is peeling off the outside, there is a smell of mouldering carpets, the menu is exactly the same boring and limited one as it was last May, and as badly cooked. The weird waitress is still here. Each time one catches her eye she flashes an enormous grin, raises one eyebrow in a significant manner and bobs in a sort of half curtsey. I don't know why. Perhaps she is an idiot. The trouble is, I can't resist a furtive glance now and then, and she must be watching me like a hawk, because I always catch her eye and she then breaks out into her odd little routine.

27 January. The hotel-to-hotel tourist bus is almost full when I board it at the crack of dawn so I go and sit on the long seat at the back, which is empty. Most of the people seem to be American, which is not a bad thing, they are almost always friendly and polite and at least one can understand their language. The bus stops at the final hotel and the last two people come aboard and force their way up the aisle to sit next to me. I take an instant dislike to them: the elder, in his fifties, is burly and muscular, his shirt is unbuttoned almost to his navel so one can see an assortment of charms and pendants nestling in the thick black hairs of his chest. He wears a gold wrist-watch the size of an ashtray, shorts and a baseball hat with its brim turned up. His companion, a surly looking youth of about twenty, would probably be handsome if he wasn't cultivating an Arafat-style six-day stubble.

Having sat, the elder one rummages about in a bag and produces a large cigar and a gold lighter. He lights up, exhales a cloud of vile fumes and looks about.

'Hi,' he says to me, 'I'm Franklyn and this is my son, Ike. Folks call me Frank. Say "Hi", Ike.'

Ike says 'Hi.'

'And, so, what's your name?'

I tell him, somewhat reluctantly.

'Well George, have you been white-water rafting before?'

'No.'

'It's easy George. All you have to remember is to stay aboard.' He laughs merrily. 'That's what I keep telling you, isn't it Ike?'

'Sure Dad,' says Ike wearily.

'Where are you from, George?'

'Oh, England, huh. Last time there I was in Coventry and it rained for two weeks, then Mom got some sort of dust allergy in the hotel at Stratford upon Avon. Didn't she Ike?'

'Sure did, Dad.'

'I'm American, first generation, my parents are Romanian Jews. That makes me a Jewish Romanian-American, doesn't it Ike?'

'Yeah, Dad.'

'Mom's a first generation American too. But her parents are Polish Jews. So I guess you're an American Jewish Romanian-Pole, aren't you, Ike?'

'If you say so, Dad.'

'You know, George, the trouble about Jews is that if you get two of us together, you gets three opinions. Now . . .'

He prattles on until we reach the river.

With disparagement, the head guide looks at us assembled under a large tree by the banks of the Reventazon River. We are a motley crowd of trippers ranging from the young and fit to the old and obese: the former includes three young honeymooning couples, Ike, and a couple of Costa Rican youths who think each other amazingly witty and fall about with helpless but irritating merriment at each remark; the latter includes the Two Little Tubs, American women about 60 years old. They are so short and dumpy that they are almost completely spherical; they are wearing T-shirts, shorts and gym shoes. One cannot help admiring the Great American Momma, she doesn't know when she's beat. There is also a middle-aged French Canadian couple on honeymoon, both having married for the second time. He has his hair done up in a pony-tail with a gold and black band, and wears pink-framed spectacles. She is in shorts and a T-shirt and is quite pretty in a faded way but has rather skinny legs and the most amazingly protruberant knee-caps; it is as if she has glued two lightly baked buns halfway up her legs.

We are standing next to the rafts. I am rather disappointed with them, they are merely large inflatable rubber boats. I had presumed that they would be made of logs and tied together with rope.

The head guide speaks: 'Don't try to keep dry, you'll get wet in the first 30 seconds and stay wet for the next five hours. Don't forget that what you are about to do is dangerous. If you fall out, lie on your back and try to keep your feet out of the water, else they may get jammed between rocks and you'll either drown or get broken legs.'

Three people quietly leave the group and tiptoe back to the bus.

'Each raft will have an expert guide at the stern. He will give you orders WHICH MUST BE OBEYED. Your raft shall be divided to right and left, each side takes its own orders. The orders are what to do with your paddles and will be either "forward", "back" or "stop". You must sit on the side of the raft, not in the middle, and jam your feet under the sides – if you don't, you will probably be flung out at the first rapid.'

I find the Two Little Tubs standing near me and edge away, I don't want to be the one who will have to save them, or give them the Kiss of Life.

We are issued with life-jackets. Frank makes a fuss, telling all and sundry that a swimmer as good as he is merely hindered by the restrictions of the garb. Ike sighs and looks imploringly at the leaves above. We then have to put on yellow crash-helmets. Luckily they meet Frank's approval: 'Hey, how do I look in this?' he asks. The helmets have large air-holes at the top, so when donned they make the Two Little Tubs look like salt and pepper pots.

'Right, choose your raft,' calls out the head guide. I look about with alarm, I am standing next to the Two Little Tubs again.

Frank calls out: 'Here, George, we've kept a place for you.'

I hurry over.

The guide for our boat is Fernando, a sinewy youth with an aquiline profile and a large Adam's apple; he'll look like an impressive old admiral when he gets old. Right now he cannot get a word in edgeways.

'George, this is Fernando our captain, and this is Michelo, the only other member of the crew. We're lucky we've got only five in our boat, all the others have seven. Michelo is 21, he is not married and has no children that he knows of; he works for the tourist industry and is learning his job. Michelo, this is George. George is English. He is married with four children and two wards. He lives on a farm where he grows wheat and has willow trees and sheep and six dogs and two cats. He likes cats more than dogs. His wife breeds ponies. She has twenny-seven of them. George, you and Michelo sit at the back here, Ike and I will sit up in front, as I've done this before and can show you what to do. Don't forget to jam your feet under the sides and keep paddling in time with me and Ike.'

The Reventazon River varies in width from 50 to 300 yards. The water is a cloudy grey, partly because of the volcanic dust in it and partly because of the tumbling and grinding of its large blue-grey boulders. These boulders gather in shoals where the water shallows, sometimes they spread across as weirs from one bank to the other. These we nego-tiate with a rush and a splash and the controlled dabbing of our paddles; more exciting are the stretches where the river drops and narrows: rocks rear out of the water like the snouts of whales and the water turns silken as it squeezes and swoops past them. Even more dangerous are the rocks only just submerged; the water builds up in large humps before them and hollows out in deep troughs after. These are the most exciting bits. We have to paddle like mad while Fernando screams orders; the spray soaks and blinds us, the raft undulates and bucks as it passes over the heaving waters, we drop into troughs with stomach-churning sudden-ness and rear up so that Frank and Ike hang several feet above the rest of us. What makes it all the more exciting is that Fernando keeps for-getting his right and left so we get a torrent of instructions such as:

'BACK LEFT
                    FORWARD RIGHT
        NO I MEAN BACK RIGHT FORWARD LEFT
            FORWARDLEFT FORWARDLEFT FORWARDLEFT
I MEAN RIGHT
            stop
                    STOP
                        STOP!!!
FORWARD LEFT BACK RIGHT I SAID BACK RIGHT I MEAN
LEFT STOP STOP!!
    LEFT EVERYONE!'

As a result we descend half the rapids backwards.

Usually, when we have shot the rapids, Frank reproves Ike for not paddling in unison. Ike is a good son and says nothing, but I have noticed that for half the time Frank does no paddling at all; he sits rigid with horror, gaping at the white fury in front of him.

We swirl round an eddy and glide into a side pool. Another raft thunders past in a smash of spray and a flurry of foam. There, side by side in the stern, bent low over their paddles which dip and flash in perfect simultaneity, their teeth bared in snarls of effort and concentration, are the Two Little Tubs. I feel a wave of exaltation at the ridiculous, inspiring sight.

Between the hurly-burly of the rapids we drift in the peace and tranquillity of the deep, slow waters. The placid appearance of the water is often illusory, a second glance will show that the surface is boiling and seething with the strength of the currents beneath. The scenery is enchanting, and of great serenity, all still and silent in the blanketing heat. Venerable trees dip their mossy beards of Spanish moss in the waters, butterflies flit amongst the foliage. Sometimes the banks become great rocky precipices several hundred feet high and we are immersed in cool shade. In spite of their steepness the rock faces are completely clothed in vegetation: mosses, grasses, ferns, bushes, saplings and forest giants, some of the trees grow at peculiar horizontal angles away from the cliffs.

A toucan just flew over us, it looked like a large, yellow, flying nose.

Someone fell out of another raft: a young, tall Costa Rican on honeymoon. His little brown wife made an almighty fuss, cackling and waving and shouting advice; he merely floated past us and rapidly out of sight, followed by his paddle. He smiled imploringly at us as he went by, but didn't say a word. We caught up with him after about 400 yards, his face had turned pale green, the colour tanned people go when we pinker ones go grey. Ike stuck out a paddle, the floater grabbed it and swung round to me, Fernando and I grabbed each side of his life-jacket and tweaked him out of the water. He seemed a merry sort of fellow and within a couple of minutes he was laughing and chattering about his adventure; but he said his knees felt quite badly bruised.

We have travelled for about three hours and have reached a large bend in the river. Our rafts are beached on the shoally bank on the inside of the bend and most of us are bathing in the deeper waters on the outer curve. Frank is standing up to his waist in the water, trying to light a wet cigar. Ike is chatting up a girl from another raft. The Two Little Tubs are splashing about in the shallows; their wet T-shirts and shorts, clinging to them, emphasise their rotundities. Having waded upstream and swum downstream with the current several times, I espy a wild banana growing about 50 yards in the jungle and decide it would be an apt thing to eat one of its fruits. I force my way through the tangle of rushes that line the bank and meet, at eye level, a large spider. Something rustles suddenly in a clump of tall reeds nearby. I remember Frank's stories of the snakes he has dealt with in this part of the world, and return to the river. On the way back I find a beautiful little beetle on a stem of sedge: it looks like a small ladybird but has no spots and is a deep ruby red, like an animated drop of blood.

Frank is waiting for me on my return.

'What did you think of that rapid which Fernando called the "Big Sow?"' I ask.

Frank ponders, hesitates, then decides to be honest: 'I reckon my asshole won't unpucker for a week,' he admits.

We rafted for about five hours. Then we showered and changed into dry clothes and lunched in a game-lodge whose open balcony overhung the river. Now we have embussed to be driven through the twilight back to San José. Most of us are tired and sleepy. Even Frank beside me has exchanged his conversation for a peaceful rumbling snore.

The bus is dropping us at our different hotels: first to go are the Two Little Tubs, waving goodbyes to us all and then toddling into the foyer of their hotel. It is now my turn. Reluctantly, I bid farewell to my boisterous extrovert chatterbox friend and his son, Ike, and go in to change and have dinner; then early to bed, I will have to rise at 6.30 tomorrow morning.

The odd waitress is definitely mad. She crept up behind the book I was reading during dinner and suddenly peered at me over the top. It gave me a regular turn. She then laughed and skipped off.

30 January. *The driver who meets me at Heathrow in the early morning says that there have been terrible tempests and floods. Reach the office and telephone Dominie. When I hear her my heart sinks, she's not one to make a fuss but her voice breaks and she says 'Oh thank God you're back, we've had an awful time: the storms have done dreadful damage and George and Fiona are no longer engaged.' I hurry home – or try to, the train dodders from suburb to suburb and hamlet to hamlet or just sits hissing and smouldering for no apparent reason. Dominie meets me in the Land Rover. She looks careworn. I am very disappointed about George and Fiona; we had already taken her to our hearts as one of the family. The storm damage is bad: a lot of old friends have gone, such as the oak by Wastewoods Drive, a huge branch from the great wild pear of Pear Tree Corner; we lost the weathercock on the clock tower and many roof tiles off the house and most of the cottages; the old barn at World's End Farm has collapsed. Worst of all was the poplar avenue: twelve trees fell right across the road, it took Tony, Kerry and Tom two days to clear.*

4 February. *Terrible wind and rain and even huge flakes of slushy snow during the night. I love to lie in bed with the windows open, listening to the trees roar and the rain teem and the gutters chuckle; Dominie and the cats hate it, and cower and snuggle up amid the sheets and blankets. The garden pond overflows, the roads are like rivers and the river is getting dangerously high.*

I had a vile reveille for a Sunday morning: a telephone call at 7.30 and a female voice, rather disapproving, saying 'Pardon but I think your sheep are going to drown.'

Out of bed in a flash, dress, grab Kerry who is just starting breakfast in his cottage, into the Land Rover, dash off to Spowarts Field. Sure enough, the Colne has burst her banks during the night and the sheep are huddled together in the middle of the field, which is slightly higher than the rest, with water up to their stomachs. Kerry drives back to collect tractor and sheep waggon, I wade up to the animals and try to haroosh them to the field entrance, which abuts a small area of dry land. The fools can dart about like minnows. Soon I am soaked and enraged and fifteen of the sheep are perched in a row on the bole of a big balsam poplar which fell in the gale last week. Soaked to chest-height, I finally manage to herd them into the gateway. The sheep and I stand shivering, staring at each other until Kerry arrives with tractor and trailer. We truck the sheep to Park Field, where they start nibbling as if nothing has happened.

I hang my trousers and socks on the rail in front of the Aga, put on dry clothes and boots, walk into the garden to see how deep the pond is, and fall into it. 'Your zodiac sign should be Pisces rather than Taurus,' says Monk, arriving with the dogs.

I put on a third set of clothes and go to feed the ponies in Black Barn. I do not feed Chive, a stallion, fast enough so he has the damn cheek to whirl round and kick me in the thigh with both rear hoofs. In rage and pain I kick him in return, chuck the bucket of food at his head and hobble rapidly out of his stall.

I return home, lay and light the hall fire, brew myself a cup of coffee, pick up the stack of Sunday papers, sit in the leather wing chair, put my feet up on the stool — and the back door rings. It is the Robinsons from Brickhouse Farm: 'You have three ponies out by Rooktree Farm.'

F****************************K!

The boys are still in bed, Dominie is two miles away with the other ponies in New Wood Field, so off I go alone to catch the little bastards. Having caught them and returned them to the field, I have to repair the gap through which they escaped, by the big holly; it was felled in the gale and has flattened part of the fence. It takes an hour to repair.

8 February, Muscat and Oman. The Embassy is all ship-shape and Bristol fashioned with its flagpole and cannons. Our gardens beside the harsh blue sea are overlooked by the battlement's of the Sultan's palace. The general scenery seems as if all flesh has been seared off the land by the intense heat, leaving only bones and a few sinews: angular mountains, some as sharp-pointed as steeples, cut-edged valleys so deep that the sun seems unable to penetrate their depths, and arid, gravel-strewn plains. The steeply angled faces of the mountainsides are pitted with innumerable caves or blotched with colours: reds, browns, purples, greens – not the soft greens of vegetation but the stark colours of mineral. Some mountain peaks have fortresses, sited so that they can look down the cliffs and mountain slopes.

I visited an archaeological site within a sea cove: an abandoned city. It was very frustrating not to know what I was looking at: the ruins, mostly strewn as rubble, though there were a few arches and walls with windows remaining, must have been at least four centuries old and of a mercantile and fishing port. However, some of the graves on the outskirts looked newer: perhaps the descendants of the townspeople come back to be buried here, as my family returns to Gosfield: elephant's graveyard syndrome. The heat was so intense that I expected to hear my sweat sizzle off my face; the hot sand burned through the soles of my shoes so that I had to dance with the dust-devils which were born and leaped and died in the shimmering spaces between the graves.

12 February. Dominie's brothers gave her a birthday party in Buck's this evening. All six of them and their wives or girlfriends were there, also most of the grown-up children: 24 people in all. Jonathan, as eldest brother, stood up at the end of the feast and gave a nice bumbling speech saying how super Dominie is and what a warm and loving nature and how she holds the family together and that 'George is the luckiest man in the room': none of the other wives looked particularly gruntled. The brothers have handed round a hat and are giving Dominie a large urn for the garden. I am giving her a fountain. The basic design is of a bowl which overflows into another bowl which, in its turn, overflows into the pond. The height is about eight foot from the surface of the water, and it weighs about a ton. Tom will have to build a brick plinth to put it on, he should have that ready when they deliver it next month.

16 February. Land on Kai Tak airstrip in the late afternoon. Nice to see the familiar faces waiting for me at the entrance of the aeroplane: Lee Yick Foon, small and dry; Yan Man Loong, young and bland; Moses Lam, thin and sombre. But even Moses is smiling. He has stuck 'NO SMOKING' signs inside the mini-bus and has carefully stencilled extra notices on each sign; one says 'Pigs Smoke', the other 'Except Dogs smoke in Car.'

After I have delivered the bags at Osborne Barracks I go onto the island to stay with cousins William and Caroline at their house in Turtle Cove. As I walk from the Star Ferry to the taxi rank I see a beggar sitting on the pavement beside a rickshaw. He is appallingly deformed with a wry neck, a hunched back and a withered arm. He has taken off his shirt, the better to display his woes. A Japanese tourist goes up to him, squats so that they are face to face, photographs him, and walks away. He has not left even a penny.

I have just bought a book of Chinese poems. One says:

> The rat has teeth,
> some men have no decorum;
> the rat has a skin,
> some men have no manners.

Now I know what it means.

My cousins have a dinner party in the evening. One of their guests is a charming Hong Kong Chinese business woman. Last time I met her she was perturbed: 'I love my new office, but my necromancer says I must leave it, as it has the wrong vibrations for me,' she had complained.

'Then keep your office and change your necromancer,' I said.

'What an ingenious proposal! You must have a back-to-front mind!' she exclaimed.

I remind her of this.

'Yes,' she sighs, arching her lovely eyebrows, 'that was a good idea of yours, but it was not practical.'

20 February. Collected at 10.30 in the mini-bus by Man Loong who drives me to Osborne Barracks. Steven is already there. He has vile toothache, poor fellow. Apart from that he has had a good weekend, bird-watching with an ex-army friend in the Mai Po Marshes.

I am lucky to be travelling with Steven who was a friend even before I became a Queen's Messenger. In fact it was he who introduced me to the Corps. It was at a cocktail party. 'What are you doing now?' he had asked. 'Nothing much,' I said, 'I have left Courtaulds as a full-time employee, it is no longer a family business, I am not on the board and never likely to be; nevertheless people keep writing to me with remarks like "I have just been fired and my family have worked for yours for 200 years so what are you going to do about it?". I am pretending to be a farmer but most of the work is being done by other people. I have written a couple of books but writing is a hobby, not a job, so I am looking for something to do. I suppose I could work for some charity but having been a District Councillor for twenty years the Milk of Human Kindness is beginning to curdle within me.'

'Do what I do,' said Steven. 'The pay's pretty meagre, but it's very different from being stuck behind a desk, you'll see the world, it's reasonably useful and yet you'll have more time at home than you would as a commuter.'

So here we both are, halfway round the world, in the NAAFI, buying provisions for the 2000 miles of train journey.

Peking is cold and dank. It is around freezing point, there are hard scabby patches of snow and all is pervaded with the foggy and smelly emanations of millions of coal fires. The Jianguo Hotel is as comfortable as ever, but the atmosphere is so dry that sparks shoot out of the key-hole when unlocking the bedroom door. I have just got a bad shock whilst turning on my television.

During the long drive from the aerodrome to the Embassy I did not notice much difference in the general attitude of the populace to that before the Tien-an-men Square riots: the people still look more colourful and less dour than four years ago; I have seen no soldiers standing in the street intersections, with arms at the ready, like last summer; nor are many children fancy-dressed in military uniform. But the television is different. At present, in my hotel room, it is dominated by a father figure in a blue Mao suit buttoned up to the neck. He has a pear-shaped face bisected by a huge, fixed smile, made extra twinkly by several steel teeth. His eyes also twinkle. But his finger jabs sharply and dogmatically at the camera and his voice is clipped and harsh. However, Mandarin speakers often sound aggressive when they are not; a conversation about the weather can sound like a dog fight. For all I know he could be giving out the recipe for chopping and roasting parsnips. A line of police come on, unarmed; they are given large bouquets by smiling schoolgirls. Then a line of soldiers arrives, they are armed but still get flowers. The picture fades to be replaced by a typically communist one, a huge hall crammed with thousands of grim-faced politicians listening respectfully to a professional wind-bag on a rostrum.

Being bored with the television, I knock on Steven's door to suggest we hire bicycles for an hour or so. However he has awful toothache and wants to stay in and nurse it. He won't go to a Chinese dentist, 'They might put a bug in my filling,' he says.

*

My horrible rented bike has bad brakes and a seat which keeps tilting up, I already hate it, after five minutes. However Peking is a superb city to bicycle in: as flat as a pancake, and with the motorised traffic well experienced in bicyclists' sudden foibles or absences of mind. You learn to proceed on the pavement side of the cycle-paths; spitters gob the other way, towards the traffic.

I am admiring a well-shaped pair of 180 denier polyester tricot-knitted stretch trousers in front of me, and recalling Betjeman's excellent lines:

> Oh how I wish, oh how I'd like
> To be the saddle on her bike

when the bicyclist suddenly stops and I run into her. I get a cold, scrutable, oriental look and she swerves down a side-street.

I bicycle down some other side-streets, pleasantly avenued by acacia or poplar trees, and branch off into a maze of little alleyways, from six to sixteen feet wide, and full of bustling life. Probably most of the people think that I am a Nosey Parker, invading their privacy, but one old boy, when cycling past, pats me on the shoulder and gives me a beaming smile. It is cold. Two old men sit by a brazier as they play chess(?) with pieces like large flattened buns with characters painted upon them. Smells are intense: the sudden, nose-wrenching stench of a lavatory, the velvety aroma of cooking, the subtle sandalwood tangs of a cabinet maker.

Dusk is glooming through the streets, the harshness of coal smoke is making my throat sore, my behind aches from the wretched seat; I shall go back and meet Steven in Charley's Bar.

21 February. We are issued with 'cold-weather' clothing at the Embassy, we collect the diplomatic bags and the stores and are driven to the station. A little portress bossily helps us load her trolley, box-shaped with bicycle wheels, and squawking with complaints she hauls it to the carriage. Before our train leaves Peking station at 7.40 I stroll up and down the platform, past the huddled, rather nervous groups of

Europeans who are preparing the start of their multi-thousand mile adventure, standing guard by heaps of tightly packed rucksacks; past stacks of hessian bags holding the mail; past crates of food – duck to dog; past the stark branches of the foxglove tree [paulownia] which surprisingly grows at the end of the platform; up to the two mighty diesels which will haul us for the next 40 hours, grumbling to each other, their great grey metal hands clenched together in a sailor's grip.

My cabin is the normal cosy little panelled box with bed, table and armchair. The loudspeaker near the ceiling emits some twangy music, then a voice says 'Welcome to the 7600 kilometre journey to Moscow, via Ulaan Baatar.' I am on my seventh journey up this track. The scenery is becoming familiar, only the seasons show any change: it was summer when I last was here, now there are thin patches of trodden-in snow; ponds and rivers are frozen with ice which looks like congealed mutton fat; at the level-crossings, cold, quilted people stand patiently by the barriers, holding on to their bicycles; babies are wrapped up like parcels; there are a few coal-laden tumbrels pulled by donkeys or mules, their heads hanging as they trudge into the cold wind, their breath smoking; in the towns, the balconies of the blocks of flats are crammed with baskets, bedding, barrels, boxes, clothes-lines, all sooty and hazy in the coal-smutty smogs.

We clatter very, very slowly past one small village. I see two dogs and a pig going for a walk together up the earthen street. They are obviously friends: whilst they stroll you can see their heads turning to each other as they chat; when a dog stops to cock his leg, the others stop and wait obligingly, if the pig wants a brief rootle, the others stand by until he has rootled, sometimes they all stop to inspect something small on the ground and then they talk about it. I feel a twinge of sympathetic friendship for them.

22 February. We leave Dzhamine Ude, the Mongolian border post, at about 1 o'clock, and finally I can make my bed and lulled by the 'clackety-clak, yackity-yak, rockety-rock' I will go to sleep. Few things are more luxurious than sleeping in a train.

*

The morning: a cold clear light over the snow fields of the Gobi desert. Few things are less luxurious than a train loo which has been used messily for several hours and in which everything has frozen solid and there is no loo paper and footprints are on the seat and horrible stains and blotches are everywhere and someone has puked into the tiny sink and oh my God.

Breakfast: sandwiches, bloater paste with pickles, cheese with pickles, sardines with pickles – this a bad idea; boiling hot coffee.

Steven thinks I am being vamped by what my father, who was in SOE, called a BFS (Beautiful Female Spy). Actually, although tall and blonde, she is not particularly pretty, having that spatulate snub nose Scandinavians often have, but she has a nice square face and a jolly, schoolgirly manner. She was walking past my cabin and espied me looking through my binoculars at a glum raven in the snow. 'Ah!' she cried excitedly, 'another bird-watcher.' She hurried in and sitting beside me took my binoculars and whilst inspecting the raven said: 'I am Finnish.'

'Hüver pyver.'

She was even more excited. 'Ah! You speak my language so well!' she exclaimed.

I didn't disagree, I am pretty good at the two words I know.

She prattled on – in English, fortunately, flicking through my bird book and explaining she had not brought one as she had only become a bird-watcher two days ago. Through the open doors of our washing-cubicle I could see Steven sitting on his bunk; he kept raising and lowering his eyebrows at me, and mouthing silent cautions. After the girl left, promising to visit me again soon, Steven beetled into my cabin. 'Watch it,' he said, 'there's something fishy about all that.'

'Why?'

'She's after something. No normal girl would voluntarily speak to a large, middle-aged, balding Brit whose breath smells of sardine and pickle sandwiches.'

'I'm probably her type.'

Steven snorted and went grumpily back to his cabin. When she returned and sat down beside me later, Steven hurried through with *his* bird book. Doing his job as my escort, no doubt.

*

We draw into the station at Ulaan Baatar at 13.20. The reception party
– including the ambassador – is waiting on the platform. I go in the
Land Rover with the diplomatic bags, Steven follows in the Range
Rover with the provisions. We drive past the place where Stalin's statue
had loomed, a token of the Russian presence and the government's
inclination. It was taken down an hour ago; only the plinth remains, a
shattered block of greyish cement.

7.30, dinner with the ambassador and his wife. The other guests are four
Mongolians, two of either sex: very pleasant but rather shy to start with.
They speak English well, all having been to Leeds University.

'Didn't you find Leeds a bit grey and dull?'

'After Moscow University, where we each spent five years, *nowhere* can
be grey or dull.'

The head of the Mongolian People's Literary Consortium is particularly amusing and interesting: tall, as some Mongolians are, with dark
twinkling eyes and a beaming smile. He is trying to collect Mongolian
folk tales and legends before they disappear and quotes:

> The sky is rich in stars.
> The earth is rich in names.
> And each of them
> Has its own legend.

'I will be a Brother Grimm or the Hans Andersen of the Steppe,' he
says, going on to tell me How it Came about that the Camel tumbles
into Ashes, Why the Kahn's Daughter did Marry a Bald and Shabby
Commoner, of The Maiden with the Golden Dung Fork, How Baadai
did sell his Horse, of The Seven Khodzhgors and one Lone Modzhgor,
and of the Foals with Golden Chests and Silver Buttocks.

As we leave after dinner for the twenty-yard walk back home to
Greyhound Cottage I look at the thermometer on the back door: it
reads minus 28°C. At about this temperature, if you spit, it freezes
before it hits the ground; you are unadvised to have a pee. The ambassador stepped outside, last week, when it was even colder. He held a cup
of coffee, recently brewed. He raised it to his lips. There was already a

film of ice upon it. Annoyed, he emptied it to the ground: it landed with a clunk as a solid chunk. He told me that he once opened a bottle of beer and the froth froze as it seethed out so that it ended up looking like a candle stuck in the neck of the bottle. They say that one Queen's Messenger was a hairy man, even his ears were hairy. They itched in the cold, so he put his finger into an ear and puggled it about. The hairs in his ear, frozen stiff, snapped, and fell onto his ear drum, causing an even greater itchment. The ambassador's wife had to whoosh his ear out by blowing down it with a drinking straw.

I must tell that to the Mongolian collector of lore and legend.

23 February. Very cold, there is no wind so it does not feel too bad, but it is very dry, my lips are cracking. Steven is staying in Greyhound Cottage this morning to write a report and fret over his toothache: I have arrived at 'Harrods', the general store, for the felt boots which Candy has asked for. The bleak grey corridors are packed: long queues stand patiently on the cement floors for there are some shoes recently in from Moscow. I am just about to buy the felt boots – they look a bit like ordinary rubber boots, but are made of thick grey felt – when I see the hair boots: vast and fluffy, each must have been cobbled from half a yak. The shop assistant tries them on, they look charmingly ridiculous, as if she were the daughter of an Arctic Pan, so I've bought them. I will now have to lug them all the way back from Outer Mongolia to Colne Engaine.

Dominie wanted me to buy her a fur hat. As she would not be with me for a fitting I devised what I think a most ingenious idea. I have brought with me a piece of string and a child's balloon. The string has two knots on it, these mark the circumference of Dominie's head. I shall inflate the balloon to a large size, put the string around it, and deflate it slowly until the knots meet: the balloon will then be the size of Dominie's head and I shall then try the hats upon it.

There are three shop assistants nattering to each other behind the counter in the hat department. I call their attention. I put my bit of string on the counter. I produce the balloon. It is red and limp; they stare at it, I suppose they have never seen one before. I start to blow it up. They shrink back together in a protective huddle. I continue to blow it up: it is one of those well-made, tough ones and my face starts to empurple with the effort. A crowd begins to gather, they stand beside me, silent and round-eyed. There is a terrific smell of mutton and damp felt. My balloon is fully inflated. I look down for my bit of string. It is not there. Someone's nicked it. I search frantically, holding the balloon aloft with one hand, feeling among all the booted feet on the floor with another. The crowd is now a multitude, but still in perfect silence. Sadly, I start to deflate the balloon. It subsides with a wet blethering. I pinch its mouth to lessen the noise, the splutters change to a high-pitched whining. The whole roomful of people emits a single groan of surprise. Embarrassed, I let go. It shoots into the air. It darts about in a series of aerial arabesques above the crowd, moistly farting. Finally, with its last snort, it lands on the counter in front of the three shop assistants. Everybody cranes forward to peer at it. Every single face is completely expressionless.

With a shamefaced grin I melt through the crowd and into the street. Whilst I stand, thinking about it and wishing it had not happened, I feel a nudge. I look down. Two children are standing beside me: shyly, one is offering me my balloon, the other my piece of string.

I go to the post office and buy 42 postcards and the 168 stamps needed to send them abroad. The Mongolians round about me jostle and barge to get next to me and help choose the prettiest stamps, the ones depicting Ghengiz Khan are the most popular; they were not allowed to mention him until the Russians lost their influence.

The temple/palace of the last Bogd Khan (the 'Spiritual and Temporal Ruler') is open, so I look around. It is a walled enclosure and contains five temples and five formal gateways. It is Buddhist, but strangely different from the smiling, floral, peaceful, childish temples of Bhutan and Nepal, and the difference suddenly makes one realise that these quiet, polite, subdued, doll-like Mongolians are the People of the Blue Wolf, the race of men who, under the command of Ghengiz Khan, Ordu of the White Horde, Batu of the Golden Horde, Tamburlaine, Kublai Khan and maybe even Attila made the kings of Europe and peasants of Cathay tremble at their very names; the people whose coming was preceded silently by the stench of Death, followed by the thunder of hoofs and the screams of arrows. The scenes painted within the temples are of terror and torture. Dismembered chunks from corpses are painted on the ceiling: lungs, hearts, eyes (in pairs and dripping blood), kidneys (also in pairs), arms and legs (gushing gore from their dismembered stumps), eyeless and tongueless heads (silently screaming), bodies (strung upside down, blood pouring from their hacked-out groins). Even more macabre is the reproduction of these bloodied bits and pieces in pink satin plush; lovingly cut out, sewn together and stuffed by some sweet little Mongolian housewife in the gloom of her winter ger, no doubt. These horrid objects hang, as if on a clothes-line, above the scenes of the tortures of hell which are painted on the walls. Hell is cold; it is of frozen, agoraphobic open wasteland rather than our claustrophobic, subterranean fires.

On my walk back to the Embassy I view the site of Stalin's statue. The plinth has been extracted. Even the hole which was made when the stump was drawn has been cemented over. Nothing remains of the vile brute, except for the thin whispers of the ghosts of the Died-too-soon and the Never-to-be-born. I stand and ponder for a bit. Each Mongolian who passes stops and stares for an instant, curious or amused. Not a single East European even glances; they hurry past with eyes staring ahead. They may not have liked Stalin, but they know that, as far as the locals are concerned, they are his confederates. Even the huge pictures of the Three Big-Wigs have gone: the President, the Prime Minister and the Head of the Communist Party. They have tiptoed away. Only Lenin's foxy features remain, on a couple of hoardings and as a statue in the bleak little park.

Steven and I sit in Greyhound Cottage for the rest of the day, listening to Gilbert and Sullivan and military marches on the tape machine, Steven writing his article on the birds of the Gobi desert while I write postcards. At 6.30 we walk the dozen paces from our front door to the Steppe Inn, where we drink and chat with the rest of the Embassy and outside visitors celebrating 'TGIF' – Thank God It's Friday – and then we have dinner with two Embassy staff.

Of the four other guests, two are youngish, palid, townee Brits from some do-good organisation, the others are a pair of Mongolians, he being tall and twinkle-eyed, his wife being short and subdued. They met, of all places, in Pudsey. There is mutton for dinner, although our hostess says that, on principle, she is against eating meat.

The young do-gooders add that they too disapprove of animal husbandry, and bring their anti-blood sports opinions into the conversation. The Mongolian and I, both as farmers and hunters, disagree vehemently. I begin to get irritated, the Mongolian exasperated, only Steven is quiet; he is a good and keen shot but the chewiness of the mutton is aggravating his toothache.

The discussion veers embarrassingly on the border between debate and argument. Eventually the Mongolian shrugs and turning to me says: 'You and I may be of different race and culture, but you are more like me than like your countrymen.' I feel very complimented.

After dinner some of us go to a new, once-weekly nightclub which has been opened in a basement near Sukhbataar Square. The effect, when descending the flight of sombrely lit stairs, is similar to that of a deepsea diver being lowered into the dark, mysterious depths of some small, submarine pothole. The next sensation is of the incredible noise: the roaring and squealing and throbbing of the band: someone shouts at me that Mongolia's favourite pop group is called '!HONK!' We are led through the gloom to a table by the dance floor and, without being asked, the waitress gives us each a tumbler three quarters full of neat whisky. The main lighting is from a psychedelic collection of beams and flashes which together with the whisky give the impression that the whole place is spinning round and round and flashing on and off at the same time. Also lit up by the light are luminous clouds of cigarette smoke. The tables are crowded: a few Mongolians, but many men with broad leather belts and the sleeves of their tartan shirts rolled up to display muscles and tattoos: oil prospectors. Mongolian girls are sitting beside or upon some of them. Two people only are dancing at present. One is an unusually short little Texan, wearing a baseball hat with the peak turned up, and dancing in a bounding, hunched-up manner with his knuckles almost trailing the ground. The other is an immensely beautiful Mongolian girl. She must be over six feet tall and has a cascade of thick black hair which reaches halfway down her legs – which are easy to admire, as she is wearing a very tight, very short mini-skirt. She looks stunningly exotic, with her slanting eyes and impassive Buddha's smile upturning her lovely mouth; as well as being tall she is willowy and her dancing seems more like the twining of a snake than the strutting of a biped. Suddenly she spins round and her hair mushrooms out into a great disk, perhaps ten foot across. As she twists and undulates beneath this great parasol, so does the little man caper and gambol beside her: they are like two strange creatures out of a dream.

24 February. Another freezing morning. Steven and I wander around for a bit. Our morale is a bit low: Steven with his toothache, me with a headache. A man wearing a heavy quilted del and leather wellington boots with turned-up toes sidles up to us. He thrusts his right hand into the recesses of his long left sleeve and produces an oval boulder. 'Dinosaur's egg, 60 American dollars,' he hisses.

'No thanks, I've already had breakfast,' I reply, quick as a flash and twice as witty.

The man presumably thinks otherwise: 'From Gobi desert, very rare.'

Steven thinks it may be some sort of trick to get us into trouble with the authorities, so we politely decline the Mongolian's blandishments, even though he drops the price by 80 per cent.

We are lent a Land Rover and we go off to the banks of the River-that-flows-under-the-Wooden-Bridge. The Ribes genus is well represented here and I want to collect some more currant cuttings for Alaun Griffiths, and I think I know a gooseberry growing part-way up a cliff nearby; I was too lazy and cowardly to collect it last time. Before we walk down the steeply sloping hillside to the river we run seven times round the Cairn-with-a-Horse-Skull-on-a-Pole. Our Mongolian driver watches, bemused that we are doing what he has been taught is an ignorant, superstitious, non-communistic ritual.

After we have finished, Steven having been excited over a flock of horned larks, me nearly killing myself by using a loose flake of rock as a handhold, we return, pausing only to wait for our driver who, sheepishly, has started to run seven times clockwise round the Cairn-with-a-Horse-Skull-on-a-Pole.

We all go out into the countryside in the afternoon to toboggan. I collide with a frozen yak pat and fall off my toboggan. Somehow, in doing so, I run over a finger and bleed like a pig, but after a few seconds the cold freezes up my wound.

You must go outside at midnight, in the depths of the steppe during winter, when there is a total hush and not even the slightest breeze will sough through the dry grasses of the sleeping plainlands. You will be at the Back of the North Wind. As you stand in the utter silence when even the air has been frozen into stillness you might hear a tinkling: a minute, silvery, tintinnabulation, like the echo of bells far away.

It is the Whisper of the Stars.

For eons, for ages, its source was a mystery: crystallised starlight shattering in the cold? the voices of people too small and too shy ever to have been seen? the ghostly echo of long-gone battles? goblin blacksmiths, fairy sleighbells? the ethereal lamentations of the exquisite Alangoa, ravished by a moonbeam?

In reality, it is the minuscule clattering of your breath which, having frozen in the bitter cold, falls crystalline at your feet.

My alarm has just woken me, it is 3 o'clock in the morning. My eyes have sleazed open. Is it really worth it? The windows have iced over. My bed is a snug haven.

I dress: two pairs of socks, pyjama bottoms, cellular vest, Viyella shirt, corduroy trousers over which I belt quilted chaps, jersey, quilted waistcoat, quilted oversocks, boots, padded anorak, underpants pulled down well over my ears (much more comfortable than a balaclava), knitted gloves. I could get claustrophobia in all this.

From a scruffy bundle of bedclothes in the far corner of the room Steven's voice drawls sleepily: 'What the devil are you doing at this God-awful hour?'

'I am going out to hear the Whisper of the Stars.'

Steven's voice sharpens in anxiety: 'My God, how frightfully twee,' he says, 'I hope this cold hasn't frozen your balls off.'

I step outside. I feel as if someone has grasped the end of my nose with a pair of pliers, and slapped my cheeks, and bitten my earlobes. My eyes begin to water. Something itches, and pricks my cheeks, my tears have turned to ice.

To hell with the Whisper of the Stars.

I go back indoors. While I undress two worried eyes peek at me from the bedclothes opposite, but Steven does not speak. I get into my bed, it is still warm, and turn the light out. I wonder if Steven has heard of the Song of the Sands. I'll ask him when we're crossing the Gobi tomorrow.

25 February. At 9.30, the train left Ulaan Baatar for Peking. We have some journalists aboard, bitterly disappointed that there has been no coup. One of them told me that they have lived entirely on cold potatoes and mutton: 'Mutton this, mutton that, every bloody day, mutton, mutton, mutton. MUTTON FAT is engraved on my heart.'

Twilight has arrived, the sun is setting over the low, cold hills. The Gobi desert seems covered with more snow than usual. We have seen hundreds, perhaps a thousand, of little gazelle; there was one herd of about 500. I don't think that they are the Mongolian gazelle (or zeren) as these need water every day, but perhaps the snow is an acceptable substitute. The Saiga antelope is another beast of the steppe, but that is very recognisable by its hideous bloated face with a porcine snout. I think it may be a sub-species of the Persian gazelle; it is found in most of the Asian continent from Iran to China, including Tibet and Mongolia. (Steven looks over my shoulder as I write this and says '*Gazella subgutterosa*'.)

There seem to be fewer birds than usual, even for the winter. However there is one bird I have not seen here before, a black vulture. It is very large and sinisterly dark. We saw about seven groups during the day, each comprising about half a dozen birds sitting hunched up in circles like witches in a coven. They were motionless, only one bird moved; it was doing a weird hopping dance in front of its cronies, with wings outstretched and bedraggled feathers hanging down like an old frayed skirt. One group was beside a pony which I presumed was thirteen hands, making it possible to calculate that the birds were two and a half feet high. I saw one flock aloft, their silhouette was typically vulturine: no visible head or neck, broad rectangular wings with splayed-out feathers at the tips. (Steven has been thumbing through his bird books: 'They shouldn't be here, but I think they must be cinereous vultures,' he finally says.)

One of the fellows on this train is typical of the exotic type one meets in these far-off places: he told us that he is a carrot farmer from Lincolnshire and is using some of last year's profit to see the world. I was thunderstruck; he is the first farmer I have met who has actually admitted to making a profit. He seems to know his birds and insists we have just seen 'white-collared jackdaws'. Are there such birds? They looked a bit like ornamental pigeons to me. (Steven says they are probably the jackdaw *Coloeus dauricus*.)

26 February. It is mid-morning. We are at Da Tung. Several magnificent steam engines are puffing around, heaving waggons laden with cargoes of logs or coal, or spartan carriages full of humanity. There is a woman on our train with a dog: she, French; the dog, a wire-haired terrier with a shifty way of looking out of the corner of its eyes. She takes it for walkies on a lead. She smiles at the passers-by who are looking appreciatively at it; she would not smile so sunnily if she knew they were thinking: 'Hmmm, very nice, very fat, very juicy; braised, I think, with crispy noodles and fresh shrimp's balls.'

27 February. Peking: Steven and I stroll through the Forbidden City. Steven is publicly reprimanded and fined the equivalent of a penny three farthings for smoking in the Garden of Floating Greenery. I take a photograph of him thumbing through his wallet, watched by a stern little official with a fine-collecting bag hung from his shoulders, and a small crowd of derisive onlookers who stare and snigger. We continue, through Tien-an-men Square. No sign of 'the troubles'. No soldiers around; everyone looks as placid and contented as is possible in this dank, soggy weather. An old man sits on a low wall. He has a cage beside him. It contains a starling-sized, brown bird. Steven stops and having worked through the pages of the bird book he is carrying decides that it is a white-browed thrush. He shows the picture to the old man. The old man is pleased and excited and calls some of his friends over. The book is passed from hand to hand, Steven and I are nodded and smiled at and talked to and we finally depart in high good humour, having not understood a word.

A bit of capitalism is in evidence, a man selling puppies on the pavement. He raps them with a twig occasionally to remind potential customers that dogs are more succulent if they are beaten to death.

3 March. Land at Heathrow on time: 05.25 hours. Back home in time for breakfast. Everything looks lovely. It has been very warm and the crocus and daffodils are flowering in the garden; in the hedgerows the catkins and pussy willows are out, blackthorn is in flower, may is budding and birds are singing. But also there have been terrible tempests. Branches and leaves are all over the lawn and float in the ponds. The kitchen chimney is swathed in scaffolding.

As I am walking round the garden I meet Monk with the dogs. I tell him about running into a frozen yak pat with my toboggan. 'Some people would say that story is "a load of bull shit",' he says.

11 March, Bonn. It seems a place with very little personality, and what little it has is of neat and tidy dullness. Having delivered the bags at the British Embassy, a modern rectangular shoebox-type building in keeping with the general style of architecture, I strolled up the street for a bit. There was nothing much to admire except some well-planted municipal shrubs, cotoneaster and barberry and other berrying types, and even they made me feel bored and dispirited: they were so immaculate, every berry was spaced exactly from its neighbour and no leaf had misbehaved and consorted with a caterpillar or lost its gloss. So I made my way to the park. This is attractive: well laid out with lakes and groves and aligned alongside the Rhine. I am sitting on a bench by the river: huge barges are chuntering past, some so heavily laden that the wavelets are sloshing right up to the gunwales and they look more like barely emerged submarines. The air all about smells of river, damp leaves and the slight balsam scent of poplar trees. I hear argumentative quacking from a large flock of mallard in a nearby lake. It is lunch-time, and several joggers pass, looking fitter and panting less than their British counterparts; there are several unpleasantly beefy dogs being led about, Alsatians, Rottweilers, boxers and Dobermann pinschers. A sweet old Hansel and Gretel dodder past, arm in arm. I wonder what they did in the war.

It is always fascinating to fly over Berlin and see the remains of that macabre wall zigzagging in its crude vandalistic way through buildings, across streets and over parks. On the Eastern side it is still marked by a wide strip of bare land and sentry towers, which from the air look like rather charming pepper pots. The East is discernible also by the contrastingly small number of cars in the streets. Both sides are built with unattractive post-war utility blocks, faced with grey or beige cement and plaster.

Some people are fond of Berlin: people who remember the hectic days of the early 1930s or who served here have nostalgic memories of a life long past and friends far gone. My memories of Berlin are the fear and awe associated with its name: it was the place the Germans lived, and the Germans were the people who sent aeroplanes overhead to drop bombs on us, to kill us all, even the King and Queen. Berlin is an ugly, morose, depressing place; the horrors and remorse of its history and those who died still haunt the streets, a feeling of menace and gloom reinforced by the files of bleak buildings with their facings of cement or grey-brown plaster.

My driver is the friendly Berliner with a black beard and high sing-song accent. He whitters about the flood of Easterners coming daily into the West: 'It was all right at first, we even gave them money so they could buy the things they had only ever heard about – they all wanted bananas – but now they fill the roads with their horrible little cars and you cannot get into the underground and the shops are all emptied and now they are getting jobs this side of the border where the pay is good and going back to live in their side where the rents are cheap . . . it costs me this . . . but it only costs them that . . . and moan groan grizzle . . .' The staff at headquarters are also in a state of sulk: they are no longer called the 'British Military Government'; their name has been changed to the wishy-washy 'British Mission in Berlin', 'like a load of poncy padres,' one of the security staff complains.

12 March. After breakfast I take the underground railway from Kaiser-Damm to Zoologischer Garten and then walk down to the erstwhile Checkpoint Charlie. The registration plates on the massive array of buses parked alongside the streets show that they come from East Germany, Poland and Czechoslovakia. Little groups of East Europeans stand around looking bemused. They are recognisable by their dusty, drab clothes: the men wear tubular-legged jeans, the women wear frowsty dresses and headscarfs. They all carry bags bursting with fruit and bottles of orange juice. Groups, mainly female, gaze wistfully through the windows of dress shops, gangs of young men hang around outside video shops. None of them seems to go in. None of them smiles. They just stand and stare.

The wall each side of Checkpoint Charlie is being bulldozed down. With expressions of awe and wonder, people gape at the machines at work. The entrance through the wall is bounded by movable barricades. People plod between them in a continuous stream, cars drive through and as they come to our side some break out into an exultant cacophony of tooting and hooting and cheering and waving. A family walks through and stops, thunderstruck. There are three American service men walking past, black men. The East Europeans gawp at them with intense curiosity, as I did in 1944, aged six, when I saw my first black man (driving an American army lorry full of bombs).

I have been instructed not to cross the boundary, so all I can do when I have arrived at an edge of the wall where it has been bulldozed down is to put my arm round it and feel the other side. It is only about five inches thick, strange that such an apparently frail structure could be the cause of so much human despair. But it is not frail, the concrete is reinforced by iron lattice, and the cement is too hard for me to prise off a bit as a memento. The whole wall is pockmarked from ground level to eight feet, chiselled away by souvenir hunters. People are still at it, busy pecking away with hammers and crowbars. Some, mostly East Europeans, are introducing a bit of capitalism into the scene by selling chunks, neatly wrapped up in transparent plastic bags and aligned on the open lids of suitcases. Pieces from the Western side are the more expensive, they are the ones coloured and scribbled with graffiti – no one on the Eastern side could get near enough to deface the wall – except with their blood and brains. Apparently a Japanese trader bought several tons of the wall last week. As Dirk Bogarde wrote: 'Today the dreadful wall lies in designer-chunks all about the coffee tables of the West . . .'

I walk along the wall towards the Brandenburg Gate. Here and there it is penetrated by large gaps; youths excitedly jump through, from one side to the other, or photograph each other standing in between, with a leg in each sector. In one of the gaps I finally find a bit of the wall loose enough to prise off, it is about the size of a bean. At the Brandenburg Gate the scene with its milling crowds and holiday atmosphere is like a market fair: there are pedlars and stall holders selling bits of the wall and Red army badges and Russian hats and hot-dogs and ice-cream and postcards (some pre-wall or even pre-war); there are children running about with balloons or getting lost and howling; there is a man with a monkey and a barrel organ (he wears a pink spotted tie, like the monkey, but the monkey has been stuffed); there are tourists crowding on top of the wall, which is lower but wider here, and photographing each other.

From the Brandenburg Gate I turn back 'home' onto Strasse des 17 Juni. Whatever happened then? Something to do with Fred the Great I suppose. Why do foreigners so love inflicting their streets with dreary dates? At the Ernst-Reuter-Platz the name changes to Bismarckstrasse. I absent-mindedly stray onto the red part of the pavement which is reserved for bicyclists. One of them charges me: a bearded weirdo dressed in tight black clothes like a widow's corsets, he screams something aggressive and guttural as he approaches and only just dodges out of the way as I remain rooted to the spot – through astonishment rather than bravery. It is considerate of the Germans always to be correcting the little sins of other people.

I am now sitting at the bar of the Officers' Club, writing this, drinking Guinness and eating sausages and chips. The barman has just said: 'I hope you didn't buy any bits of the wall, most of what are sold are forgeries.' There are red squirrels in the Scots pine outside the window; I had forgotten how large their ear-tufts look. They had better watch it, the grey squirrels have taken over at home.

14 March. Dominie's fountain and urn arrived yesterday. They have been dumped beside Monk's log and ferret shed. Dominie excitedly took me to see them at the crack of dawn (in spite of my complaints about having to get up early, because of jet-lag. 'People don't get jet-lag flying to Berlin,' she said). They look huge; God knows how Tom will manoeuvre them into place, particularly the fountain, whose sections will have to be stacked one on top of the other in the centre of the new pond. It was lucky that I had the foresight to have a concrete pad made there.

On an impulse, in the evening, I opened Great-Aunt Min's diary to see what she was doing here exactly 100 years ago. Pretty terse: 'Friday the 14th of March, 1890. Planted two trees on lawn, plum and copper beech. Mr C. P. Wood, Evangeline and Captain White came up in afternoon and looked over farm.' The plum has gone, but I went up to the copper beech, now about 60 feet high and with a girth of 94 inches, and wished it a happy 100 birthday.

27 March. The streets of Monrovia are unlit and silent, all is dark and sinister. The car lurches over potholes, shadows slip round corners when our headlights sweep past. There is a heavy smell of decay and humanity. My escort tells me that there is considerable amount of unease at present as a rebel army is marching upon us and is expected in about a month. Everyone is packing and frantic. They think the rebel army will win, as Doe's tribe, the Krahn, has become very unpopular and his army is notorious, even in Africa, for its indiscriminate brutality. The Embassy's life has not been made easier by a 'friendship' visit by one of our ships, the first time the Royal Navy has been to Liberia for 29 years. 'Why now, for God's sake?' moaned someone to me.

They have put me up in the converted brothel. It is rather bleak without the girls leaning over the balustrades round the great stairwell. My bedroom reeks of stale sweat. There are horrible stains on the bed cover. I rip it back and see that the lower sheet is caked with dried blood.

The soap in the sink is so matted with wiry black hair it looks like a pot-scourer. What appears to be a fluffy toy hanging from the ceiling turns out to be a spider. The air-conditioning has been torn out of the wall and the temperature is in the high 90s, with a humidity of about 100 per cent. Outside, in the alley, people are taking turns to fight or fornicate – I prefer the fighting, it is quicker and not so squelchy. Someone has just knocked over the dustbins, the acrid stink of stale garbage is wafting through the hole where the air-conditioning unit was. At least the mosquitoes are being kept at bay with the anti-insect coil given me by [Queen's Messenger the Captain] David Bloom: ten minutes after I light it there is a great thud as the spider, dead, falls off the ceiling onto the linoleum. I insulate myself from the bedding with a layer of shirts and, using my forearm as a pillow, sweat out the night.

28 March. I walk to the Embassy and whinge about the brothel. They tersely say that the only decent hotel, The Africa, is full; there is a conference of African states about South Africa's apartheid, and all 400 rooms are taken. I take the 50-minute taxi ride to the hotel. As I presumed, there is plenty of room as the conference was cancelled a fortnight ago, so I book myself in.

There is a curfew after 4 p.m. so I am just dawdling in my room, scribbling this, but at least it is comfortable and clean.

29 March. After breakfast I walk up the beach. It is idyllic in a stereotyped way: sun, sand, blue sea and coconut-palms, but the waves are large and aggressive and smack angrily at the boulders piled up as breakwaters at the far boundary of the hotel garden. No-one is bathing, no-one is even wandering along the strand. It is sweltering, the sunlight glares off the sea, the mild breeze has no relief in it but is blood-hot and muggy so that I feel as if I am inhaling beef broth. There are no interesting shells. The jetsam includes a couple of intriguing species of seed case. They are both hard and woody: one type is about the size and shape of a bantam's egg, containing a single wizened stone which makes a rattle; another is tri-lobal with a pea-sized seed in each lobe and a pretty herringbone pattern to its exterior grain. I collect a sample of each.

After a mile I come upon a group of seven locals slouched under a palm. One holds a guitar but he seems too lethargic to play it.

'Good morning,' I chirrup. There is no reply, just the slow raising of eyes and cold, unblinking stares.

Another mile: a small shipyard of dug-outs lying at random in the dunes. The biggest boat looks newly finished. She is called *Sweet Mother Nyame*. She measures fourteen paces long by five feet at the widest. Her bottom is one huge bole, shallowly scooped out and heightened by a couple of thick strakes to either side; these meet at 'clipper-bowed' stem and stern posts. She is very graceful in spite of being so crudely built. An even larger bole lies nearby, half hewn and full of dried palm fronds – do they speed up the process by burning? A man is chiselling away on a small dug-out. It is about the size of a Canadian canoe. His tool is a short-hafted axe; he'd do better with an adze. He is a friendly man and we converse with gesticulations and grunts and laughs, a communication as primitive as the craft he is making. The gist of our messages to each other is that I should buy his dug-out so that I can go fishing and he can relax under the shade of that palm.

I wander back. The little group still lolls under the coconut-palms. This time they do not look at me at all, they look away. It makes me uneasy. There are some small translucent pebbles which glow when wetted by the surges of the incoming tide. Could they be diamonds? Very unlikely, but I'd better collect a few just in case. It would be sickening to hear, later, that the sands of Liberia are as rich in diamonds as are the beaches of the Skeleton Coast further down the west flank of Africa.

On my return to the hotel I scratch at the window of my hotel bedroom with one of the pebbles. If it is a diamond it will leave a scar.

It leaves a scar.

Well, this is rather exciting. But perhaps other minerals can scratch glass?

I put the seed pods in my bathroom sink to wash them. Something fast and hairy runs out of the tri-lobal one, over my hand and down the plug-hole. I am nauseated with shock. And I've had the horrible thing in my pocket for a couple of hours. When I float them, and turn the tap on them, the tri-lobal pod is held in the flow and spins rapidly. Is that accidental or is it something designed by nature for a specific purpose? Could this be useful for some machine? Couldn't we start from nature and work backwards, sometimes?

30 March. On the journey back to the aerodrome in the afternoon we drive through a market, crammed with people. None of them seems worried that there is a rebel army on its way. The women are very grace-ful, even the fat ones waddle with elegance. They wear attractive printed cottons, mainly of large designs with a dominance of yellows, greens and orange-rusts. Many carry enamelled basins on their heads. I see some maidens, bare-breasted and daubed with white. My driver is descended from those who emigrated from the United States when Liberia was founded for liberated slaves during the last century. He is contemptuous of the girls. 'They are from one of the ignorant primi-tive tribes, who were here before we came, it is something to do with their religion, when they circumcise their young ladies.' He says that some of the 'original' people still have their own language, but they usually mix amiably enough with the newcomers, although, between them, there can still flare up intense inter-tribal rivalry. There are sixteen tribes, but I cannot make out if they are all from the original people, or if the incoming Afro-Americans created some additional tribes, or if they married into them. Whatever it is, the present rebellion is basically tribal, even though the leaders of the opposing sides have American names: Doe and Taylor.

The taxis, and some of the private cars, have messages or names printed upon them. I will write them down as we pass: MANY ARE CALLED . . . UNTO THY HANDS . . . GOOD FRIENDSHIP . . . THANKS & PRAISES TO GOD . . . SOLOPOGEE [?] . . . MY FAMILY GIFT . . . LOOK UP TO GOD . . . THE LORD IS MY SHEPHERD . . . MOTHER'S BLESSING . . . HONESTY LEADS TO SUCCESS . . . DO GOOD AND YOU WILL PROSPER . . . DO NOT THINK, BECAUSE [because what?] . . . NO JOB, NO

RESPECT . . . GODS GIFT . . . RESPECT YOUR SUPERIOR . . .
TRY YOUR LUCK [I wouldn't be catching that taxi] . . . DONT PLAY
FOUL . . . ONE WIFE [is that a boast, or a complaint?] . . . TAKE IT
EASY . . .

We are now in the open countryside. This road was built by the
Americans, and is lovely: a raised causeway through the jungle, past
glades with beautiful palms and clumps of greenery, sometimes there is
a farmstead with a few bananas and some chickens. The traffic acci-
dents here must be appalling: one does not see one or two wrecked cars
by the road, but groups of them, as if they had suddenly been massa-
cred, or died in a great plague. I think we have passed more wrecked
vehicles than mobile ones.

*3 April. When we went on the rounds yesterday to check the livestock we noticed a
mare in poor condition: her head down, her eyes partly closed and her nose runny.
Dominie dosed her. She was no better in the evening so we called the vet. He peered
down her throat and up her behind and said she had a blockage and if she was still
ailing tomorrow morning we would have to take her to the special horse hospital in
Newmarket. He then gave her an enema at one end and a massive laxative at the
other, and quit. The mare is still lank and listless today, so we have had to box her
and truck her the 36 miles to Newmarket.*

*The vet is youngish and bustling and surrounded by a group of admiring acolytes.
They are all female and nubile. It is strange how so often it is women who are good
with ill animals; less irritable and impatient, I suppose, and with a kinder nature.*

*He starts poking a tube down her throat, via a nostril. It makes me squirm to
look at it. Having peered down it, he says he thinks there is a blockage in her gullet.*

*'See,' he says to me, 'I can look down this, right into her stomach, there is a light
at the end to illuminate her interior. I can pour medicine down it. I can even suck
things up.'*

*Then, to my utmost nausea, he proceeds to suck until I can see green gunge going
up the transparent tube towards his mouth. I speed off, before I hear him swallow-
ing.*

*I inspect the other invalids looking over their stable doors. There is one particu-
larly pleasant horse, of the kind I like: with an amiable, fond expression; huge, and*

almost square. He is surely mostly cart-horse. An old man and an adolescent girl go up to him.

'Now Henry,' says the girl, 'we won't be long, the doctor says you're much better. Mum and the kids send their love. Hettie has laid some lovely eggs in your manger. Dapple and Patch say they miss you. We've got you a lovely new blanket with "H" for Henry on it. Now say "good-bye" to granddad.'

The horse says nothing, just pricks his ears forward and stares down at them, with great friendliness.

'Bye-bye, Henry,' calls the girl as she walks out of the yard.

'Bye, Henry,' calls the old boy, 'see you tomorrow, mate.'

We are back home. The mare looks better already: the vet found the blockage, a spent cartridge case, and pushed it down into the mare's stomach with his tube.

Now one of the ewes is on the wrong side of the fence, separated from her twins, so I will have to catch her. Why on earth does anyone keep livestock?

7 April, Santiago, Chile. I have just had a walk to get a feel of the place. The general effect is attractive: it is late autumn, the trees have turned and there is a smell of damp leaves. The roads are light and airy and many of them are avenues, mostly edged with a gnarled tree with masses of small yellow berries, or with a type of plane. Chile's surprising versatility can be seen in the variety of flora and the cosmopolitanity of the people. On the one hand I have walked past birches, planes, olives, weeping willows, cork oaks, magnolia, oleander, elm, a small nasty palm, bottle-brush, crab apple, casuarina, evergreen oak, judas, mimosa, pomegranate, date-palms; on the other hand the names scrawled on a 'lover's wall' included Darwin y Nora, Karen y Frederick, Carlos y Francia, Claudia y Nelson, I love Jim Morrison, Flor y Mario, Yoyo y Jaime, Marcela y Ruben, Cindy y Lisa (eh?), Veronica y David, Mabel y Petro, Carol y Yuri.

The Mapocho River runs through Santiago. There is a chain of parks and gardens along the town-side embankment: it makes a pleasant hour's walk from the Plaza Atria at one end to the great covered Central Market at the other. One's perambulation passes under fine trees, alongside fountains and pools, and past statues. The statue I have named The

Finger is the first one, in the Plaza Atria. It is a personification of power, an acme of muscle and effort. It is in five stages. The first stage is the base: a massive concrete lump which, like the bastions of a castle, slopes out to take the weight of its load; upon this lies a massy, rectangular block – of bronze, like the remainder of the erection. The next stage is a nude man whose body is bent and whose knees are buckling with the weight of the burden he is carrying. This is, as stages three and four: a bowl, which is borne on the nape of his bowed head and held uncomfortably in place on the rear of his back-stretching arms, and another nude man, standing in the bowl. This man is concentrating all his attention and muscle in doing one thing: his body is arched back like a strung bow with the effort of it, his buttocks clenched as tight as walnuts, his stomach muscles banded, his biceps knotted, the sinews of his neck as tightly strung as piano wires . . . and the aim of all this effort? It is stage five: the positioning of his right index finger. This he points straight up into the sky. Unlike the contorted bending and undulating and leanings of the rest of the construction, this rigid digit, as straight as an arrow, is at exactly 90° to the ground. Like the man, the finger is bursting with effort, with concentrated power: it is swollen, tumescent, disproportionately large; even its tip, far above ground, is broad enough comfortably to take both of the wide, pink claws of a roosting pigeon.

8 April. I have been wandering around the centre of Santiago. It is a pleasant city, although earthquakes have obliterated most of the early or grandiose buildings; even the cathedral is reinforced with bricked-in windows and iron staples. The general atmosphere reminds me of Vienna. The buildings are smaller and more shabby, so are most of the people. There are, however, many streets from which traffic has been banned: families stroll up and down them; youths ogle pretty girls who mince about in giggling groups; there are stall holders selling snacks or magazines; pedlars with junk jewellery spread before them on the pavement; groups of musicians, scraping away with fiddles or tootling on flutes, surrounded by admiring audiences; cafés with outside tables by which one can sit and have a glass of beer and eat something sweet and sticky. All good-humoured and relaxing.

I went into a couple of museums. The local civilisations produced a more attractive and kinder art than their northern counterparts, but there is one particularly beastly pottery statue of a man wearing the skin of another chap. His hands and feet stick out of the loose sleeves and britches of the other fellow's arms and legs; his lips pout and his eyes peek out of the mouth and eyelids of the flayed face. The thing which intrigued me most had nothing to do with the indigenous population, it concerned the Spanish invaders. The museums contain several portraits of local worthies, rather stilted and naive, but with a solemn charm. The men are usually in uniform: magnificent creations intertwined with gold braid and all adangle with swords and lanyards and decorations. The women too are in their best, mostly evening dress by the look of it; all the women, whether young or old, beautiful or plain, proud or modest, have one thing in common: a small, dark moustache. Probably these were once reckoned elegant, like the shaven foreheads of Elizabethan England or flat chests of the 1930s. (Later it was suggested to me that the moustache emphasised the European origins of the sitter, the indigenous Indians being Mongoloid and having almost no facial hair.)

The fish and vegetable market is a charming place. It is a great glass and cast-iron hall slightly reminiscent of Liverpool Street station. I have rarely seen such a variety of fish: not only ones which look like our cod, herring, halibut, bass, mullet, eel, sardine, flounder, whiting and rays but also huge swordfish and tiny anchovy, blue crabs, many different shrimps and prawns (including an interesting fresh-water prawn which spawns in the sea but then goes to live upriver), sea-urchins, cuttlefish and octopi, shellfish of many kinds. There are four types of mussel alone, scallops, clams which are round and brown like baked potatoes and many others I do not recognise. The fruit and veg section is also packed with a huge choice: although only averaging 180 kilometres in width, Chile is 4600 kilometres long, and its climate varies from the freezing Antarctic in the south to the torrid desert in the north. The different varieties of local produce illuminate this versatility: there are nectarines, melons, apples, olives, pears, cherries, grapes, cabbages, carrots, radishes, persimmons, oranges (costing about £1 per 15 kilos), tangerines, passion fruit, chillies (of course), strawberries, raspberries, horseradish, garlic, onions, prickly pear, leeks, asparagus, beans and masses more. Some of the radishes are as big as hand-grenades – and perhaps as deadly. The potato and the maize originated hereabouts and there are many species of them. Some of the maize is as thick as a forearm, other types are long and pointed like marlin-spikes, some are little thingies not much bigger than cotton reels; potatoes come in all shapes and sizes and can be blue, red, yellow or beige. In the meat section there are stacks of cattle feet, brains of different sizes, a crate full of bright yellow chicken feet and a wooden box all asquirm with snails.

9 April. It was interesting flying over the Andes: volcanoes, snow-topped ranges, deep valleys with torrents, arid gulches and cliff faces. However the area round Montevideo is as flat as a pancake: a dull, but not ugly plain dotted with trees. Closer to the city there are many small farmsteads, not much bigger than allotments, all hedged in and looking very English. From my aeroplane window I can see over the city to a vast brown expanse. I cannot understand what it is, it seems too level and even-coloured to be a desert. A passing stewardess says it is a river! It is the surface of the River Plate stretching to the far horizon. The river is about 200 kilometres wide here.

The houses we are driving past are modern 'executive' residences. They are all different and mostly charmingly eccentric, many are thatched and have a 'Ye Olde Englishe' look.

The city, as we near its centre, also looks English, a bit like a down-market Torquay with an esplanade lined with wrought-iron lamps and ragged palms: people walking about, well wrapped up and leaning against the cold wind; one old man striding out, wearing long shorts; stoic fishermen sitting on a wall, not minding not catching anything; an Austin car of the 1950s; a dog wearing a tartan waistcoat being taken for a walk by an old woman in a camel-hair cape.

The riverside beaches are sandy and seem reasonably clean. We are about 100 kilometres from the sea. I ask my escort if the water is salty. He doesn't know, but when I ask if we can stop so I can go and dip my finger in it to taste, he says I will probably poison myself with pollution.

They are fond of ornate and florid names here. We pass a park called the 'Parque de las Instrucciones del año XIII'. Not a name which trips off the tongue; perhaps they just call it 'XIII'.

It is getting dark but, as in Chile, they eat late here and the restaurants will not be open until 8.30 so I go for a walk up the main street – the Calle del 18 de Julio. It is almost midwinter and it feels like it. The wind is chilly, the shops are brightly lit, a smell of charcoal and roasting nuts wafts from the many braziers which are alongside the pavements. I come to the Plaza de los Treinta y Tres, a pleasant market square full of stalls; most sell home-made jewellery or second-hand books. There is a relaxed, unaggressive, rather cosily unexciting atmosphere. I look at my map and am tempted to walk up the Bulevar del 21 Setiembre which leads to the Parque Dr Juan Zorrilla de San Main, but decide it will take too long, so wander back to the hotel.

15 April. Staying over this Easter weekend are Charlie and his attractive, auburn-haired girlfriend, Lucy. I insist that we all go to early Communion at 8 o'clock. Charlie asks if Lucy can be excused as she has been working late so I try not to be a tyrant and say 'OK'. The new parson seems pleasant but young and shy, quite a good sermon, not addressed to us as if we were morons.

Dominie had supervised the laying of breakfast before church: she had put an Easter egg beside each place, and little nests made of wicker and straw and filled with tiny eggs in the middle of the table.

Now lunch. There is a mighty squeeze round the table as there are eighteen of us. The parson had nattered on about the Paschal Lamb during his sermon, we have three saddle of lamb set before us. They are all Matilda's great-great-great-grandchildren; I tell the assembled multitude and there are cries of 'don't' and 'shut up, Daddy.'

24 April. We took off at 14.35 yesterday and landed here in Bangkok after a twelve-hour flight: it says 2.30 in the morning on my watch, but the local time is six hours later. I could not even doze in the aeroplane; now, at last, I am feeling sleepy.

My old Company Sergeant Major used to extol something he called 'class'. It was not entirely snobbish, it meant something that was above the average through a combination of pride, tradition and efficiency. Many British Embassies or High Commissions do not have class, not any more; they are undistinguished buildings with the presence of an office of a firm in sanitary ware. But the Embassy at Bangkok has class. A Gurkha soldier snaps to attention and salutes at our entrance. A huge Union Jack flaps from the tallest flagpole in Thailand, a converted ship's mast. The grounds are immaculate and full of flowers; the building smells clean and uniformed staff help unload and carry the bags.

I am standing in front of the statue of Queen Victoria. It is a great heavy thing of bronze. Her Majesty is slouched on a throne with her knees sprawled apart, enveloped in a blanket. But she is impressive, partly because of her elevation, partly because she looks down at one with imperious, hooded eyes. She used to be on the pavement, placed there in the days when we could, with impunity, plonk our potentates in other people's public places. She had to be moved to her present site, within the Embassy compound, because her bronze lap had become embarrassingly shiny: the locals, having heard that she was the 'Great White Mother Queen', and impressed by the mighty fertility symbols in her hand – the orb and sceptre – kept touching her pubic area as a fertility charm. The area between her parted knees gleamed like a cave of gold. But still, even today, three flower garlands lie at her feet.

Nearby, there is a war memorial. Whether it was the tersely named Robert REID, or the resounding Robert Thomson Consterdine CONSTERDINE-CHADWICK, their deaths were probably pointless and heartbreaking.

I am now in my hotel, The Imperial. This too has class. My room is light and airy and contains a large and tempting bed. Although I now feel half drugged with sleepiness, it would be stupid to sleep through my short stay in a city I have always wanted to visit. I am having 'brunch' before I sally out. It is swelteringly hot. Yesterday was the hottest day in Bangkok for 24 years, and today is not much cooler – so I am not eating outside, but within an air-conditioned terrace whose huge plate-glass windows reveal a garden of lawns, flowerbeds, palm trees, ponds and rills. I always try to eat the local food: this sounded good on the menu, 'river prawns with rice', but it is steeped in curry powder and made even hotter by tiny chopped-up bits of chilli. After one mouthful the eyes glaze and start out like organ stops, the face turns scarlet and sweat beads the brow. I have to cool each mouthful down with a gulp of lemon juice. There are pots of different sauces and powders on the table: most of them are hot; one of them, an attractive amber liquor, is made from the 'distillations of fermented ditch shrimps'.

I do not like going in tour buses: it is humiliating to be associated with a lot of men wearing shorts and silly hats and plain women with blotched complexions, all of us being shepherded in docile flocks by strident guides; but if one has little time it is the easiest way of getting an overall view of a place. I have decided to go on a tour of some of the 'wats', the temples: they are the buildings most typically Siamese, and the journey from temple to temple will involve meandering through the streets. We are in a mini-bus. There are six of us trippers, also the driver and the guide. Our guide, at first sight, is beautiful. On second sight, her face is as flat as a shovel, as if it had been painted on a shield with a fine brush: a couple of arcs, tapering upwards at the tips, for eyebrows; two similar but fainter lines below for her upper eyelids; a couple of dots for a nose; and then a mouth, also turned up at the tips into a Buddha's smile. Other people in the bus include two thin-lipped French women in crumpled linen suits who spend much time grumbling to each other, the chief cause of complaint being the inability of the guide to speak French. There is a weird British pair with Lancashire accents, he is in his late twenties, with stocky legs encased in baggy shorts; she is in her fifties and wears a horrible blouse, loosely knitted from a very heavy yarn so that it looks like a string shopping-bag containing a couple of quinces. She has his bun-like features but with fading ginger hair rather than his mouse. They walk about hand in hand; presumably they are mother and son – perhaps he is her youngest, her nestle-cock. The last passenger is a Japanese, armed with the normal Japanese camera. He is a business man taking the day off.

Driving through Bangkok has been a bit of a disappointment. It is not that different from any other Eastern city: high-rise office blocks, cheap lodgings and hotels; dual carriageways and fly-overs; garages, cinemas, junk-food dispensaries; advertisement hoardings and boarded-up building sites; buses, bicyclists, hurrying shoppers; the occasional intriguing glimpse of temple, shrine, bustling side-street or market, a ramshackle slum or contorted beggar. It is regrettable that squalor, poverty and obsolescence are often more interesting or picturesque than their converse.

The traffic congestion is the worst I have met anywhere in the world, even Cairo or Istanbul. Our bus is more frequently immobile than moving. Most drivers seem resigned to this and live in a special sub-world of their own: looking down from the bus windows, I can see inside cars where people are pouring thermos flasks of drinks, eating, reading, working; perhaps in some of the big, dark-windowed cars they have got the television on, or are having cocktail parties.

The temples are charming: enclosures crammed with shrines and chortens and pavilions and pagodas and bell towers, all dotted about at random in the stone-flagged yards, like pinnacled islands in fossilised oceans of rock; roofs of ascending tiers, fish-scaled with brightly glazed tiles; symbolic flames that glow and flicker in their gilding of gold; mosaic dragons and flowers and rosettes made from chips of mirror and slivers of porcelain in whites, greens, blues, reds and yellows.

Wat Pho is typical of these. We walk past its spindled spires and tiered shrines to enter the Temple of the Reclining Buddha. It is a hangar containing a bloated, golden Zeppelin. The bulbous bulk of Buddha fills the whole building; there is a narrow walk around him, so one can look up and stare. He is 150 feet long and 50 feet high. His head is propped up on one arm, and the ends of his mouth are curved up in the familiar smile; he is contemplating 'his imminent escape from the interminable chains of earthly existence'. In such a circumstance, I wouldn't look so happy. In spite of his colossal size, he is still a personality. The soles of his massive feet depict dainty scenes inlaid with mother-of-pearl.

Next is Wat Benchambobit (my subconscious transliterates it into What Bed-chamberpot?). Inside, swathed in saffron robes, three lines of kneeling acolytes are being confirmed. They have shaven heads and serene expressions. Apparently it is customary for a youth to volunteer to become a monk for at least three months: 'It is a sign of respect and gratitude to their parents,' says our guide. If they want to stay as monks longer, they may be excused National Service. As we watch in discreet silence at the chanting, the bowing and the exchange of ritual items, there is a squeezing and a jostling and our Japanese co-tripper barges through the crowd of relations and onlookers and photographs the monks slap in their faces, making them blink with the sear of his flash bulbs. Perhaps some Japanese spend so much time learning the intricacies of their etiquette that they forget that politeness has two parts, the ritualistic knowledge of accepted customs and taboos, and consideration for other people's feelings.

There are cloisters in which sit or stand a line of life-size bronze Buddhas. They show his 54 different stages of divinity, and they vary from the fat and effeminate to the emaciated and grim. Whatever the stage, the general effect is of pensive dignity. How very different from the Buddhas I have seen in the Himalayas or Mongolia: squat, bow-legged creatures with fearsome fangs, starting eyeballs, adorned with necklaces of human skulls and hurling thunderbolts. Here, every Buddha has a serene smile and even the gross figures have grace.

I am so sleepy, having not shut my eyes for two days, that my head keeps lolling about as we are driven through the streets and I am missing much of the general scene.

Here, at last, we are at the final temple to be visited: Wat Trimit. So? I'm getting sleepier and sleepier and more and more bored with wats: I'm getting temple fatigue. Buddha is pretty large here also, and mighty heavy: five and a half tons of solid gold. I suppose, in the long run, that the gold has been of more use as an image, giving comfort and inspiration, rather than as a pile of bricks in a bank vault.

Back in the hotel. It is early afternoon. I must keep moving. If I lie on that oh-so-tempting bed I'll fall asleep and then wake up at midnight and spend the rest of the night twitchingly awake, to fall asleep at 8 o'clock in the morning, when I should be checking out of this hotel. I'll go for a walk. I'll make it easy, I'll walk down the high street by the Embassy, it goes straight towards the old palace complex about eight miles away.

*

Notes scribbled as I walk: appalling pavement, potholes everywhere, some big enough to engulf a rickshaw, every sort of manhole cover and grating of every size and material; the pavement busy with serene and pleasant people, the girls so pretty, lots wearing mini-skirts, the men neat in dark trousers and white shirts with ties; people cooking, frying, boiling, charring things on skewers, roasting maize and bananas; a woman ladles out food to a customer who holds out a battered aluminium bowl, her chopsticks are deft with something fibrous and flaccid and whitey-grey; there are costers selling melons, loquats, oranges, and rambutans which look like red sea-urchins with dishevelled green spines; sudden smells, the rancid stink of urine drying in the heat, the scent of newly sawn timber from the furniture maker's, the waft of joss-sticks; the latter smoulder in the shrines – one sees these every so often, they are of many-armed Buddhas below pagodas, surrounded by entourages of other Buddhas, some large and bronze, some tiny, in moulded plastic, they are accompanied by strings of elephants, and heaped about with chains and circlets of flowers and buds; you can buy these lucky wreathes from stall holders who thread them as you watch; a building site – the workmen wear straw hats with high crowns and wide brims; everywhere the writing, the letters resemble arches scattered with little rings and embellished with curlicues, they have no division between words so a sentence looks like the long arcades of a bridge or railway viaduct; beggars, hands meekly out in a prayer position before the face; a big shrine in an enclosure, people are hurrying in to buy the flower garlands and having prayed they lay them before the multi-armed god, many of them then hurry over to the sellers of lottery tickets; in one corner, under a canopy of fabric, wearing the traditional tall, tiered, pointed hats, four pretty dancers sway and undulate, their arms as fluid as snakes, as I watch in admiration the twangy music stops and they sit down to be fed tiffin by a deferential crone in a blue dress; some military officers pass by, you can tell that there is an American influence, they have that odd, bandy-legged strut that American soldiers affect, and even the female amongst them, pert and pretty in smart khaki mini-skirt, sports more medal ribbons than the average five-war British General; there is a traffic policeman, just off duty, for he is still pig-snouted with his pollution mask, but he has folded his white gloves neatly and tucked

them into his belt; there is a small fat monk whose shaven head emphasises his huge ears, if he should trip he will not hit the ground, but will
glide over the pavement like a pink-winged bat; the houses are now
becoming smaller, the street narrower, shop after shop of Buddhas,
congregations of them, in garish gilt or mass-produced bronze, the
larger 'Titan'-sized peer through transparent plastic shrouds, the smaller
'mannikins' are shrink-wrapped like cucumbers in a greengrocer's.

I've walked for one and a half hours, perhaps it is time to turn back.
But I can see ornate gables and spires spiking above the dilapidated
buildings that enfilade the street, a wat perhaps. I've seen enough wats
to last a lifetime, but it will make a good turning-point for my walk.

Wat Saket, the Golden Mount, was 'built on order of King Rama III
to his Commanding Officer Sriphiphatratanarajakosho'. Perhaps they
just called him 'Phaty'. It houses relics of the Buddha and is built on an
artificial hill. There are 318 steps before you get to the top. Why am I
doing this? It is appallingly hot and clammy, I am pouring with sweat and
tottering with tiredness.

The climb has been worth it, if only for the panoramic view over roofs:
steep-pitched and tiled if old; of red-painted corrugated iron if middle-
aged; or flat 'black-tops' if new. The central spire chorten is plated with
golden mosaic. Within, it is a bit of an anticlimax for a non-Buddhist: a
small round cell dominated by what seems to be a ten-foot high, golden
wedding cake.

I must go back to my hotel. I am almost sleeping as I walk.

6 May. *The scents of honeysuckle and roses were all about. I was sitting in the
warmth of the late Sunday afternoon sun by the ornamental pond, listening to the
(annoyingly) green waters splashing from Dominie's fountain and reading the newspapers. Dominie called to me from the door of the verandah: 'your cousin James
[Butler] is on the telephone. His doctor advised him to take up a sport so he has
bought a hot-air balloon. He says if you lend him two strong people to help launch it
he'll reward you by letting you have a ride.'*

*Before they could gather their wits and make excuses I had recruited George and
his friend Peter Wylie as launchers, bundled them into the Land Rover and had*

driven the four miles over the Colne Valley to James's house. Now, attired in hats and asbestos gloves, they are apprehensively holding the mouth of the balloon open, waiting for the pilot to turn on the fire blower. The balloon is red and yellow and slightly shiny and when we first took it out of its bag and stretched it out on the pasture it looked like the monstrous after-birth of a colossal dinosaur. Now that it is a quarter full of hot air it is billowing and bulging as if baby dinosaurs are back inside, fighting.

There is a terrific roar; George and Peter flinch as a huge jet of fire booms into the bag. It swells with a vast inhalation. The pilot turns the jet off, re-aligns it, and fires again. The bag lurches and reels and rears up, swaying drunkenly. Suddenly it is upright. The pilot, a sharp-faced fellow with burn peelings on his bald head, hops into the basket. 'You in next,' he says to James's friend, who is learning how to fly. The friend climbs in.

'Now you,' he says to Jane, James's stepdaughter. She pops up, over, and in.

My turn. The wickerwork basket has footholds woven into it, so it is easy to clamber up the side, over the leather-padded gunwale, and in. It is quite crowded with four of us and three gas cylinders.

The pilot instructs: 'Hold on to these rope loops — all you have to do is hang on to them — remember to remain inside the basket at all times' (silly ass). The jet roars again. We remain rooted to the spot. More roarings, like a frustrated bull. Suddenly I realise that James, George and Peter are having to hold the basket down by leaning on it.

'Right . . . let go!' shouts the pilot.

They stand back and instantly they recede below, their upturned faces shrinking from round plates to buns to buttons. The roof of Gladfen Hall swims into sight and immediately diminishes; its garden dwindles as the fields crowd round it and then, looking ahead, I can see the rolling farmland and woods turning to blue far away into the horizon. To the north-east, on the top of the plateau, I can see my house, nestling amid all its trees, and further south I see the shaggy primitive back of Bullock Wood half tucked away in the rolling folds of the Bourne Valley and, closer by, the meticulous rectangles of Coppins and Elms Hall woods and the rooftops of Westwoods and Abbotts Shrubs. Everything is so green, and so many greens: the lush blue-green of wheat, the lighter, feathery green of barley, the amber-greens of budding oak and the darker greens of ash and sycamore, the smoky silver-green of bat willows and the billowing green, splotched with white, of hawthorn hedges. Here and there, vividly, but in co-ordination with the greens, are great yellow patches of rape. Everything is so busy yet so unplanned and higgledy-piggledy: fields and wood-

lands are of all shapes and sizes; lanes amble and brooks meander; and the Colne River winds and twists through its willow groves and osier beds and between its watermeadows.

Our course is north-west-by-north and so we are now floating over Halstead. It looks like a toy-town, 600 feet below: the neat little rows of red-tiled shops each side of the High Street leading up the hill to the grey flint of St Andrew's church, the white-painted weatherboarding of our old watermill weaving shed, the tidy rows of council housing and the random clutter of the back streets. I can hear the piping voices of children as they call up to us, and dogs barking.

We are now veering further west and are drifting right up the Colne Valley. Our speed is four or five knots. The river keeps passing beneath us. When we go over it its warmer air gives us a lift, and we can see a blaze of colour as our red and yellow are reflected in the waters directly below.

We are lower, and are almost hedge hopping, going down as low as 80 feet, level with some of the tree tops, then sailing up an extra 30 or 40 feet to bound over them. There is a sensation of really flying: one leans out over the waist-high edge of the basket and sees the landscape gliding beneath and the trees sailing by and the little houses appearing in front and disappearing under one's feet. I always knew that this was a pretty part of England; from up here it is beautiful. The river is placid and edged with rushes and spangled with the pads of lily leaves. Mallard and moorhen skitter in panic across the water; now there is a pair of Canada geese lumbering below, ploughing the water with V-shaped furrows; sheep hurry bleating across the pastures, away from our silent shadow – those ones are Wullie's; the little villages look idyllic, neat and spruce and cosy as in a child's picture-book: we have passed Great and Little Maplestead to our right, now Sible Hedingham is rising out of the fields in front; the great tower of Castle Hedingham is floating past, almost at eye level – it looks like a rock crag sticking through its mound of trees. A flag flies from one of its towers, the cross of St George I think, but the wind is too mild to make it stretch out and display. Particularly pretty are the watermills, all in white weatherboarding; I did not realise there were so many, nor did I realise how many geese there are, almost every riverside cottage seems to have its little flock. They waddle about and honk and gape up at us.

There is a deer, a roe, showing its white scut as it bounds in the horse-tails and rushes of the marshland below. The marsh has now developed into a carr of alder and willow. The birds seem to glide beneath, more as if they were swimming than flying. Some children, fishing or picnicking, are shrilling up at us and waving excitedly.

*

We have been going for over an hour and the pilot is looking for somewhere to land. I tell him that if he waits for half a mile, and if we continue in this direction, we will fly directly over the park of the house where James's stepmother lives.

We are there. There is the white shape of the house at the end of its drive; sheep are panicking in the parkland below, but they have lambed so no harm is being done.

'Don't forget to keep your legs slightly braced for the shock of landing,' says the pilot.

There is a bump, a surprisingly hard one – we rebound up and come down again, with a softer bump – a small skip – down for good. We stay in the basket. The balloon still looms above us, swaying slightly. A small blond boy bicycles out of the lodge and up to us and stares, mutely. The car and trailer suddenly appear down the drive and race over the grass. James leaps out.

'What fantastic navigation,' he cries, beaming.

George and Peter crawl out. They look resigned.

James says 'I'll go and have a word with Mollie' and disappears towards the house.

The balloon gradually deflates. We pull its top lanyard so that it stretches its full length on the ground as if it were lying down to die. As it subsides it exhales a hot stale smell of gas. We start to coil ropes, unscrew bits and fold up the balloon.

'James is being a long time,' I say. 'Either he is getting a large gin and tonic or a reprimand.'

The small bicyclist speaks at last: 'Her ladyship won't be giving him no gin and tonic,' he opines.

12 May. It is pleasantly cool as I set off on my walk for although we are on the equator, we are 10,000 feet up. Quito, the capital of Ecuador, is a mixture of the grand and the cosy: a background of the snow-capped peaks and volcanoes of the Northern Andes, an abundance of little cottages and bungalows. These are strewn at random over the mountain ridges and valleys in groups and clusters; from afar they look like banks and spits of pebbles dumped upon the lush green slopes. The people here are small: tiny. Even the Hispanics toddle about with the tops of their heads below my chin, the Amerindians are another half-foot smaller; they waddle, rocking from side to side as if they have no legs. But this is the only place in the Americas where I have seen the indigenous people at ease, even happy. A young woman, dressed in the local rig of heavy black curtains emblazoned with vivid bands of red or green or yellow, has just stepped out of a smart car, her own. A quartet of men sit on a bench in front of me: from behind they are four dark trilbies, four long pig-tails, four archetypal silhouettes, four puffs of nicotine smoke – and, unusually, four chatterings and laughs and gesticulations.

A man is walking in front of me with an old-fashioned gramophone (complete with brass horn and winding-handle) balanced on his shoulder. He has only one record; it is so scratchy that I can recognise no tune, no-one pays any attention to him, nor gives him money. Is he doing it for personal gratification, like someone with an antique walkman? Along the pavement are stalls from which are sold rugs, panpipes, dolls, brightly coloured cloth bracelets (or head bands?), sun-glasses, heavy (but very attractive) knitwear from coarse, woollen-spun yarn, mainly with an ecru colour base, sweets, cigarettes, sugared buns of a dough-nut type, veg and fruit, including pears, bananas and limes; there is a man holding a bunch of ties, a woman holding a chandelier of plastic baby dummies, sellers of lottery tickets. The public telephones are placed on tables on the pavement. Attendants sit on rickety chairs besides, and collect the money and listen to the conversations.

I can look up some of the side-streets, here in the centre of the city, and as they ascend they abruptly stop to reveal, spread on the mountain slopes, patches of vivid green: pale green if farmland, darker if wood-land. The houses are whitewashed and have balconies, overhanging eaves and heavy doors; streets are cobbled with rectangular blocks and sometimes echo with the voices of children which shrill out with that brittle intensity you get between walls.

I have reached the cathedral. It is shut, they are still building it; they must hasten, it has already started to disintegrate. It is in a bogus Gothic style and constructed from a gritty, harsh, white stone which resembles breeze-block. The central spire is the best feature: it is of ornate tracery and wears a ringlet of angels who, with their spiky silhouettes, look more like dragons. Gargoyles loom above me. Several are of American animals, exaggerated to monstrosities: an armadillo, iguana, a Galapagos tortoise. More familiar are the weeds growing between the flagstones and on the already crumbling walls: groundsel, dandelion and mother-of-millions.

13 May. Leave Ecuador early morning – land in Peru a couple of hours later.

The first sight of Lima was horrible. We flew over an opening scene of burning rubbish dumps, several miles of them spread along the shore. These were followed by a massive shambles of flat-topped shacks; as we approached the centre of Lima the shacks looked as squalid but were aligned more neatly. Now that I have sallied out into the city I no longer feel tired and travel-sleazed and am much more cheerful. The ugliness of the place no longer depresses me. The buildings may be plain and dull, when not downright seedy, but the people show character and vivacity; besides, here in the area called Mireflores, there are several streets of small, attractive houses with pretty front gardens. I am sitting beside a small table on the pavement of the Avenue José Pardo, sipping the local beer and digesting luncheon (which was a bit drab, being a shrimp salad made with four shrimps in an incompatible blend of pineapple chunks and cold macaroni, and sea bass, well cooked but boring). The early afternoon is warm and balmy, with a pleasant breeze from the sea. The traffic toots and jostles past, people wander or bustle, according to temperament or intention; on the flagstones I hear the 'click-clack' of high heels, or the 'squidge-sponge' of crepe soles, or the 'shuffle-shuffle-drag' of broken-down sandals. The pedestrians are of every sort of racial type, mainly Caucasian-Latin, but also Negroid and many of the indigenous Amerindians. It is interesting how the latter's squashed-nosed profiles are similar to those of the stele and other carvings of Inca, Aztec, Mayan and Toltec. They are small and thick-set with dark, ruddy faces and the straight, heavy black hair typical of the Mongoloid. Their clothes are colourful, with many yellows and reds; this is the only thing about them which shows any élan – they seem expressionless, their faces set into lines of stoic sadness.

A huge water tanker drives past, slowly. Now and then it stops and from a large, wrinkled, dangling hose it stales a huge flood of water onto the flowerbeds which have been planted between the two lanes of traffic.

I have now walked for nearly a couple of hours up the beach. The sea is warm but has large patches of yellow froth. On my right there are low cliffs of compacted cobbles and shingle, on my left the dour and gloomy strand consists of blackish sand and various sizes of stone, ranging from shingle to boulders; there is also litter. The litter has been increasing greatly during the last half hour and it has finally dawned on me that I have been walking into a vast rubbish dump. The acrid smell of refuse has overwhelmed the tang of the sea. All about me I can see the stooping figures of poverty-stricken peasants sifting through the trash. Suddenly I remember that I was told not to walk about with my watch or signet ring exposed, nor get out of shouting distance from a police-man.

A lot of the needy peasants are looking at me.

I turn on my heels with what I hope is a casual and unconcerned mien and retrack my steps. I hope my gait appears as unhurried as before, and they cannot see that my strides, though as apparently languid, are considerably longer.

Not much flora, the sea and the litter have blighted most of that, but I have seen a small brown humming-bird, an osprey-like eagle, a very attractive brown and white dove, something which looks like a wax-wing and a few gulls, too far off to identify.

I am back in my digs, eating dinner of five avocado pears bought from a barrow boy. They are laced with some dressing I made from oil and vinegar I found in a cupboard. The oil is rancid.

I turn on the television: the Flintstones, an unfunny American cartoon. The dubbing is in Spanish, which I cannot understand. I suddenly realise what I am doing: it must be the height of futility and boredom to sit in a dark and poky room trying to lip-read Fred and Norma Flintstone.

I also cannot comprehend the next programme but, from her expression, the dear little old lady on a rocking-chair is enthusing over the charms of the guinea-pig which is nestling in the cosy contours of her lap. She is stroking it. It is looking appealingly up at her with its boot-button eyes.

The picture fades, to be replaced by a new one: the same guinea-pig, and the same dear little old lady; but the guinea-pig has been skinned and has a wooden skewer up its arse, the little old lady is holding it by the skewer and is roasting it over a charcoal fire. Two children await, greedily.

20 May. Dominie very tired from looking after her mother, who spends all day giving her a stream of fussy and irksome little orders: 'turn up the television – let in the pigeon, it wants to go to its nest in the vase – get me a newspaper – clear up that dog's mess – a tap is dripping in the bathroom – comb that dog – change the television programme – tell Mrs Julian that I don't want crust on my cucumber sandwiches – let that dog in – close the window again – my eiderdown is not on straight – pass another newspaper – where's my brush?' Dominie says that every Friday evening, when one of her brothers can take over and she can come home, it is just like end of term.

We lunch in the verandah, to the sound of tinkling fountain and fighting pekinese. Henrietta has been told by her gynaecologist that her baby will be a boy (a boy's heart-beat is 120 per minute or less; a girl's is 140 or above) and small (caused by her smoking, I complain). She and Jimmy have not yet decided on a name. We suggest many names, from Aaron to Zzebedee, via Eggfrith and Wilfred. What one parent likes, the other doesn't. It will end up with some drear name like John or Edward.

24 May. Few places live up to their reputations. Rio de Janeiro is one of the few which even exceeds it. It is beautiful. At first sight, anyway. The city is spread along a series of bays and inlets whose beaches, almost snow-white, are interrupted by isthmuses; these break up into an archipelago of islands, some only large rocks, others, such as Sugar Loaf Mountain, exaggeratedly pointed and simplified like a child's drawing. All of this is backed by a massive range of irregular mountains. The total tableau is a mélange of sea, islands, mountains, valleys and buildings, the whole lot dominated by the 1300 feet of Sugar Loaf Mountain on the shore, and, above all, floating with outstretched arms amid the clouds, the colossal statue of Christ on the pinnacle of the Corcovado. Round about His head, as small as midges, wheel and swoop buzzards and their marine counterparts, frigate birds. Everywhere you go in Rio you will suddenly see this statue, hovering 2000 feet overhead; for a moment it may be hidden by a skyscraper or a grove of palm trees or one of the strange steepled knolls – but then, again, above you once more, there is Christ. And he has to be busy here, for as a local saying has it: 'Never has Christ blessed a happier and more lovable brothel.' But I don't think it is happy: the poverty here is appalling, and it is riddled with AIDS.

The beach of Copacabana is expansive and white and often has large rollers and clouds of spray, but few men go there to swim; they go to admire the stunning girls who sashay about in giggling groups, the bottom halves of their bikinis so minutely tailored that all that is visible from the front is a tiny pubic triangle of cloth and from behind a bit of dental floss or, with the more modest, a bootlace. In contrast to this attractive femininity, the speech of the Brazilian is a guttural gabble, more Teutonic than Romance in sound.

A Queen's Messenger's job has elements of danger: we have been killed, hijacked, beaten up and harassed; but generally our dangers are those of a conventional traveller, and of these the most likely nowadays is mugging, and the most likely places to get mugged in are Kingstown (Jamaica) and Rio. However, an even more common hazard in Rio is a bus ride. This one, from Flamengo Bay to Copacabana, is packed with every conceivable human type: Negroid, Mongoloid, Caucasian; rough, hairy, smooth; fat and thin; rich and poor; the sane and the demented – the average is small, dark and cheerful. A little fellow who is too short to reach the overhead rail is clinging to my arm instead. He has a slightly greenish face and a tiny moustache which fans out from his nostrils: if a frog had pubic hair, it would look like this. The rest of us are hanging on like monkeys along a branch; we swing out in unison with the centrifugal force as the driver corners; he too swings out and has to grasp the window-sill with one hand whilst steering with the other. Halfway round a hairpin bend he has managed to extract a cigarette packet from his pocket, open it, remove a fag from it and light up. For no reason except, possibly, cussedness, or to keep us on our toes, he will suddenly brake and send us all piling up behind him; he will then accelerate and send us hurtling towards the stern. He jams on his brakes, for a reason this time – we are at a bus stop. About a dozen passengers squeeze in. The driver is bored by this hanging around and charges off before the last and frailest is able to board. She is a little old lady. She has one foot on the lowest step, the other on the pavement. We are overtaken by a red Mazerati. This annoys the self-esteem of our driver, who accelerates after the sports car. Considerately, he keeps the door open for the old lady. She hangs on to the boarding-rail with one hand; with the other she grips several shopping-bags and a crutch. She is now hopping on the foot which is still on the pavement, it must be her better leg. We accelerate; her hops lengthen. The passengers cheer her on. She has to let go, and mouths curses at our departing rear. The man next to me is proud of all this. He is lean and bald with spectacles and a well-ironed and darned suit, perhaps a run-down professor or a member of the political opposition.

'You have been here before, to our beautiful Rio?'

'Yes.'

'Then you have already experienced the passion of our bus drivers?'

'Not until now.'

'Ah! My friend! My friend! Our bus drivers are the most audacious in the world. To qualify as a bus driver in Rio, it is very difficult. You must be a paranoid with suicidal tendencies. You start by doing your service militaire as a Kamikaze pilot. You beat your mother-in-law in the evenings and tease the lions in the zoo at weekends.'

Those around me, the ones who understand English, nod proudly.

I walk along the beach. A small urchin runs up to me and points worriedly at my shoe. On my toe cap reposes what seems to be a huge turd. The urchin summons a youth who is carrying shoe-cleaning equipment and who drops on his knees to start cleaning my shoe. I leap back, enraged, having met this little charade before, and angrily point out the artificial-turd dispenser which the smaller of the little swines is hiding behind his back. Grumbling, I scrape my shoe clean on the number plate of the nearest parked car. The owner, a tubby fellow in shorts and an open shirt, comes rushing up and whinges at me. I give my foot a final scrape, scowl at the urchins and curl my lip at the expostulating car owner, and plod off.

*

I return to the Hotel Gloria and look at the brochure on tripper's tours which the concièrge has given me. Remarkable: one tour is of the 'famous Borel Slum section of the city'. How can people sit in an air-conditioned bus in their expensive clothes and stare at other people's poverty without feeling embarrassed? Poverty may be picturesque, as I saw in Bangkok, but one need not be salacious about it. Some of the people here are so decrepit and miserable that it is a wonder why they bother to stay alive, far less shuffle from one pointless place to another.

25 May. I have just been handed a telex:

UNCLASSIFIED
FM FCO
TO IMMEDIATE RIO DE JANEIRO
OF 240940Z MAY 90

PLEASE PASS FOLLOWING TO QUEEN'S MESSENGER COURTAULD:

10.45 HRS ON 24 MAY, GRANDDAUGHTER, 8LB 12OZS, MOTHER AND CHILD WELL.

Well, it won't be called Wilfred or Eggfrith. Nor is it small. I hope Henrietta didn't have any trouble. I wish I were back in Essex. There are still 10 hours, 33 minutes to go. I am ragingly impatient to go home. How is Dominie? How is my new grandchild? What is her name? Did Henrietta have a difficult time? How has Ranulf taken to his sister? Are the other children alright? And Violet and Monk and all? How are the sheep? I hear it has been very hot in England. How are my new trees doing in the dry weather? How are the crops? Why do I do this silly job?

26 May. *Home! Arrived here mid-afternoon. House empty, Dominie away, at her mother's. It is interesting to see how our absence is marked. Mine is simple – the lawn needs mowing, the fountain is not playing, the stable clock is ten minutes slow, the*

Oak Room smells unused and musty, the post and newspapers and magazines are heaped on the back slab. Dominie's absence is more subtle. The place feels as if it has no heart. The dogs were pleased enough to see me, and ran round the garden in front of me, but now they are lying about in the kitchen, looking lethargic. The cats haven't even bothered to move. Flowers in the vases are withered. Dead blue-bottles are on the window-sills. There are no smells of cooking; no bubblings from the oven. The telephone hasn't rung for three hours. There is a numb silence. The house is holding its breath, waiting for her return.

I hurry round to Henrietta's. My granddaughter looks exactly like her other grandfather; I am surprised she is not smoking a pipe and wearing spectacles. She is to be christened Charlotte.

Dominie has just telephoned from Brewhurst. She is well but longing to be home. She says George and Fiona are re-engaged: I am very pleased but a bit bemused.

13 June. Arrived at Delhi at 9.00 a.m. The British Compound is tidy and efficient: smart Gurkha guards salute me as I enter; the flowerbeds are weed-free; the central fountain is spouting before the main entrance; gardeners march behind lawnmowers; the file of vultures perched on the roof ridge of the hospital wing are neatly aligned. The Security Officer helps me organise a trip to the Taj Mahal tomorrow. Now I am jet-lagged, and it is debilitatingly hot, so I decide to relax in the morning and tour Delhi in the afternoon.

I have a sneaky feeling that I have made the wrong decision. There are four main ways of being driven around here: in buses – packed with people and involving much queuing and queue-jumping; in taxis – old and rickety and as uninterestingly like taxis anywhere; in bicycle rickshaws – I would not like the sight of some poor bent back in front of me, and spindly shanks straining at the pedals; or in scooter-tricycles – these are friendly little yellow and black beetles. They are powered in front by a Vespa motor-bicycle. Around this a small body has been built; it accommodates the driver who sits in front, steering with handlebars, and a little sofa at the rear, just big enough for two small people. It is roofed and walled with a fabric and frame cover, rather like the hood of a pram.

As we bounce and bobble over ruts and potholes, or race up avenues or dart under the wheels of lorries, I feel as if I am in an animated bowler hat, a hat pulled well over my eyes so I have to sit slouched to peer under the low fabric awning. We started off with such a hopscotch of jerks and jumps I had to brace myself with a leg wedged in the far left corner, the other foot jammed beneath the partition in front, one arm holding a strut above my head and the other the back of the seat. My driver is a frenzied Sikh in a pink turban. A manic grin flashes in and out of the depths of his beard, like lightning in a storm cloud. I see it often as he turns to me to complain about other drivers. He is appalled by their incompetence: 'Oh my goodness, sir, did you see that unobservant fool?' he exclaims as a huge pair of front wheels just miss us as we cut across the growling snout of a petrol tanker. He presumes that the best method of defence is attack and charges other vehicles shouting 'Confounded fool, not looking properly at other road users . . . absolutely no traffic sense . . . never never never are they looking where they are going, sir . . . always getting in the way, these rickshaws . . .' A holy man crosses our path. He has thick spectacles, a baggy umbrella, a white beard and a surprising nimbleness when leaping out of the way – his holiness is not that of the Sikhs so of no interest to my driver. The vehicle contributes to the racket; the angry gargle of its motor, the roar and rumble of the back axle beneath my feet, the rattle and squeak of the bodywork, the flap of canvas, the adenoidal bleat of the horn. The driver likes the horn: he uses it on anyone or anything which meets his disapproval; he has just hooted at a stop sign. It was the only indication he gave of having noticed it.

Delhi is a satisfactory blend of the old and the new, the archaic grace and beauty of the Mogul architecture, the pride and stateliness of the British Raj, paradoxically co-ordinated by the shambolic human bustle. We potter down wide avenues and parade-ways, past the magnificent public buildings of an Empire Where the Sun Never Sets, designed by Lutyens, past domed tombs set in brushy wildernesses of abandoned gardens, predecessors of the Taj Mahal, along narrow alleys where people jostle and craftsmen squat holding hammers or cutters or welding torches, past open stalls selling fruit and vegetables and sacks of pulse; lesser traders sit on rows on the pavement, their miserable wares arranged on sheets of newspaper – no-one seems interested, perhaps they have to sell to each other, like the spiders in my fly-free cellar who make a precarious living eating their neighbours. There are elegant and beautiful women in saris, fine bearded men in turbans, sad scruffy men in rags, groups of neat schoolgirls, disorderly mobs of ragamuffin schoolboys; porters, drivers, pedlars and shoppers and people merely ambling or standing about gossiping; an elephant lurches down a street, on its back a ramshackle howdah of poles and carpets; there are six huge pots under an awning, nestling together like a clutch of gigantic terra-cotta eggs; a group of bearded holy men, looking grave and impressive and saying nothing; a wall is being built, the hod carriers are graceful girls with bricks on their heads; there is another girl with an enchantingly beautiful face, she bears a polished brass ewer on her head and wears a scarlet sari with gold edging; a hairdresser snips and combs under a tree; a peacock, a living jewel, nicely picking its sacred way through the litter of a stagnant ditch; a muddy pool, dotted with the seal-like heads of water-buffalo; sitting by a clump of pink-flowering oleanders there are some snow-white Bramah cattle, painted with orange spots; we squeeze past another herd, they need worming, they are so thin that you can see every bone in their tails, dangling like long, skeletal fingers. The gusts of smells are intense: cesspits, curry, cattle, diesel fumes, spice, sewerage, something dead, hay, diesel, burning charcoal, cattle, oleander, corn, diesel, tobacco, cattle, hot iron, cardamon seeds, sewerage . . . Everywhere, forcing themselves between the mass of man and beast, are the vehicles: bicycles, rickshaws, scooters, tumbrels, carts, traps, waggons, cars, buses, lorries. Many of the lorries have signs on the back which say 'BLOW HORN' or 'HORN PLEASE' or annoyingly, divided by the reinforcing struts, 'HOR NPL EASE'. Some lorries look like huge mobile pillows, their cargo containers being over-stuffed, over-bulging bags; perhaps they are carrying cotton, or fodder. There is an abandoned lorry by the wayside, it is so old and decrepit it has just crawled there and died.

I see almost every type of beast of burden: the hump-backed cattle plod in pairs, their yoked heads sway from side to side; the mangy little donkeys scuttle with pitter-patter steps; tall camels stride, their super-cilious eyelids drooping high above the mob; elephants shamble and swing; horses canter, trot, limp or hobble, depending on decrepitude; with head stretched out the water-buffalo steps its measured pace; stolidly, the men who pull barrows haul and trudge; women glide, lithe legs invisible inside saris; everywhere dogs scuttle and cower, or slumber, or are dead.

14 June. I started off at the crack of dawn to be driven the 125 miles to Agra, the site of the Taj Mahal. My driver is a Kashmiri called Rajab. Like my Sikh scooter-driver yesterday he thinks that a continuously sounding horn is as effective as a bulldozer in getting people out of the way. Perhaps he is right, we are here, after all.

The main impression of the drive was one of ceaseless bustle. Much of the area transversed was built up: Delhi seemed to continue for miles, then there were many small towns and villages. In every high street several dramas seemed to be happening at once: a market day, a religious holiday, an exodus from something urgent and a work area where everyone was desperately active to earn the daily bread.

'Busy, busy, busy, everyone always busy,' said Rajab disapprovingly.

The Taj Mahal: the very name seems to have a sob in it, and so it should, for it was built by a widower who himself had made many widows – the grandson of Akbar, Shah Jehan, who erected the tomb for his beloved queen Mumtaz Mahal. It took 22 years to build, between 1630 and 1652. It is in pure white marble. It was to have been complemented by a twin in black marble for Shah Jehan. But that was never started and he lies beside his wife under the great bubble of polished marble above the central hall.

The rectangular enclosure in front has, in addition to the chain of ponds up the centre and formal layouts of gardens, now rather threadbare, a side-walling of cloisters, with fort-like doorways in the centre of each. All of these are built of pink-red sandstone. I tiptoe up the steps of a deserted gateway. It grows darker and darker, steeper and steeper, narrower and narrower, more and more musty. The door at the top is locked. There are squeaks all about me. Then a dry rustle. Suddenly I remember that this is the country of Kaa, the snake, and hustle down and out.

Ideally, the approaching chain of formal ponds should reflect the Taj Mahal on their surfaces, but there is a faint hot breeze today which ruffles the waters. I climb the steps onto the platform on which the tomb is built and before entering walk past it and look over the balustrade behind. A wide river valley spreads below. The shallow waters are full of water-buffalo, grunting and roaring like sea-lions. To the left, half a mile away, I can see the red walls and battlements of a great fortification.

The outer walls of the tomb are embellished with arabesque tendrils and flowers made from semi-precious stones inlaid into the marble or, on the lower stages, into some panelling of pink marble. Within, all is dark. The graves, placed primly side by side rather like marble twin beds, are lit only by candles. Around them is a screen of marble so intricately pierced with a design of creepers that it looks more like lace than stone. It too is inlaid with semi-precious stones. Awed, people speak in whispers; we silently shuffle about, our shoes muffled in cloth galoshes.

A few miles from Agra there is Fatehpur Sikri, a city that has lain desolate for nearly five centuries. It was built by the Great Mogul Akbar in 1569 and abandoned about 13 years later – no water: bad news for his town planner. Akbar had a nasty temper.

I walk in the great echoing courtyards, under arches, beneath domes, past the façades of palaces and pavilions, alongside colonnades and up and down flights of steps. A dry, empty shell of a city, utterly dead; its people totally gone, not even here as ghosts or as the faintest of whispers. It should be mysterious and tragic but is not because of the pestiferous attentions of guides and hawkers who dog my every footstep:

'I am a fully accredited guide. Look, here is my licence, sir.'

'You are going the wrong way, come with me . . .'

'Photographs and postcards, sir? Look, beautiful cards, only 50 rupees.'

'. . . a personal service, sir . . .'

'I am just learning English sir a student sir no charge . . .'

'I will show you around and leave my fee entirely up to you . . .'

'Paperweights: here, in alabaster, inlaid with lapis lazuli, jasper and malachite, only 200 rupees each, 150 then, 100, look both for 120, very well, for you alone, 50 rupees . . .'

And now, when I thought I'd shaken the last of them off, and am peering into a deserted enclosure surrounded by colonnades, perhaps an elephant stable yard, a very humble, very small, very quiet voice behind me:

'Can I help you, sir? I take you to the bathroom? *Please* sir? Sir, I am the Toilet Man.'

On our way back Rajab decided to take a short cut. Soon it became obvious that we were lost, but he denied it, presuming, perhaps, that I was too stupid to understand why he kept stopping and saying to strangers: 'Dilli? 'Dilli?' 'Dilli?' 'DilliDilliDilli?'

At first, people pointed and jabbered in a reasonably confident manner, but later questionees began to shrug and move off and I really became worried. Then, going down a lane, we came upon a stationary convoy of lorries. Rajab drove past them all, pompously waving aside their gestures to turn back. After about a mile we reached the cause of the stoppage, two lorries who had locked bumpers in a bullish attempt of passing at a place too narrow for the manoeuvre. Rajab and I got out and joined the crowd who were watching the lorry drivers arguing. The driver of another lorry, a good-humoured fellow in spite of beetle brows and a sardonic expression, and fluent in English, advised me to tell Rajab to back out of it, 'before another damn fool like him comes up behind and bottles you in.'

'Won't the police come soon and sort this out?'

He laughed at my naivety: 'They are too busy, elsewhere, collecting bribes.'

'Bribes?!'

'Sir, you could buy a policeman here for the price of a cup of tea.'

I told Rajab to reverse out. Grumbling, he did so, to derisive cheers. Halfway back we met, as presumed by my sardonic confidant, a line of twerps in cars coming towards us. We all stopped and gesticulated. I saw a field entrance and track a short way off and told Rajab to get onto it. Moaning gently, he did so. The track joined other tracks and after a mile or so became quite a reasonable bridle-path – just as well, for looking behind I saw, half hidden by the huge pall of dust of our progression, a line of a dozen cars.

We motored along the headlands of several more fields.

'We are lost,' grizzled Rajab.

'Nonsense,' I said, 'aim for that distant factory chimney, there must be a road near it.'

Our car led our long, dusty convoy through the factory yard. We were watched by a variety of staff and workers who goggled at us in bemused surprise. Sure enough, having driven through the factory, we came upon a main road. I told Rajab to turn right, so that the setting sun was to port, and within an hour and a half we were back in the turmoil and bustle of Delhi.

21 June. Having navigated myself round the Indian continent with no drama, I enter the late-evening home-bound train at Liverpool Street and within ten minutes of moving off there is an excitement. Several people are in the carriage, mostly home-going commuters: grey-faced, tired and quiet. The most noticeable of these is a young woman. She is very pretty, with a prim, slightly ironic mouth and thin curved eyebrows, though with an uncommonly small head, made smaller by her dark hair strained back into a severe bun. She is immaculately dressed in a navy-blue suit of 14-ounce fabric, dobby woven with worsted merino warp and slubbed linen-spun weft, and has an expensive attaché case and good shoes. There is also a huge, churlish, watery-eyed yobbo who slings himself in the seat opposite me. The train judders out of the station and dodders up the track for a dozen miles and then the yobbo suddenly pukes about a bucketful of beer-rancid custard on the floor between us. He chunters on and on, I have never seen anyone do it so often, or with such quantities.

'You filthy, disgusting bugger,' I tell him, when he has paused to pant.

'Yea, filfy wuddy animal, an' I bet you ain' e'en go' a First Class ti'itt,' reprovingly pipes up the pretty business woman, all glottal stops pulled out in cockney outrage.

The yobbo staggers out at the next station and for once, instead of the quiet rustle of newspapers, from all about can be heard comradely chatter as we exchange our indignations.

28 June. Arrived here in Washington yesterday evening. This morning I have my routine breakfast at Pearsons Drug Store.

The Americans are very polite to each other, with an almost old-fashioned courtesy. I hear this conversation between the wrinkled old waitress behind the counter and a customer, also black, with huge muscles straining his jeans and T-shirt:

'This is very nice, 'cept I also asked for potatoes, ma'am.'

'What's that you're saying, sir?'

'I said, ma'am, that I asked for potatoes.'

'No sir, you did not.'

'Yes ma'am. I did.'

'No sir, you sure did not.'

'Yes ma'am. I sure did.'

'Sir, you did not ask for potatoes.'

'Ma'am, I always ask for potatoes. Fried potatoes, ma'am.'

'This time, sir, you did not ask for potatoes.'

'There was no exception to my rule, ma'am, and that rule is that I always eat potatoes with my breakfast.'

'I will give you potatoes, sir, but you did not ask for them.'

'And I will eat them ma'am, 'cos that's what I always do.'

He slowly drags out that last 'ma'am' and that 'always' in a great deep drawl so that it sounds as if he were crooning a sleepy Southern song. I suspect that in some subtle way he is being cheeky.

As I will be leaving early this afternoon for Canada I have decided to use up my short stay here with a visit to the cathedral church of St Peter and St Paul. Outside, it looks pristine in its newness: the pretty, pale yellow Indiana limestone from which it is built shows no smoothed out ageing in the sharpness of carving and masonry; there are no shrapnel scars or bullet holes or vandal gouges which you see in European cathedrals, nor their mixture of architectural styles and additions and embellishments and lean-tos. Over the door there is a pleasant carved scene of a gathering of nudes disporting in a bubble bath. It is called *The Creation*. Within, it is impressive: a leaflet says that it is the sixth largest church in the world and the view from the west end of the nave to the altar is a tenth of a mile. The basic effect is spoiled by the stained glass, much of which is garish and harsh. In the same way as my local 'wool' churches bear memorials to Essex or Suffolk merchants of medieval and Tudor times, so one can see memorials to the rich merchants who helped pay for the place to be built: the Duponts, the Rockefellers, Kelloggs, 'Andrew William Mellon, Banker & Industrialist', etc. Round the base of a large statue is the following inscription:

'PATRIOT + FREE MASON + FIRST CITIZEN + CHURCHMAN + PRESIDENT'

It is of that toothless old traitor to his King and Country, George Washington. Another memorial, rather charmingly, is to Abraham Lincoln:

> 'whose lonely soul
> God kindled
> is here remembered.'

I am pleased to see that there is a place set aside for Huguenots.

29 June. Conversation in the lift in my New York hotel:

'The 32nd floor please.'

The lift boy is youngish, brownish, scented and sleekly plump: 'Are you from England?'

'Yes.'

'I am from Pakistan, from the Punjab.'

'Aha, a fellow Briton!' I exclaim with bogus bonhomie. 'Why are you in America?'

'I have to be, haven't I? I could not get a visa to the United Kingdom. I did not have enough money to bribe the peoples of the British High Commission.'

I grit my teeth and change the subject. 'I have just seen your Benazir Bhutto on the television. Very beautiful, very intelligent.'

'Not at all beautiful, not at all intelligent. Paints her face like a lady who sells herself. All ladies look nice if they paint themselves. And she is not at all clever.'

'But she got a very good degree at Oxford.'

'Oxford, Cambridge. All the same. You pay money, you get a good degree.'

I am narked: 'I was at Cambridge, and I can tell you I had to work to get a degree.'

'No. You are rich. The rich can have anything. The Bhutto lady paid. And ladies. Ladies should not be in politics. They must stay at home looking after their husbands. They should not mess with other things. That is the place of we men. You and me.'

As I look at his round, bland, smug, guileless, childish, opinionated, bigoted, utterly stupid face, it suddenly dawns on me that we are only on the 17th floor and I just have time to pulverise the little bastard into a pulp.

No-one would believe him, if he complained.

My father would not have approved: *one must be courteous to all one meets, and especially civil if they are our kindred from the colonies.*

Just this one, Papa?

No.

All right then, but it would do him good.

'Goodbye. Thank you. I hope you'll get to England, somehow.'

I am so nice, sometimes, that I nauseate even myself.

30 June. As I have about three hours before I leave our United Nations office for the aerodrome I have decided to see if I can find my great-great-great-grandfather in the first US census. He was apparently a man of immense charm and had terrific drive and initiative. Unfortunately he could never finish anything, having a butterfly mind, and he seemed to be born unlucky; perhaps he was too early for his innovations to be successful. He was an idealistic socialist, with a passionate belief in opportunities for all and a dislike of the 'Establishment', especially church and monarchy, little realising that socialism with its inherent bureaucracy and insistence on compulsory 'equalisation' is potentially far more tyrannical than any other régime. He founded a 'communist' settlement in Ohio. It failed: once the settlers started making any money, they left, not wishing to live in the restrained conditions. However his efforts helped – perhaps even inspired – Robert Owen in the early Owenite Settlements (there exists correspondence between the two). He kept writing letters to his eldest son, Samuel, saying 'come here to the land of the free, and make your fortune' (his socialism was flexible). He died almost penniless in the United States, but happy; Sam died one of the richest men in Europe, but sad.

The census is filed in the city library. Having wandered about from wrong room to wrong room, I finally am in the right place. I am holding a copy of the 'first census of the United States, taken in the year 1790.' According to the introduction, the total numbers of 'free' people living in the United States was 3,933,539.

I know that great-great-great-grandpapa's name was registered in Caughnawa Town in the Montgomery County, and that his name was mis-spelt, so: . . . . here!

CORTEAULD, George,
Free white male of 16 years & upward including heads of families –   1
Free white male under 16 years –   1
Free white females including heads of families –   *
All other free persons –   *
Slaves –   *

[*=illegible]

Slaves! – after all that pious waffle he wrote about the 'Land of Freedom and Opportunity'! Maddening that he could not write legibly, but I know that he was married by then to the beautiful and hot-tempered Irish girl, Ruth [nee Minton], but their first child had died and none of their other seven children was yet born, so I do not know who the 'other free persons' could be, probably some of great-great-great-grandpapa's poor deluded disciples.

1–3 July. I arrived home to find Dominie gone, back to her mother's. House very empty. It seems to be rather futile without her here, perhaps this is what she feels like when I am away: vague discontent and a suspicion that whatever one does is probably useless and transient. I have been busy about the garden, farm and estate, but it all seems routine and lack-lustre; Henrietta fed me a couple of excellent meals but I ate at home most of the time, boiling together the staling contents of the fridge into stews or soups.

Today is a medical day. First at the dentist, who pokes about with prongs and picks and buzzing things, and reams out crevices and scrapes off bits of chalk. He says my teeth are good. Secondly at the osteopath, whom Dr Cutts has recommended for my neck-ache. He is in Colchester. He fools me at first by laying me prone on a comfy couch and kneading and fiddling about with soothing hands and murmurous talk and then his warm, gentle fingers clasp about my neck and SUDDENLY he wrings it as if I am a chicken. There is a dreadful crack and my ears sing. Then, before I can collect my wits, he hurries to the other side of the couch and does it again, from a different angle. Then he flips me over, arse uppermost, and gouges his thumbs into my shoulder muscles. Throughout all this I am mute with astonishment and pain. Then he does more soothing things, this time with some sort of electrical pads; I keep a wary eye on him, lest he should unexpectedly send a couple of million volts through me.

Much to my surprise it seems to have worked.

10 July. Landed at Islamabad at 5.30 yesterday morning. This morning I have come to Murree. It is about 60 miles from Islamabad and relaxingly cool, being in the foothills of the Himalayas. It is where the British used to go to get away from the muggy heat of the plains. My driver, although a Pakistani, has a drawling public-school accent. His taxi is not allowed into the town of Murree, so he and I are toiling up the long flight of steps which starts at the car park, goes up the wooded flanks of a steep hillside and ends near the entrance of Murree High Street. There are a few beggars squatting on the steps, not many, for most people seem to prefer to sell something, the women scarves and shawls, the men slices of coconut or roast maize cobs. The air is snappily sharp and there is a smell of resin, mostly from some long-needled trees with pendulous cones, the Bhutan pine. There are also many Indian chestnuts. I planted a couple of these in our gardens at Wastewoods: the young leaves are pink and the flower panicles can be over a foot high, but sometimes a tree will take 50 years to flower. There are also wild pears (*Pyrus pashia*) with tiny fruit and a poplar (*Populus cilata*), labelled with their botanical names. Some donkeys are beside the road, being loaded with stacks of bricks. One donkey, a grey, has its forelock dyed red. Does that mean it has been to Mecca? I ask my driver. He says he hasn't a clue.

*

Having walked through the town I am now on the further outskirts, looking over the road wall at a long sleepy view of mountain ridges and valleys with terraced fields and small farmsteads. My driver points down. Below us there is an old man, picturesquely swathed in robe and turban and sacrificing a goat on a blood-spattered slab of rock.

I had presumed a sacrifice would be something reverent and ritualistic and redolent of the awe of ages, not an incompetent old bugger sawing away with a blunt penknife whilst a stoic goat, about to die, reaches out lethargically for a tuft of grass.

He's done it. That goat don't 'alf bleed.

We sit in a small eating-place by the high street. There is a narrow alley just below us where I can just see five small open-fronted shops: one is of a seller of pulses whose lentils, beans and chick-peas are displayed in the rolled-back tops of sacks; another shop sells nothing but hurricane lamps; next, side by side, in the shade of their alcoves, is a cobbler hammering at his last and a tailor whirring away with a sewing-machine; finally I can see the smallest shop, right at the end, where squats an old man selling doughnuts. My driver sits opposite me and eats some grainy things soused in a yellow oil, which he swabs up with poppadoms, using his right hand only, of course; I have a chicken biryani. It is very good. We don't talk much: the exotic parade of humanity walking past is entertainment enough. Most people seem cheerful, there is a bustling and a gesticulating and much laughter. Even a couple of beggars, who stop to chat beside the doughnut stall, punctuate their conversation with laughs and arm-wavings. One of them is a burly man with a thick beard and a withered leg so that he has to use both a crutch and a stick; the other seems fit enough but is old and grey and ragged and has bare feet. A business man struts past, his prominent belly jutting prosperously before him. He is followed by a drift of womenfolk with pale faces, kohl-dark eyes and heavy lipstick. There are children, some of them Afghans, selling plaited leather belts and leashes; others are local girls immaculate in chuddars and long-skirted school uniforms of blue cotton, an unfortunate boy with a hare-lip so deep that it has made his front teeth splay out into tusks, a gang of youths all smiles and pushing each other and shouting. There is a tall man with bare feet and a long-tailed turban, carrying a huge tea-urn on his back; a small man pattering with quick little steps under the weight of a huge bundle of faggots (a slightly less poor man would have a donkey for that); a lanky north European tourist with bony legs in shorts, shepherding a small uneasy boy whose vivid blond-ness draws curious stares; a huge soldier, almost six and a half feet tall, with many medal ribbons, a green beret with a cockade and a large, grey, jutting beard; two old men shuffling hand in hand; a ragged woman of grandmotherly appearance carrying a swaddled baby; a very elegant woman in high heels and with her gauzy voile chuddar held in place with a jewelled band, followed by a maidservant carrying what seems to be her laundry; Afghans, Kashmiris, Pathans; drovers, pedlars, merchants, soldiers, wives and concubines.

My driver tells me a most melancholy story: 'I had a passenger once, when I was driving at Gatwick Airport. Fellow who was completely kitted up for Hawaii or some such place. Wore a huge straw hat, a T-shirt printed all over with guitars and parasols, and a pair of shorts even more ghastly than his shirt. Sun-glasses and sandals and wristbands of terry towelling. Complete peasant. Still, one must try to be friendly, so I asked him if he'd had a decent holiday. Poor fellow burst into tears. Absolute floods. Deary me, I thought, I've made a boo-boo here, 'spose the chap's wife's a gonner – scoffed by a shark, or something. Actually, it wasn't quite as bad as that. Turned out that he had this terrible fear of flying. Took a course of hypnotism. Lot of mumbo-jumbo, staring at swinging watches and going into trances and so forth. Convinced he's cured. Decides to celebrate by going to the jolly old Isles of Paradise. Kits himself up, drives to Gatwick, clambers into the Jumbo – suddenly, wham – he throws a wobbly and has to be chucked out. Jumbo flies away leaving him to weep his little heart out in my cab.'

4 August. Four Colnes Show – [Earls Colne, Wakes Colne, White Colne, Colne Engaine]. Many 'folksy' stalls, including that of a woman to whom I had given four different-coloured fleeces: the white of Matilda, the chocolate of the Stare-Eyed-Ewe, the ginger of Uncle-Torquil-Look-Alike and the black of Second-Blackie. I gave them to her after last year's show, having admired some fabrics made from her home-spun yarns. Today, as a 'thank you', she presented me with a scarf she had knitted from all four colours. It is very attractive, and soft – the wool being almost pure Shetland. As I don't like wearing scarfs I gave it to Hart, who was there with his mongrel Penny. Henrietta showed off Lottie, lying in her pram. 'Thass a nice little tiggywog, that is,' said Hart, gazing fondly down.

'What's a tiggywog?' Hen asked.

'A tiggywog is a small, fat baby,' he said.

That's a good word.

There was a charming exhibition of 'Stationary Engines': little old machines which coughed and spluttered and turned flywheels or pumped water from one bucket to another or puffed out smoke rings or snorted steam or just trembled and hummed. Beside one there was the sweetest man who had settled down like a fisherman, upon a folding stool and beneath a green umbrella: he sat by his little panting engine and stared and stared at it; he smiled at it and smiled at us looking at it and then looked at it again with the utmost love in his eyes.

Thence to Halstead to shop. I park my car next to the bank in the High Street. As I step away from the market stall selling fish I see the traffic warden starting to write down my car's particulars. 'Oh fuck!' I say, involuntarily, then notice a biddy nearby looking disapprovingly at me.

'I do apologise,' I say. 'Still,' I add tactfully, 'I'm sure you don't know what that meant.'

'I reckon you reckon wrong,' snaps the old girl, miffed.

'Do you know that you are parking on a double yellow line?' the warden asks when I reach him.

'Yes.'

'Don't you know it is not permitted?' he asks.

'Yes.'

'Then why d'y do it?' he asks.

'Because I didn't know you were around.'

'That's not an excuse,' he says, indignant.

'I know that isn't, that's a reason.'

He doesn't seem to appreciate the subtle difference and goes off shaking his head and muttering.

10 August. I arrived in San José yesterday morning and hurried up Central Street to see if the Brussels sprouts are still growing in the garden there. They are, but the house is for sale. I hope the new owners will continue to grow the sprouts as charmingly odd adornments for their front garden.

Today I have booked a tripper's tour to Braulio Carrillo National Park which 'lies in one of the most rugged zones of the country. Typical of the park's landscape are tall mountains with steep slopes covered by dense forest and numerous rivers that carve deep canyons.' It seems that I am the only person to enrol so instead of a mini-bus I have a car and driver to myself. My guide/driver is Alfredo Gutierrez, a pleasant youth with a long thoughtful face. He is, in fact, a thoughtful sort of fellow. Amongst other things he tells me of his theory of the different work ethic between the Northern peoples and the Southerners. 'You Nordics work so hard because you have to plant and harvest your food in such a short while, and then preserve it and store it, but here in the Caribbean for example we have four crops of potatoes a year.'

He calls humming-birds 'honorary insects'.

Many of the mountain ranges that we traverse are very wet, the steep slopes dripping with condensation, the vegetation soaking and steaming: the lacy fronds of tree ferns, the huge round 'poor man's umbrellas' of gunnera, the orchids, plantains, lianas and trees.

We walk through the rain forest for nearly three hours. It is dripping and smells blowsy. Much of the way is along a slippery track which has been machete-hacked along a ridge. This is a strange elevated walkway, often only six feet wide with an almost sheer drop of several hundred feet to either side. It would be terrifying were its steepness not disguised by a heavy camouflage of luxuriant growth which climbs up to cover the slopes and eventually tower over our heads. Alfredo says many of the trees are different species of fig. He points to one. 'Surely that berry is not a fig?' I say.

He breaks it open. There is a small maggot inside. 'A fig is not a normal fruit, it is really a swollen flower bud. It can only be pollinated by a miniature wasp who crawls into it to lay eggs.'

We see some American swallow-tailed kites, beautiful piebald birds with long, graceful scissor-shaped tails. We meet a crab. There he is, 60 miles from the coast, several thousand feet above sea level, scowling at us in the middle of the path, his claws held up like a boxer in defence.

We see many Morpho butterflies. This is one of the most lovely of them all: huge, and of lacquered, iridescent turquoise. It is sold in America, set in plastic. Alfredo had one bus load of Yanks, whenever they saw a Morpho they all shouted 'There goes another 50 dollars!'

After our trek we stop at a roadside place run by a busy, jolly family and gulp bottled lime juice and eat pork cracklings; the skin side is good and crunchily brittle, but the other side is encrusted with inches of crumbly fat. Alfredo picks the leavings off my plate and nibbles them.

Now we are in his car again. He stopped on a bridge over the Rio Sucio (dirty river) where a grey volcanic river and yellow rain river meet and mingle, and after we had inspected this junction he is driving through varied and attractive countryside to Limon.

The port of Limon is seedy and run down with a lot of people slowly milling about doing nothing. Alfredo and I sit at a beach restaurant and have a rather nasty meal of sea bass chunks steeped in brine (rubbery and sour) and red snapper (fried and dry).

11 August. Today, again, I am the only person on the organised tour, so once more I have a guide and a car to myself. We start off badly: the guide arrives late; he then loses the car key so that his office has to come with another car. He is as young as Alfredo, but has a round face, a small black moustache, buck teeth and hasn't shaved for a week. He is called Georgio and is needlessly thrilled that I am called George. He is better at his birds than Alfredo, not as good with the flora.

We drive north-east, much of it along watermeadows and marshland. The birds we see include the pleasingly named black-bellied whistling duck, great kiskadee and chestnut mandibled toucan. There is a particularly beautiful tree called a ceibo (saybo). It is massive, very tall with a clean bole for a hundred feet or so, then the branches splay out in a semi-dome, with long tendrils of aerial roots hanging from them. Sometimes we are assailed by a strong smell of sulphur. Georgio says it is from a volcano; there are about five active in Costa Rica at present.

I notice that many of the churches have small parks immediately in front of their entrances. Within each park there is usually an ornamental bandstand. Georgio says that it used to be a custom in the little towns and larger villages that, after church on Sundays, all the women and girls would walk round the park one way, and all the men and boys conversely. Whilst this perambulation was taking place the town band would play in the bandstand. People would then bow or ogle, depending on social class and age. Sadly, this tradition is dying out: the bandstands are being demolished, the trees uprooted and the parks being grassed over to make football pitches.

The first sight of the Arenal volcano is of a perfect cone. Its sides are dotted with spouts of steam from fumaroles. There are two or three clouds which encircle the upper part of the cone like the rings of a hula-hoop. Another cloud normally hangs above it: a huge lid like a flattish mushroom. Sometimes a bulge swells up in its centre to transform it into a cardinal's hat; on occasions, about every ten minutes, it will expand into a vast billowy grey-white ball of smoke and smuts and steam. A few moments later one will hear a muffled thunder, a guttural grumbling of mighty discontent. Then there is a metallic hammering as boulders bound downhill, leaving trails of smoke. At night you can see them glow in the dark, Georgio says. He keeps whinging that we are going too high. Maybe he is right, but I think he is irked that I can outwalk him. He started off like a bolting stag but after a couple of hundred feet he kept making excuses to stop to pee, or to listen, or to look at the view.

I think that perhaps we have now gone far enough, we are being drizzled on by fine grains of lava and the sparse vegetation is petering out to be replaced by beds of ashy clinker: also my right foot hurts.

We have had an excellent but vast lunch at La Vaca Muca ('The Cag-handed Cow'), in sight of the volcano and now Georgio is driving me back through some mountain passes.

12 August. The British Embassy is playing football against a team of local farmers. They are playing in an experimental farm which the British have founded and are funding. It is an hour's drive from San José. I am rarely interested in watching other people playing games so, with four other similarly inclined people, three being female, I go for a ride through the estate. My horse is a grey mare. She is a bit thin, but looks healthy and is the largest beast they have, as I am the largest rider. When she saw me approach she put her ears back with disgust and assumed the sour expression of one who is thinking: 'Cripes, I hope that beefy-looking bloke is not the one I'm having to carry about.' The stirrups are huge and of toughened leather, the saddle is of the cowboy style with a high pommel and back. It is not nearly as comfortable as it looks; the stirrup leathers are very long and one is not meant to rise to the trot, just jolt and joggle in the saddle. The high back flips you forward so that your crutch slams against the pommel. I can understand why cowboys and gauchos have such shrill voices. I haven't ridden for three years and the nipping muscles at the top of my thighs soon remind me of their presence. Not wearing boots, the stirrup leathers have started to chafe my calfs. However whenever anyone looks at me I smile brightly. Our leader is a local gaucho type who probably spends more time on a horse than off it. He is riding a nasty-tempered pop-eyed stallion who prefers to proceed sideways, snorting and frothing. I do my best to keep my mare and myself out of reach of his hoofs.

The ride is attractive. Some of it is through woodland, but mostly alongside the fields of livestock. I see sheep, the first I've seen in this country. The cattle are mainly hump-backed zebu, or zebu crosses. They have long floppy ears like basset hounds. How pleasant it is to see them fat and contented and glossy, rather than the worshipped but starving toastracks of the Indian streets.

We return to find that the British have lost three to one, so everyone is happy: the farmers, because they wanted to win; the British, because we were not utterly humiliated and by losing we did our duty of diplomatic courtesy.

20 August. *I hate it here: the presence of suffering and death; the sharp smell of disinfectant not completely hiding the sour stink of blood; the murmur of voices behind* *closed doors; a sudden yelp of pain or fear. Bertie hates it too, I can feel his dirty little body trembling on my lap.*

We are a despondent, woebegotten group in this waiting-room: an old woman with a cat in a basket, it mews non-stop; another woman, holding a covered cage; a mother and small daughter, the latter hugging a lank kitten; Jack the shepherd from Rotten End with his collie, it has a bandaged paw, he is engrossed in the pages of the 'East Anglian'; an old colonel type, rather threadbare but still stiffly smart, sitting bolt upright on the pew, a blear-eyed and very aged terrier between his polished brown shoes; a smartly dressed woman stroking and murmuring to something pop-eyed, I think it is a King Charles spaniel.

She says something to the colonel type, he does not deign to reply, just sits there, staring straight ahead: pompous old fart. But perhaps he is deaf.

The door opens and he is beckoned through. He tries to get his dog to follow him by tugging at its lead, but it sits, hunched up and abject. Picking it up he marches out.

Two children tiptoe in and shyly sit down. They have something small in a cardboard box.

The thing in the covered cage suddenly gives out a great screech. We all jump, then smile sheepishly at each other.

The girl's mother talks to the two boys. They take the lid off the box. She looks inside. Something rustles and squeaks. She cringes back: fastidious.

I've read the 'Farmer's Weekly' I brought with me; I've looked at the posters showing the types of sheep and the different breeds of dog, and I've scanned the notices exhorting injections or medicines for distemper, worms, brucellosis and swine fever. I'm bored as well as depressed.

Ah. My turn. I pick up Bertie and quit.

As I walk down the corridor towards the surgery I pass the old colonel type. He is carrying a lead, but no dog.

Odd that women are meant to be the 'weaker sex', it always seems to be the old men who cry.

'Bertie not any better?' asks Mr Whippletree's assistant.

'No, he coughed all night and was sick twice.'

She puts him on a table and feels about. Bertie trembles and turns his blind-eyed face imploringly my way.

The vet speaks: 'At twelve he is very old for a pekinese. Being blind and fat, he is bored. His heart is very weak. He will die within the month. What do you think?'

I think that he is old, blind, fat, bored, bad-tempered, smelly and greedy; I think that he is one of my best friends; I think that he belongs to Candy, thousands of miles away, she was eight when I gave him to her and she named him Bertram which she could only pronounce as 'Bert-worm' and we all called him that; I think that I have more days away than at home for the next month, and that Dominie may be with her mother for the whole time and that I don't want Bertie to die alone and afraid; I think that I will miss little old Bert-worm and that Candy may never forgive me.

Bertie is lying in my arms, very still. But not still enough.

'Some of these ancient hearts don't know when to stop,' the vet complains, as she gives Bertie a second injection.

I buried him under a cherry in the Wild Garden, so that I can say 'Good morning' to him when I do my early morning round of the garden.

2 September. Sunday. Diplomatic bags are delivered to many places in the world where we have political enemies or terrorist foes, but I reckon 'friendly' New York to be the most dangerous for delivery, not for any political reason, but because the bags look like money bags. We have to park our car outside the office in Third Avenue and lug the bags over a pavement infested with potential felons.

So. Here I am, with my driver. We are standing by my car, waiting for the Security Officer who is late. Annoying Man hoves into view. He is middle-aged, unshaven, stripped to the waist, wearing baggy trousers and huge sloppy boots with no laces.

'Hi, Babe,' says Annoying Man.

'Hello.'

'What y've you got in those bags?'

'Hot air, mainly.'

'You're losing your hair, Babe.'

'Yea.'

'I kicked Tony Curtis in the ass.'

'Really?'

'Yep. Right in the butt.'

'Oh.'

'You're losing your hair, Babe.'

'So I've been told.'

'I kicked Tony Curtis in the ass.'

'Gosh.'

'Right in the butt.'

The Security Officer emerges from the office door. 'This personage is not being an aggravation, I trust,' he says.

'No, no,' I reply, 'he's been telling me how he kissed Tony Curtis in the ass.'

The reaction is even more than I had hoped for. There is a screech as loud as St Ursula with all eleven thousand virgins.

'KICKED!' howls Annoying Man. 'You Goddam NUT! . . . I *kicked* Tony Curtis in the ass, I did *not kiss* his ass, I *kicked* his ass, are you deaf as well as bald, you Goddam nut, I did not *kiss*, I *kicked* Tony Curtis's ass . . .'

Even Screaming Sheila, the IRA supporter who squats with banners on the pavement outside the office, seems amused, but the Security Officer and driver are alarmed. They hustle the bags and me through the doors: 'For Goodness sake you shouldn't inflame that psychiatric case, you mustn't aggravate that character, he's egregious he's . . .'

Having a couple of hours before I go off to catch the Washington 'shuttle' aeroplane, I am sitting in the little square off 51st Street, admiring the waterfall and spooning out a plastic mug-full of chilli con carne. Various other people are eating or reading or just relaxing by the tables scattered about under the locust trees. All except one: she is a fat woman in tight stretch-pants and is crawling on her hands and knees towards me, holding out a piece of bread to a pigeon which has taken refuge between my feet.

Why is it always me? Perhaps it is because I stare at people, thinking about them.

3 September, Washington. After breakfast at Pearsons Drug Store I wander through the narrow brick-cobbled lanes of Georgetown and the wide paved streets of the commercial and governmental sections of the city, past the museums on the Mall to the National Gallery of Art at the far end.

On my way I meet a fellow toiling up Wisconsin Avenue. He is tall, with long grizzled hair and beard; wiry arms and legs protrude from a ragged shirt and a pair of jeans which are cut short above his knees. He has a long bony face and a long bony nose. He also has three large suitcases, bound about with an unnecessary amount of cordage, and a big bundle made from a sheet. He walks uphill about a dozen paces, puts down his load of two baggages, walks down to the other two, picks them up and carries them uphill to the first two, puts them down, picks up the other two, carries them a dozen paces uphill, puts them down, goes downhill . . . My work-study training is irked by this incompetent footling. I catch his eye as I walk past.

'Morning,' I say.

'Good day my friend,' he replies agreeably.

'Excuse me,' I say, 'it is none of my business, but wouldn't it be quicker if you carried what you are holding past the ones waiting rather than stopping to change them?'

'Probably,' he said, just as agreeably, 'but I'm not in a hurry.'

There is another odd fellow, a bit further on, a middle-aged man who stares at a lamppost and complains to it, in loud angry tones, about God.

In the West section of the National Gallery of Art there is an exhibition of Edvard Munch, all etched or daubed or puddled in sombre blacks and greys, the landscapes murky, the people bent and hollow-eyed and in the latest stages of despair or disease. I too am thoroughly depressed by the time I have examined about 80 pictures with such titles as *Anxiety, Two Lonely People on a Beach, Separation, The Sick Child, The Death Chamber, Rotten Stump in Moonlight, Death Kissing a Woman.* However the East section is much more cheerful, showing the 'early' (to Americans) art of George Caleb Bingham, an artist whose painting was focused on the frontier lands around the River Missouri between 1835 and 1877. Some of his election scenes are almost Hogarthian in their busy assembly and jolly red faces and depiction of corruption and greed – he has an interesting little quirk in making dogs silent critics: asleep below the dais of a pontificating bore; with contemptuous lip, looking at a liar; slinking tail down from a scene of bribery. The landscapes are evocative, with vast pale skies and early morning mists clouding the forest glades or prairies. Best of all are the river scenes of the Missouri and the Mississippi: stranded paddle boats, punts gliding on unruffled waters, raftsmen poling and canoers paddling. Great-great-great-grandpapa must have known scenes just like that, alone in a little skiff he sailed down the Ohio and Mississippi to New Orleans, about 2000 miles.

Then I go to the Gallery of Twentieth-Century Art and am filled with amazed indignation at the blobs, dribbles, splotches, or even blanks. At least Klein's *The Blue Night* has some use. The picture is one single colour, the catalogue says that the viewer 'is encouraged to create his or her interpretation of the blank expanse of blue'. My interpretation is that the people who bought it were stark raving bonkers but another view, female, is pleased to discover that it is the only 'picture' with glazing and she tweaks her wiry hair in its reflection. Another picture is even more boring, a mere expanse of white. This, aptly enough, is called *White Painting*. Mr Rauschenberg, the artist, 'wants the viewer to participate actively in establishing the meanings of his work. *White Painting* might stand for silence and purity or might mirror the ever-changing environment, functioning as a surface on which the shadows of passing viewers are cast.'

Bollocks.

I am in a 'garden restaurant'. The 'garden' is roofed over with plastic sheeting. I started lunch with a 'Crock of soup – created daily from our homemade stock' and then having deliberated between 'Steak 'n Fries' or 'Chicken Sonoma – grilled and washed in white wine, a light and flavourful dish' – (and they call *us* quaint!) – chose the former. The steak is vast and rather tasteless, the potato chips like huge yellow scabs and the 'onion rings' tough and elastic enough to castrate a bull moose. But the beer is a relief after all the walking in the muggy heat.

I meet the bearded suitcase-lugger once more. He is still in Wisconsin Avenue, but this time he is on the opposite pavement, and going downhill.

'Hello, again,' I say.

'Greetings, good friend,' he answers, 'I wonder, er, if . . ?'

My dollar disappears amongst his rags, as if it has never been.

He seems worried, not the blithe spirit of this morning. While he talks, he strokes his beard with long downward sweeps, like an anxious Confucius; he doesn't look at me, his eyes are of a pallid blue and although the pupils are pinpointed they are not focused on anything, just directed to something vague over my shoulder.

'We are having revolutions. Your country and mine. The whole of the Western world as we know it. In turmoil. Being destroyed. I don't know what we can do. Mrs Thatcher warned the Queen, but she only listens to the Archbishop of Canterbury. Our problem here is different. Separate from yours, but connected. We are running out of resources – oil – and I don't know what to do. There will be a revolution. The people will have to go back to Nature, but you see they don't really want to go back, though many say they do – I try to tell them but they won't listen, so they will have this revolution – they must, you know, it's inevitable – and when they finally run out of gas for their cars and oil for their heat – and I don't know what to do you should tell them the Queen might listen – but you've already had one revolution and now this other one – the whole of the Western world – and of course I'm so helpless I wish I knew what to do – perhaps I should learn a language, but I don't know, you know, there is no time, so little time . . .'

I sidle off muttering 'Gosh, really most interesting – yes, I know, very worrying – I'm afraid you must excuse me I have people waiting well – goodbye then . . . Byee – Goodbye – See you then . . . Yup. Yup-yup. Yup. Byeee.'

5 September. Arrive in Heathrow at 6.55. Ring Dominie from the office, expecting to hear the dreaded, but Granny Smith still alive although been semi-conscious for most of the time. When awake, she has hallucinations. One was that a man came into her bedroom with a card saying 'Bargain Offer: one human being and ten dogs put down at half price.'

She is dying hard. Although she is too weak to hold a spoon – Dominie or one of the nurses has to feed her – often she suddenly starts up, bolt upright in bed, with her eyes glaring around to make sure that she is still alive. Dominie says her terror of death is horrifically infectious.

Go to the saw-mill at Burton's Green to help slice up the elm. Some of the planks which the saw cuts have to be four and five inches thick, for they are to be the legs and stretchers of the new dining-room table. As we remove each plank off the body of the trunk we disclose the most lovely grain: in rings and whorls where there have been burrs, in convolutions where there have been branches, in rows of squiggling contour lines on the main body of the trunk. The colours range from pale gold through ambers, coffees and chestnuts to dark mahogany. Every plank is infinitely superior in artistry, beauty and interest to all of the pictures in Washington's Gallery of 20th Century Art put together.

9 September. Of all the places to land at night, the cities of Arabia are the most beautiful. The desert background is velvety black. Upon it have been heaped and strewn the world's diamonds: in great piles where the houses congregate, as long thin necklaces for the minor roads, as many-stranded chokers for the dual carriageways, as glowing brooches for the roundabouts; amid the blaze of diamond the occasional neon twinkle of ruby, sapphire or topaz, and the emerald cabochon glow of a football arena. Above it all shines the moon, lying on her keel with her stem and stern pointing up, sailing across the sky.

I land in Riyadh at their 19.30 hours. Usual muggy heat. Surprising lack of military bustle: a few more soldiers in the airport and the diplomatic enclave — particularly round the Iraqi Embassy — but that is the only evidence that the country could be at war any second. I deliver and quit — fast.

11 September. An evening meeting for the committee of Great-Aunt Ruth's educational charity. The old girl would be pleased to see how much the schoolchildren enjoy the travels which her money sends them on. I last saw her when she was 97. She was sitting up in her chair as usual, her white hair cropped short, her beady little blue eyes twinkling beneath the green eye-shade she always wore. Her mind was still as sharp as a needle. Dominie and I brought Henrietta. She was aged about eight months and lay swathed in white lace in her wicker basket. We put her at Aunt Ruth's feet and after staring at the baby for a bit Aunt Ruth leaned forward and very slowly put out a veined, wrinkled, bony little claw and touched Henrietta's fat little hand. I think that she was somehow passing on some of the memories and friends and things that had happened for nearly a hundred years. I think she thought I thought that too, for she suddenly looked up and embarrassed me by seeing me smiling down at them and when she died two years later she left me her house.

I would like to see her again, to thank her. Perhaps I will.

*12 **September.** Dominie rings at 6.30, her mother died an hour ago.*

Collect sloes and make sloe gin.

Dominie arrives early this evening. She is subdued: mentally drained. Her elder brothers are at Brewhurst, dealing with the bureaucracy of death: certificates, licences, undertakers, solicitors, executors and the press.

14 September. I felt very guilty leaving Dominie. Her mother's funeral will be on Monday the 17th, and I will not be there to support her; but our children will, and so will her six brothers; and I cannot let down the other fellows by getting one of them to take my place at such short notice.

I am escorting Craik on this journey. He is a copper-headed, peppery, amusing fellow, and like Steven was a friend before we became Queen's Messengers.

We arrive at Peking at 11 a.m. and after lunch we traipse about the streets, Craik full of stories of what it was like last time he was here, when he and Mike arrived via the trans-Manchurian Express on the worst day of the Tien-an-men Square uprising. They had to run the gauntlet of tanks and soldiers in a couple of Shanghaied rickshaws; people kept stopping them to point out pools of blood, or scatterings of empty rifle cartridges.

Excellent dinner in the Chinese section of the Janguai, go to bed bloated and flatulent; I think that part of the problem is that one inhales a lot of air when using chopsticks.

*

19 September. We have been on the train for an hour and are entering the foothills of the mountains which will soon be hunching up their shoulders to carry the Great Wall in serpentine undulations along their backs. Autumn has arrived, but there are several flowers evident, especially a type of ox-eye daisy and bell-bines with large blue or purple trumpets.

Five hours later. We are now past Yan K'ou and are travelling along the wide river plain whose name is not on my map. We are in Inner Mongolia. It is harvest time, the crop is mainly maize and millet, but there is a strange cereal Craik and I cannot identify, even though we are both farmers. It is tall, and resembles maize but has sparser leafage. The seed presumably comes from the head which is a drumstick-shaped cluster at the very top of the stem; it is of an attractive rich dark brown.

An English-speaking Chinese has overheard Craik and me talking about it as he passes us in the corridor and says it is sorghum, mainly used for making a sort of porridge; some species of sorghum are used for livestock feeding, he says, and other types are used when brewing a kind of beer and some of the canes can produce sugar.

Every village has its threshing-floor at work. These are circular, and seem to have no other foundation than beaten earth. Most threshing is done with heavy stone rollers, dragged by mules or donkeys in circles round and round the floor, but there are a few people using flails: strange that they are not jointed, like European ones, so that they can lay the length of their 'forearm' across the seed-head, but are mere sticks, whose only working surface is the very tip. There are many other labourers working about the threshing-yards: sorting, sieving, raking and winnowing – this they do by tossing the corn up in the air with flat-bladed wooden spades and letting the wind blow away the chaff. The heaps of corn are of three basic colours: golden, reddish and greyish. It is hard to identify them from a moving train but we presume that they are, respectively, the maize, sorghum and millet.

Eight hours later. We have passed Da Tung, where the locally made steam engines, great, black, dirty, panting beasts, flex their mighty muscles to haul huge cargoes of coal up and down the railway lines; we have travelled alongside the river Yu Ho, meandering in the flat lands of its river valley; now, further into the grey-skied north, it is almost treeless – the occasional belt of poplar, and the villages merge mudcoloured into the surrounding drabness. The thin soil has been harvested but threshing has hardly begun and the fields are dotted with stooks, the crop looks like rye, or perhaps bearded wheat. Some people are digging up potatoes, using cromes and mattocks. A man is ploughing with a team of oxen; he pauses to stare as we clatter past and his oxen immediately stop, no longer nagged into action by his voice or his goad.

Nine hours later. We are pausing in the lonely railway station of Ji'Ning. Autumn is becoming wintry. The sky is bleak and grey; the wind is fierce and swirls up veils of dust from the platform and shakes the straggly hedge of dwarf elm; chimneys stream horizontal veils of smoke; scraps of paper whisk through the air. People are motionless and hunched as they stand waiting for the down train; they clutch their bundles closely to their chests as the wind tugs at their jackets and trousers. They gaze at us with faces which, if they have any expression at all, is one of mild dislike.

We have started off again. At the end of the station there is a waterpump. Seven steam engines are queuing beside it like patient beasts of burden waiting to take their turn to have a drink.

The wind has freshened even more and is blowing so much dust off the surface of the bleak, undulating countryside that the effect of the sheet erosion is that of a sandstorm: sheaves are trundling over the fields; a heap of grain by a threshing-floor is streaming its golden contents like smoke before the wind. The poor villagers will lose much of their harvest if they don't do something quickly.

We were at the border post of Erlian from 21.35 to 23.15 hours. Craik and I had dinner in his cabin between frontiers. We started with an avocado pear each. Then I had sandwiches made of a combination of cheese, spam, marmite, pickles and sardines. Craik had two tins of smoked oysters: he ate them finickly, at the end of a toothpick; then he spread crab-meat on little biscuits and munched those. We sluiced it all down with a bottle of claret each.

20 September. The train draws into Ulaan Baatar at 13.20. It is snowing, but the smiling faces of the Embassy staff are welcome. Greyhound Cottage is warm. Benson the cat looks old and angry.

It seems that the changeover to democracy has not been particularly noticeable yet, the most discernible thing being the withdrawing of Russian military personnel. Not many British have been bustling here with commercial intention – the Japanese have – the biggest British expedition has been a team of zoologists looking for the golden mole and the long-eared hedgehog. They found three of the latter: one stuffed in the dingy room (which is called the museum) off Sukhebaatar Square; one squashed flat on the road, perhaps run over by a yak-drawn tumbrel; and one eating a slug in the steppe. I saw photographs of it – enchanting, just like Mrs Tiggywinkle but with large bat-ears.

21 September. At about 5 o'clock in the afternoon some of the Embassy staff went off to play golf on the steppe. With its undulating ground and short-cropped turf the whole place is one huge golf course: instead of holes they stick flags in the ground and scratch yard-wide circles round them. Neither Craik nor I can play golf ('Like whisky drinking,' asserts Craik, 'not an officer's occupation unless he is a Celt'), so whilst everyone else was whacking away at the little pillocks we climbed up the mountain slopes above them. As we ascended, the soil became gravelly and only thinly covered with vegetation. Most of the flowers were over, but there were some tiny pink ones which I thought were a type of cranesbill, and a deeply dark-blue larkspur. We saw very few birds: a small flock of horned larks; a couple of pippit-types which flitted off suddenly with a twit of alarm; a brace of ravens saying 'kraak!' – as they flapped below us, a kite swooped above. I found low thickets of a rose in a larch grove and gathered some hips.

I am now building a cairn for no purpose, as a monument to nothing except, perhaps, to the passing hours of this empty afternoon. It will not even be a beacon or a guide for there will be no-one to see it and it is on the road to nowhere: to the east there are one and a half thousand miles of bleakness before the chilly shores of the Gulf of Tartary; to the west, the Baltic Sea is four thousand miles away, over the steppe of Outer Mongolia, over the plains of Turkestan, the soggy vastness of the Land of Ob and the sad, cold cities of the Ukraine and Poland; to the north, after a week's trek on yak or pony, there lies the domain of permafrost which extends far to the Severnaya Zemlya, the Back of the North Wind.

However, to the south, one thousand feet below me, the quartet of Britons are playing golf; their wives, well muffled up, lean against a Land Rover, and warm their hands on mugs of tea, and are bored; too bored even to gossip, for there is nothing to gossip about.

It is quiet up here, on the skyline of the Valley of the Tuul, but not still, for a thin wind blows and although there are no trees or bushes for it to sing through it emits a ceaseless breath in one continuous sigh. Sometimes it gusts and the dead stems and grass stalks bend and tremble and plaint out a shrill whinging. A lark is tinkling, somewhere above my head; even higher, in the washed-out pale blue sky, hangs the black silhouette of a cross, a steppe eagle or a lammergeyer. The mountainside spreads out below like a rumpled blanket. In the crease of one of the larger folds there seems to be a small crop of mushrooms, a small hamlet of gers.

The rocks that I am picking up are grey and gritty. Most of them are sunk into the ground. When I wrench them out there are insects underneath, surprisingly similar to the ones in my own rock gardens: millipedes and centipedes, sow-bugs, beetles, and colonies of ants who scurry about in confused despair at their sudden catastrophe.

Perhaps this cairn will be here for a thousand years; perhaps passersby, if there are any, will add an extra stone or two for luck; perhaps some interfering busy-body will dismantle it to see if there is anything buried underneath. If he does he will find a symbolic little bit of Britain, a pound coin with the queen's head. When it is found there may no longer be a monarch, but a committee, no longer a Britain, but a Zone, no longer coins, but bar-codes tattooed on people's wrists.

It is time to go. I put a specially large and flat rock on top of my cairn, prod the dozing Craik awake, and we start our descent.

*

On the way down I found some rhubarb growing in a bank of scree and collected some stems to eat and a couple of roots for Alaun Griffiths. We arrived just as the golfers were gathered round the last hole. We all then had tea or coffee from thermos flasks. I looked up to admire my handiwork. My cairn was an undersized nipple atop the pap-shape of the mountain. As I watched, an eagle swooped down and alit upon it. So, my cairn has a purpose after all, and I feel wholly fulfilled.

22 September. I was invited to meet some of the officials concerned with the state-run experimental farm, including Minzhigdorj Balzhirin, the director, Erdene Baatar, his assistant, and the interpreter Bayareetsogt (they all sound like Hobbits, these fellows). They were smiling and charming, like every Mongolian I have met. We sat in a bleak and musty-smelling boardroom where we talked and drank many cups of tea and ate sweets and sugared berries.

I asked a lot of nosy questions such as: 'Has one kind of livestock more social kudos than another?'; 'How do you store your meat?'; 'Why are there so many breeds of cattle, none of which seem suited to the Mongolian winters?'; 'There seem to be an unnecessary number of horses, are they used for purposes other than riding?'; 'I have seen no tumbrels or waggons, are there any wheeled vehicles?'; 'What is the difference between a Bactrian camel and a dromedary?'; 'How is it possible to reconcile the supervision and regulation that communism depends on, with a herdsman's independent and individual way of life?'

I was introduced to a 'mature' student who had been one of a group sent by the Ministry of Agriculture to see new – to them – techniques in Britain, the USA, Cuba and Russia. He had spent all his life in the tundra and the Gobi, so when I asked him what things had surprised him most, I presumed the answer would be something like television, escalators, neon lights or traffic jams. Not so: he looked nostalgic and said: 'There was something which my companions and I did not believe when we first saw it. We thought it was magic, or a circus trick, or a freak thing. We saw it first in England, but then we saw it in Wales, and then often in Scotland.'

He paused to eat some berries, unwrap and suck a sweet, sip some tea, write down some notes and scratch.

By now I was rapt: 'Well, what?' I asked.

'Sheep dogs. What you British do with your sheep dogs. There is a shepherd. And he blows a little whistle, and he points. And the dog runs off and brings back the sheep. And then the shepherd blows another whistle, and the dog puts all the sheep in a pen. And then the shepherd tells the dog to take out the ram and two ewes and move them into another pen. And it does. It was wonderful. We Mongolians have been herding sheep for thousands of years, and we have never done that. All our dogs do is protect flocks from wolves and lynx and leopard.'

After I had finished with my questions they grilled me. They were particularly interested in the British methods of rearing sheep, mutton being their staple diet, though they eat anything else that can be herded, from yak to camel. I read recently that the Chinese and Japanese, being of the Mongoloid race, have a digestive system which is allergic to milk and its by-products. This must be nonsense, for the Mongoloid Mongols have a diet which includes milk in many forms and from six species of livestock (cow, yak, mare, nanny, ewe and she-camel).

The director said that he was especially interested in breeding beasts with white wool, for the fleece of dark cashmere goats, of brown sheep and of tan camels is of limited colour range in the dye vat. The camel hair production is erratic, ranging from five to twenty kilos per beast. They also wanted to increase the winter hardiness of the cattle and the fertility of their sheep. The sheep store fat in the buttocks rather than in the tail. He was interested in rabbit farming and also the possibility of 'mobile' workshops, where a prefabricated weaving-shed or spinning-plant could be towed from settlement to settlement. The only problem was that he had no particular ideas on how all this was to be financed.

Before I left I had a closer look at the berries at which we had been nibbling. There were five little bowls, each with a different type of berry: two were currants – a red and a black, one a sort of cranberry, one a very tart yellow berry and one too squished and sugar-coated to identify – perhaps a sort of cloud-berry. I spooned up a sample of each and put them in my collecting envelopes to give to Alaun Griffiths.

*

It is early evening and beginning to get dark. It seems likely to snow, but here in the circus it is warm. There is the old magic: the anticipation I remember so well from childhood Christmastime visits to Bertram Mills Circus, the roundness of the ring, the smell of animals and sweat, the excited buzz of children, the festooning of ropes and soaring sails of overhead canvas, the gaudy uniforms of the band. But this band out-plays them all: it roars, it trumpets, it booms, it throbs. Some Mongolian music is pretty weird, especially the mouth-music and the nose flutes, but much is more attractive to Western ears than most Oriental music: there is none of the wailing and bleating of the Indian continent or the spasmodic clashing and twanging of China. The Mongolians have real rousing tunes of the sort which makes you want to dance or march: much of their music is intended to be in rhythm with the sound of horses' hoofs.

We start with wrestlers. They squat at each other, thump their feet like a couple of angry buck rabbits, grapple, tumble to the ground, do it again and then, the loser having walked with bowed head under the raised arm of the winner in the 'eagles-wing' ritual, they quit to polite applause; they are just the warmers-up. Then, with a roll of drums, the camels appear and bob and bow and lope around the ring, their great split hare-lips flapping at each step, their drooping eyes looking disdain-fully down; they are rare and white and brushed to fluffy perfection, they don't do much but we admire them until they are made to crawl past us on their knees which I think demeaning to such aristocratic beasts. A dejected little monkey pedals a tiny bicycle round the raised rim of the circus ring and falls off, to widespread unsympathetic merriment. Then we have the contortionist. She is a pretty girl – being a bit short-sighted I always think that women on stage look even more glamorous than they are – but, anyway, she has a long black pig-tail and a round red smiling face with full lips and arched eyebrows over huge almond eyes. She has the Mona Lisa ability of staring straight into your eyes from whichever angle you are looking. And what angles! At one moment she is standing on her arms, her legs entwined above her head; next, she may have become a weird unipod, standing on one leg but with her other leg under one arm. Near the end of her act she actually manages to stand on her shoulders – her arms keeping her off the floor, but then, snake-like, she slides her legs even further down so that her face is staring at us from between her thighs. We all sit, trying to work it out: her hands and arms are where you'd expect her feet and legs to be; her head is where you'd expect her knickers; her knickers are where you'd expect her hat; her knees are keeping her ears warm.

There are clowns. They are very, very funny. There's a couple of them, not dressed up in the pointed hats and red noses of our clowns but in deliberately baggily badly fitting Russian clothes. They don't talk much, they are basically mimics, and they mimic Europeans. In the first act one is dressed as a woman, overmade-up and with balloons under 'her' skirt and shirt to exaggerate her bum and tits. The other plays an amorous man with a portable cassette player who tries to get her to dance: he waltzes around her with a soppily beatific expression, wiggles and hops before her in a ludicrous caricature of modern jiving; and when he finally succeeds in getting her in his arms, the balloons, of course, are squeezed until they pop. Next the clowns bring on a small but very proud tabby cat. They try to pretend it is a lion, hold up huge hoops and thrash a vast imaginary whip. All the cat wants to do is stare at them and wash its legs. Everybody screams and rocks with laughter, children and adults, Mongolian herdsmen from the steppe, Bulgarian diplomats from the drab streets of Sofia, English secretaries from Bolton; it seems that there is total agreement amongst all human beings as to what is funny. Then another pretty girl: tall and willowy with a proud, supercilious face; she writhes sexily between the spinning rings of a variety of hoops and juggles some balls about. Yaks come on again and shamble around like mountainous bales of animated fur; there are tumblers, weight lifters, more jugglers, acrobats, a finale of roaring music and a parade of enchanting girls who mince and strut dressed in sequin-sprinkled dresses.

Dinner with Bob and Sheena. The meal was delicious except for the pudding. This was made from the rhubarb I had collected. Sheena was a bit dubious when she saw the bundle of stems I asked her to stew: they were dark and wiry and not much thicker than a pencil, but she kindly said she would try. She put a lot of her precious sugar in, and made an excellent pastry, but eating the rhubarb was like chewing on chunks of fibrous rope.

23 September. The rhubarb has had a dreadful effect, all of us who ate it yesterday evening spent much of the night perched on the mahogany.

We arrive at Ulaan Baatar station at about 9 a.m., the two-engined trains chug in a few minutes later. I settle down in my cabin. Craik snorts and snuffles as he rootles about next door, like a boar snuggling himself into a new sty. I put my allocation of diplomatic bags in the roof racks, my own baggage on the upper bunk; I strew out my maps, binoculars, bird book, notepad and eating-kit on the lower bunk; then I take off my jacket and tie and hang them up in the little cupboard, ease off my shoes, make my armchair even more comfortable by arranging my pillows round about it and then sit in it and look out of the window. Our friends from the Embassy are outside. They must wait until we depart. They look freezing, their hands in their pockets, their breath steaming, their ears red. Suddenly they all start laughing and pointing at me. At me? No, past me. I look round. A Japanese female has sat herself down on my bunk and is taking the hood off her camera. She is quite attractive, although stumpy and bespectacled, but her expression has a slightly dippy earnestness about it. 'Hello,' she says, 'I am from the cabin next door. I have been here since Moscow. You are new. That is strange. Do you like Ulaan Baatar? I have not heard about it. We must be friends. This journey is very long. It is cold. Siberia is not interesting. What are all those white bags? I am from Tokyo. You are English? I have been to London, Oxford and Stratford-upon-Avon. Have you been to Greece? I am with a friend. She too is a stenographer. We work for the Nitawitti Corporation. We are on holiday. Are you? Your friend has red hairs. The bathrooms on this train are not fresh or hygienic. You will make friends and laugh abundantly. I admire your Mrs Thatcher. Women have a new place in society . . .'

The desert is very green, there are pools of fresh water, but hardly any birds or animals. Most of the latter have migrated, most of the former are spread thinly over the newly available grazing. I saw a small fast duck, probably a teal, rise from a pond near Orgon.

Craik and I take turns to guard the bag and go to the lavatory. 'When

I die the word "Rhubarb" will be found engraved on my bowels,' he grizzles.

I am looking at a sight from which legends are born. It is early twilight, the far-off hills are blurring in the dusk and the hollowlands are pooling shadows. Above, many miles high, where the cold blue of the sky merges with the dark blue of space, four vast, gauzy figures are flying. They are astonishingly, awesomely, like angels. Their arms are outstretched, their feet dance beneath the swirl of their robes, they have feathered wings which stream from their shoulders. One has her head back as she leaps in exaltation, another leans intently forward; the one in front looks round at her companions. I know that they are strangely and coincidentally formed cirrus clouds, but if I were a herdsman trailing home in the desert, alone with my dreams, with those wondrous beings frozen in flight above me, I would be aghast with awe and wonder. I would become the prophet of a new religion.

24 September. I wake up in the cold light of dawn. Craik is fidgeting about next door.

'What's it like outside, Martin?'

'Not a bad day, but the scenery is covered with crapping coolies. Some idiot has probably been offering them rhubarb.'

We have come to know our neighbours: there are two Japanese girls (one being the potential squatter who came into my carriage at UB); a tall German youth with a shrill, persistent voice; some shamingly nondescript British students, who huddle together in a stale-smelling flock and complain; a family of podgy Dutch who never say a word to each other but seem to have some telepathic rapport as, on occasions, they spontaneously but mysteriously burst into roars of laughter; and a handsome, age-withered pair of aristocratic Danes in heavy, old-fashioned clothes of wool, canvas and leather. They sit on my bunk and sip my whisky and gently, in their sing-song voices, they try to persuade me to loathe the Swedes as much as they do. We discover we are related through the Arendrups and Rosencrantzes.

*

Arrive in Peking mid-afternoon. Miss Fang Fang checks me in at the hotel. Small and pearly are her teeth teeth.

25 September. A taxi called CEDRIC has threaded through the fleets of bicycles to take us to a restaurant near Tien-an-men Square.

The menu has none of the mealy-mouthed prevarication you get in Hong Kong where, for example, dog flesh is described as 'Fragrant Meat'. Craik grumbles and mutters through the list, reading out items which meet his disapproval: 'Jelly fish in oil, vinegar and soy sauce'; 'Goose's paws (boned) in white wine sauce'; 'Buddha Jumping over the Wall' (a mixture of abalone, fish maw, sea cucumber, squid, bird's egg, chicken and scallop); 'Spiced donkey meat'; 'Saucy dog meat' (twice-cooked, with soy sauce and crispy noodles); 'Stewed dog slices with sauce'; 'Spiced elbow'.

'What is "Spiced elbow"?' asks Craik.

'It is Number 72,' replies the waiter, as quick as a flash.

'No, dammit, I mean what is it made from, what does it taste like?'

'It is Number 72,' repeats the waiter.

'From which or whom does this elbow originate? Of what are the species?' elaborates Craik.

'Number 72,' persists the waiter.

I think I might try a bit of dog, but when actually faced with the choice I realise I cannot eat one, not on any moral or gourmet grounds, but for the first time I realise that dogs are my friends — even though I don't like most of them. So I settle for Peking duck, accompanied with a lot of other little things in bowls which Craik has ordered. For the pud, the waiter suggests Number 155: 'Steamed glutinous rice flour cake with mashed red beans'. We choose the ice-cream.

A pleasant Scotsman, eating alone near us, turns round and says: 'I heard you talking about the menu; for a real surprise you should have tried the "Deep-fried nest-lings".'

'Why, what are they like?' asks Craik.

'They get young birds from the nest, when they are still too young to have feathers, and they dip them in boiling fat. You hold them by the legs and eat them head first. You have to spit away the head, after you have sucked the brains and eyes out, because the beak is bad for the lining of your stomach. But the body is crispy outside, and squidgy inside.'

'Can you tell if it is a bird which has been fed on worms, like a black-bird, or if it is insectivorous?' I ask.

'Yes, worm-fed is juicier. But grain-fed birds are best.'

'A bit like haggis, I daresay,' says Craik.

We are walking back along the wide pavements of the main road.

Capitalism is a human instinct: an inherent impulse to trade and barter and swap and sell and haggle. You can see it in its infancy here. There are still only a few shops. They are state-run and you have to buy from them whether you like it or not, so they have little or no window-dressing. But some stalls have appeared, mostly selling clothes or fruit and vegetables. People are peddling on the pavements. Some of them are furtive, hissing 'American dollars?' at you as you pass, or whipping out a Ming bowl from under their shirts and saying 'Antique, very old, very valuable, but for you only . . .' Others overtly – a man and wife team cutting panes of glass; a man with a small stack of eggs; another with a sheet of damp newspaper on which he has arrayed a dozen crabs; a youth plaiting toy crickets from slivers of bamboo. There is a noodle maker with his cauldron of boiling water and hot plate; within seconds he has deftly transformed a lump of dough into a many-stranded rope of the finest noodles. Is that man who is selling tooth-paste and combs the founder of a Chinese Boots the Chemists? Will that man selling knickers and the other selling shirts unite to become a Marks & Sparks? That man selling puppies, will he found a McDonald's food chain? Is the man fiddling through dustbins a future commodity broker? Two men, a few yards apart on a busy crossroads, are merchandising air. One will be more successful than the other for he pumps up your bicycle tyre for you, the other makes you do it your-self. Bicycles are also catered for by the seat repair and sales man: on the curb, he has lined up a row of spanners by four new bicycle seats; he has already traded this morning for he squats beside a small pile of used seats which show bursting springs and splitting upholstery. They must have been agony to sit on.

A sign outside a new nightclub says: 'APPRECIATE XI SHUANG the BANNANA LADY'S BEAUTIFUL DANCING.'

We are off to see the Qing tombs tomorrow. To get there we will have to drive over unmade roads and field tracks for about 80 miles.

26 September.

There is a bridge, in a land far away,
whose balustrades of alabaster chime:
each one a different lucid note,
so he who crosses it may beat
a strange and sonorous pealing as he walks

This bridge is in the County of Zunua,
amid the North China Plains,
from whose flat fields rise steepled mountains:
islands of crags
that seem to float in shimmering seas of corn.
Within the valleys, hidden, alone, abandoned and desolate,
are the tombs.

They are the Qing tombs,
the 'ling' tombs:
the Yu-ling,
the Xia-ling,
the Jing-ling,
the Ting-tung ling,
and the Ding-dong-ling of the Dowager Empress Ci Xi.

Whilst, from behind,
the bridge still hums an eerie dirge of dying notes,
walk up the avenue of marble sentinels:
of graven warriors with shouldered swords,
of camels with fangs, and dragons,
and frog-faced lions with tufted tails.

Aloof they stand, inscrutable their stare
stone-faced above your bobbing, questing head;
invasive, shy intruder.

You pass through screens:
great porticos,
roofed with tiles of rust-hued glaze
and hung with doors of ox-blood red,
into yards whose grass and weeds between the flags
reveal a long rejection.

Some tombs are fine pavilions:
beneath the upswept corners of their roofs
are dragon-painted beams, and gilded pillars,
and cool and airy rooms which smell of cedar wood;
but other tombs are mounds,
mere earthen hillocks, heaped up high
above the subterranean corridors and catacombs
where massive coffins lie on lofty biers
whilst all around, meticulously arrayed
are bowls and salvers, sceptres, tea-sets, crowns and robes,
of porcelain and lacquerwork, of gold and silk and jade.

Through the smooth, humped back of one of these
there is a long and narrow shaft
piercing from the grassy, sunlit surface
to, buried far below, a room:
a cell of deathly silence, of breathless hush, of darkness.

Look down it, stare into this tomb
and presently your eyes will recognise a glow,
a gleam that time will triplicate
into three oval pearls set in the velvet gloom.

Walled in alive
were the little concubines:

these are their skulls.
Their little bony faces still stare up
at the last light
that died in their eyes.

28 September, Hong Kong. Craik is taking me to the nightclub Bottoms, telling me that it is very famous and was used in a James Bond film. It is dark inside, and smells of sweat. There are two circular bars. In the middle of them are disc-shaped mirrors, a nude black girl squats cross-legged on one, a nude blonde on the other. The discs rotate, so you can savour their charms from every angle. We sit by the black girl.

'Yea?' she asks.

Craik orders a couple of glasses of beer.

We stare at the girl. She rotates slowly before us, as if on a doner-kebab, being roasted by our hot eyes. She gazes over our heads and chews gum, ruminatively, like a cow with its cud. We sip our drinks. I feel vaguely embarrassed. A little Japanese who has been sitting by the blonde's bar bustles over and sits at ours. He wants a bit of variety. His main interest is the underneath of the girl as reflected in the mirror. He goggles down as she revolves to confront him, when she revolves away he gulps at his drink, moistens his lips and straightens his spectacles.

Craik and I quit. When we step into the neon-lit garishness of the street, a shifty looking cove comes up and mumbles at us.

'What?' Craik asks.

'Mutter, mumble, humble bum.'

'Speak up, I'm as deaf as an adder.'

'MUM-BLE, MUM-BLE, HUMM, BUMBLE.'

'Still don't understand a word you're saying.'

The cove, looking thoroughly exasperated, stands on tiptoes and shrieks down Craik's ear: 'DO! YOU! WANT! A! WARM! PUSSY!?'

Craik shys away from him: 'Certainly not!' he snaps.

We plod up the street with Craik muttering: 'Disgusting little man . . . what did he think I was . . . frightful fellow . . . that was a pimp, you know . . . good God . . . ghastly . . .'

In the early evening I meet Alaun Griffiths in the club bar in the university to give him the botanic samples I have collected. He seems a bit surprised that the berries have sugar sprinkled over them. Fly from Hong Kong at 22.55, leaving Craik who has to go to Manila tomorrow.

6 October. *Dominie seems to have recovered from the trauma of her mother's death and looks happy and bustling. Harvest Festival is tomorrow so I had to help her decorate 'our' church window, the south-west one in the nave. It is in memory of Great-Aunt Min: she having been a farmer, the theme is Sowing and Reaping. Knowing what Great-Aunt Min was like, it is appropriate that Boas, his corduroys done up below the knees with elijahs and with a soppy, floppy sun hat on his head, stands with an effete, willowy posture as he sows, whilst Ruth is butch and her stance is four square and firm; the sheaf she has gleaned is grasped in muscular arms. Placed about them are roundels which depict views of the estate and village with other farmwork taking place.*

I suggested to Dominie that we should have produce from the farm: sheaves of corn and sacks of peas, oil-seed rape and linseed; perhaps even a mutton chop and a baulk of cricket-bat willow, but Dominie told me to mind my own business and has made a huge arrangement with twigs and branches from the fruiting trees in the garden: pears, bullace, plums and elder. My 'business' was to lug them all from the car to the window, then fill the vases with water.

7 October. *I'm the only farmer here, what's happening to the parish on this Harvest Festival Sunday?*

In front, above the altar, the whole wall is a blaze of colour: the morning sun is shining through the east window. It depicts an awesome patrician sitting on a cloud. He has a beard and wears a red robe – I still remember my disappointment when told it was only God, not Father Christmas. He is surrounded by His feathered friends: flocks of cherubim, swarms of seraphim and gaggles of angels. Below, clad in golden armour, St Michael the Archangel tramples on a dragon and prods it with a sword. All the other windows are full of vases of flowers and are piled with fruit and vegetables; the lectern has been twined about with ivy and hops, the eagle at the top looks crossly out of this nest of climbers; at the foot of the pulpit there is an arrangement of vegetables, dominated by some large marrows; alternate sheaves of wheat and barley are to either side of the choir; less attractive are some stacks of tins – baked beans and what looks like pilchards. Dominie's arrangement has shed a few fruits and berries onto the pews below, there was some fussy brushing motions before the sittees sat.

We are in the Knights Farm pew – second on the left. The Sewells have lived in the village for over 300 years and take precedence in the front pew. The back of their pew is a bit wood-wormy. I have managed to gouge out quite a bit with my thumb-nail over several decades of boredom, listening to sermons, or to the repetition of prayers I know by heart. The parson is preaching now. Surreptitiously I dip into the Psalms, most of them are poems as well as paeans of praise or pleading.

Here's a couple of wonderful and strange lines, from Psalm 22:

Deliver my soul from the sword, my darling from the power of the dog.

Save me from the lion's mouth: for thou hast heard me from the horns of the unicorns.

Now the children are going up to offer their gifts to the parson.

Good, almost time to go; rattle through the last prayer, hang up my hassock, shake the parson's hand as he stands by the door, chat outside to a few people and then the one-mile drive back home.

11 October, Israel. The Arabs are chucking boulders at the Jews, and the Jews are shooting at the Arabs, and I have been advised to stay in the hotel. I have decided to risk it and am taking a tripper's bus tour instead. There are not many in the bus so I can sit alone, by a window. Over the nave beside me are an old married couple of American Jews, Samuel and Sara. His smiling beaky features and diminutive size resemble Jimminy Cricket; her square frame, beetling eyebrows and craggy features resemble Golda Meir. They are as enthralled as two schoolchildren on an outing: 'Oh look Samuel!' she keeps on saying, and Samuel stares and smiles and nods his head and says 'Oh yes, Sara, oh yes!' A little clique sits in front and natters: the driver, the female guide and a guard with a light machine gun. They look efficient and self-possessed.

Our guide hands out little cardboard skullcaps to the three Gentiles in the bus; the Jews already have their own personal ones. Much merriment is shown as I practise balancing mine on my balding dome. Samuel shyly leans across the aisle and hands me a little cup of dark velvet. 'Borrow this, I always carry a spare,' he says. I'm glad I can't see what I look like, an egg in an egg-cosy, I suspect.

Our first stop is at Hebron. It is predominately an Arab town and our guard looks about sharp-eyed and tense and holds his gun cocked and at the ready. Various people stand at a distance and scowl. Hebron is where, in a crypt, are the Tombs of the Patriarchs: Abraham, Isaac, Jacob and their wives Sarah, Rebecca and Leah. They are 'memorial tombs' rather than proper graves with corpses, nevertheless very evocative. Some of our party are very moved and I see tears coursing down the rugged furrows of Sara's face. When the Arabs owned the place they would not allow Jews entry; doubly irksome because to the Jews the Muslim usurper religion has impudently assumed the Jewish ancestors. When the guide said this she stared at me for comment. I gave none, it is best to keep out of other people's politics.

I have just been swimming in the Dead Sea. When we descended the heights it lay before us with a weird metallic glow as if it was a huge sheet of mercury. It was uncanny to think that, somewhere beneath, could be the drowned cities of Sodom and Gomorrah. The brine is so salty that no more salt will dissolve in it: one walks on a bed of salt, crystals float by like snowflakes. If you lie flat the water line is exactly along the extra-tickly central length of one's body. You are advised to move with gentle pushings of the hands: any swimming motions might cause drops to get in one's eyes, which is extremely painful. I experimentally licked a wet finger and it was like having a hot coal on my tongue. Even more painful was my entry, I had forgotten about my foot-rot, which I have had on and off ever since I went to Gordonstoun, and as I waded in I felt a burning between my toes as if I were a Polynesian fire-walker. The Scandinavians apparently specialise with their own skin diseases, types of eczema and so forth, and many come here to be cured; I kept well away from a group of blonds, looming motionless out of the water like a flock of lanky wading birds; surrounded, I feared, by a flotsam of scabs and scurf.

I *suppose* the white flakes floating round me are salt crystals.

*

The Masada pinnacle is a tall rock which stands a little apart from the main body of cliffs that edge that area of the Dead Sea. Its flat top is the site of the last stronghold of the Essene Zealots in their resistance to the Romans. Herod the Great had had it designed and equipped into a fort-cum-palace (he had nine wives, the first was Queen Doris); the remarkable water-collecting system that his engineers devised meant that the place could withstand a very long siege in spite of the environs being amongst the most arid in the world. The Zealots resisted for almost three years, AD 70–73; when they decided that they could resist no longer they killed their children and committed suicide. The Romans rather admired them for this and buried the 960 corpses in a mass grave; this is still to be discovered. The Romans piled up a huge causeway between the cliffs and the pinnacle. It is still there. Further back you can see the one built by Hollywood, when the film was made here. We took a cable car up, wandered round the ruins to the accompanying bossy babble from our guide, then I walked down a zigzag path to the bus waiting below.

We drove back via Jericho. One could see the attraction that it must have had for the mutton-eating nomads, sand in their eyes and hair, their drinking-water warm and brackish in leather bottles: the lanes we drove through were shaded by bushes and date-palms, and pomegranates and oranges glowed red and gold amid the leaves.

We arrived back in Tel Aviv during the rush hour. As we disembussed there was a terrific bang. I think it was a car backfiring but we were all a bit jumpy, having traversed several miles of hostile country. Samuel leaped in front of Sara and fluffed himself protectively out like a little bantam cock protecting his hen against a fox. The effect was a bit spoiled by the 'hen' looming behind him a good head higher and with an overlap of six inches at each side. Sara beamed fondly down at him.

20 October. *George and Fiona's wedding. There were about 400 guests. Over 100 of them were our relations, which must have been a bit overwhelming for the Hadlees; the only other Hadlee relations are the family of Sir Richard, the cricketer in New Zealand. The Knights Estate staff and pensioners and their spouses just filled the 22* *seats in the pews which were between the choir and the front pew, so they had a very good view.*

Fiona looked beautiful, wearing a tight-waisted white dress with a low front, and an enormous smile. The reception was held in a big tent on their lawn. We milled about for a few hours, drinking, nibbling, talking: all this whilst being serenaded by a 'Dad's Army' jazz band which played on the lawn. After the speeches, the Happy Pair drove off to stay in Suffolk (they got lost on the way to Lavenham) – next day they went on to honeymoon in Venice.

23 October. My driver from the aerodrome to the Embassy in Amman is Hassan. He hugged me when we met, which gave my escort a bit of a frisson. Hassan and I have a lot in common as I was a district councillor for twenty years and he is a mukhtar, a sort of local councillor/adjudicator/peace-maker. The position is hereditary. There are about 3000 people who do not think of him as a mere chauffeur but as the dominant figure in their community. His latest problem is an argument between two neighbouring households who are complaining about noise. They have become so hostile that the wives keep throwing eggs at each other's houses. I tell him that my usual problem as a councillor was also with neighbours complaining about the noise next door – but for a few exciting exceptions, such as the frightful row over 'their Kev, he's gone and impregnated our Mehalah'.

I exchanged bags with some people from our Baghdad Embassy and said it must be pretty grim being British there. They replied: 'Not a bit, many of the Iraqis are very friendly. Strangers come up to us in the street and say "you don't know me, but I know that you are from the British Embassy, and if you start running out of food or need help let us know. We think Sadam Hussein is a madman; he has already made us fight a useless war for eight years against the Iranians, now we have the whole world against us . . ."'

However, it is of course only a few well-wishers who speak thus, and Sadam Hussein has many people on his side, but much of them are 'rent-a-mobs' or embroiled in Sadam Hussein's speciality which is to 'divide and rule'. The British staff like the Iraqis, and are sorry for them. One of them says: 'Give me 100 discontented Iraqi outside our

Embassy, any day, rather than one professional trouble-making crew from the British television.'

24 October. Woken up at dawn by the ululations of the muezzin from their minarets. It always sounds impressive in Amman. The king has decreed that all buildings should be clad with the local stone so that, however hideous, they still meld with the rocky surroundings, and the steep sides of the many wadis amongst which Amman is built are made even more cliff-like with the sheer faces of the multitudinous walls. The calls of the muezzin echo to and fro in these man-made canyons and sound much more melodious than the nasal rasping through the tinny microphones of Saudi or the Gulf. The muezzin wake up the whole city: within a few moments after the first chants and wails the cocks start to crow, the dogs to howl and the first cars and trucks to rumble past.

I have decided to explore some of the 'Desert Castles'. These are not really castles, some are caravanserai, some are hunting lodges, some are large manor-cum-farmsteads, others are rest-houses based round baths, and a few can be described as 'weekend mansions'; the unifying factor is that they were built by the Umayyad Arabs within the century between AD 750 and 850. The Umayyads originated as Bedouin Muslims who defeated the Christian army of Byzantium in the battle of Wadi Yarmuk in AD 636; after that battle they established the capital of their Caliphate in Damascus. Although their civilization became very sophisticated and urbanised, perhaps they sometimes hankered nostalgically for the open spaces of their origins which is why they built their pleasure houses far out in the wilds of the desert.

I have negotiated a taxi, all day for 40 *dinars*. I probably am paying too much; I am hopeless at bargaining, being embarrassed and faltering. My driver is a charmless Palestinian called Naim. He is burly, with a greying moustache and a terse, grumpy manner. He wears good shoes, Marks & Sparks flannels and a repulsive zip-up jacket in maroon satin with 'SURPLUS PLUS' embroidered on the back. He has a keffiyeh, but took it off before he started to drive, then thoroughly scratched his head and beard and donned a pair of gold-rimmed spectacles.

We are in the desert to the east of Amman, driving through a series of arid valleys bounded by hills, sharp-edged and crested like waves in a choppy sea. The road is new and one can see vividly the bands of rock strata in different shades of grey, tan, white and brown which undulate, writhe or in the more extreme cases convolute along the raw scars of the new cuttings. I notice the occasional kestrel hovering, there is hardly any vegetation; all is desolation.

The first 'castle' has come into sight, an impressive jumble of walls on a hilltop in the middle of a plain. It is called Qasr el Hallabat. It is one of the few which certainly had some military history: this site started off as a Roman fortlet, one of the chain of watch-towers along the Via Nova Traiana (Trajan's New Road). The post was expanded by later Romans, then the Byzantines; the Umayyads demolished much of it and rebuilt a larger complex with a mosque, baths and a complicated water system. It included luxuries and works of art such as marble cladding to the inner walls, mosaics, frescoes, statues – even coloured window glass. Only a tumbled mass of ruin remains, a higgledy-piggledy of broken walls, broached by cascades of rubble which spill over to smother the cell-like rooms inside, of steps leading nowhere, blocked-up conduits and water cisterns: if you look down them you can see the relics of previous visitors, cigarette packets, scraps of paper and the item of litter you find throughout Arabia, empty plastic water bottles. One 'Moorish' arch has survived; the exterior ornamentation of the defences is still evident, with the lighter limestone of the dry-stone walling being traversed by darker bands of squared basalt. Naim gives a hiss to attract my attention and then scrapes at the gritty rubble with his toe. He exposes part of a beautiful mosaic, a bright red gamebird on a white background. Because of its colour I wonder if it is a sand grouse, but its rounded shape and stubby low tail suggest a quail. Naim shuffles at another part of the floor. I cringe, thinking of the damage this must do to the ancient stones, but am enchanted with the brace of fat little partridge he exposes.

The next 'castle' is only a couple of miles away. It is actually a bath-house and is called Hammam al Sarah. We stop outside it and the caretaker appears from a nearby hovel: she is a Bedou, tall and graceful with blue tattoos on her lips and cheeks. However she is buck-teethed and wrinkled and her dark green robe has almost turned black with age to widow her before her time. The building is charming, but very small; I pace out the two main rooms, both about four yards square. As I measure, Naim and the woman look on suspiciously, as if I was surveying the site for an Israeli missile range. The first room contains a recessed fountain pool and a small alcove with a cell to either side, each with its own latrine and plumbing; there is a barrel-vaulted changing room; a hot room, where you can see the remains of the hypocaust below and a domed roof above; and a warm room, the 'tepidarium'. Once this was full of steam and noise and splashing water; now the rocks are as dry as bones.

Now the valleys have broadened out into wide gravel plains, the hills are lower and further away, it reminds me of the Gobi desert. It is cool: we are a couple of thousand feet up and puddles of rain water shine on the road.

Naim has taken to picking his nose. He does it with his thumb.

Azraq is an oasis. There are dusty date-palms, dusty houses and a dusty castle built of dusky basaltic blocks. I have a guide, a diminutive and very old Arab. He wears a keffiyeh. Apart from that he looks like many of the old men one meets in the Five Bells: rubber boots, corduroy trousers, a collar-less shirt, an old tweedy jacket, a white moustache stained by hand-rolled fags and a pair of tiny, pale blue eyes whose rheumy wateriness suggests that they have been steeped overnight in a glass of mild and bitter.

The entrance porch has a couple of stone doors which he opens and shuts. 'One ton each,' he says proudly.

He points to the machicolation whose double slits project above the doors. 'Boiling oil,' he says meaningfully.

He takes me to a room above the porch. 'Colonel Lawrence, his head-quarters,' he says obscurely.

We go out into the large walled yard, he points to a door. 'Stables,' he says tersely.

He takes me by the arm and shows me another vast slab of stone on a pivot. 'Bigger door, three tons,' he says even more proudly.

He points to a square building plonked in the middle of the yard. 'Mosque,' he says devoutly.

His job done, he joins Naim by the mosque; they roll a couple of fags, light up and proceed to natter.

After I have explored the ruins I ask Naim if he wants lunch. To my relief he does not, so we drive towards Qasr Amra, over wide, gloomy basaltic plains. There are several Bedou settlements: long, low tents, enclosures of fabric and corrugated iron, sheep and goats, children playing, litter. No camels, they have been deposed by Japanese-made trucks.

Qasr Amra is another bath complex. From afar it looks quite big, with a triple row of humps, barrel-vaulted roofs, and a dome, but it is only 14 paces by 27. The interior walls are covered with delightful frescoes: plump, pretty, nude females, some bathing, some dancing, some lounging; musicians (including a bear playing a guitar); people hunting with long, lean hounds, salukis presumably; birds and animals such as peacocks and wild ox; wrestlers and craftsmen. Particularly fascinating is the fresco of the Six Kings, all enemies of Islam: the Byzantine Emperor, the Sassanian King Kisra, King Roderic of Spain (the last Visigoth ruler of Spain, killed by Walid 1 in AD 711), the Negus (ruler) of Abyssinia and two obscured figures who may depict the emperor of China and the Khagan of the Turks. They are all indistinct and ghostly in the shadowy room and it is frustrating not to be able to make out who is who. The complex has all the usual rooms, of which the caldarium (sweating-room) is the most ornate, with a domed ceiling, painted with the signs of the zodiac, four windows, recesses for baths and a hypocaust which is joined by a tunnel to the furnace.

Qasr Amra must have been a charming, happy place. Now it smells of pee.

Qasr el Kharanah appears as a great square block on the horizon. Like most of these castles it is not as big as it looks at first sight, only 40 paces square, but it is quite imposing, with high walls pierced with arrow slits, a tall arched gateway flanked with towers and more towers at the corners: so it really looks like a castle, but probably it was a caravanserai. There is a room each side of the entrance tunnel: large, with impressive arches, perhaps stables, perhaps dormitories, perhaps store or luggage rooms. The inner courtyard is 14 paces square. Probably, once, it contained a formal pool. The rooms round it are in two storeys; there are about 50 of them. They seem to be in 'suites' with a large central hall, often with arches, vaults and corner semi-domes, and four or five smaller rooms adjacent. They are pleasantly cool. Like all the places I have been to, there is no-one here. This is not the tourist season, and my footsteps tap out lonely echoes as I walk up and down the stairs or through the rooms.

Naim has driven me back to the hotel: we have been out for about six hours and have driven about 120 miles. He picked his nose almost all the time; no wonder he didn't need lunch. He received my tip with the first signs of animation and pleasure he had showed all day. I must have tipped him too much.

*1 **November.** To London for the Queen's Messengers' cocktail party. It was held in the marbled magnificence of the Durbar Court, in the middle of the Foreign Office. Met several old Queen's Messengers who like all old travellers were full of tall stories: the last routine journey by horse which was abolished as recently as 1949 (a two-day trek over the Himalayas from the Indian/Nepalese border to Kathmandu); the luxuries of the Golden Arrow and the Queen Mary; the discomforts of Arabian flea-pits and Transylvanian hotels; mad Ambassadors and nymphomaniac female spies, derailed trains and crash-landed aeroplanes; hijackings, civil wars and earthquakes. Also the immense varieties of Gyppy Tummy, Kenya Collywobbles, Turkey Trots, the Inca Two-steps, Siamese Squits, Delhi Belly, Montezuma's Revenge and plain old-fashioned diphtheria, typhoid and cholera. Someone told me that the tetrathon of the early Olympics in the last century was based on our training: running, shooting, riding and swimming. Looking about at the well-victualled and upholstered figures I remembered Lord Curzon's remark to a Queen's Messenger: 'Silver greyhound indeed! A fat bulldog would be more apt.'*

6 November. An appalling arrival at Cuba. I have seven bags, weighing 84 kilos, in the seats next to me. I also have two bags in the hold, too big and weirdly shaped to go in the cabin. My personal luggage is the normal small bag I always carry, plus a plastic bag crammed with ten pounds of apples, a present to my hosts.

I must ensure that I get out of the aeroplane and stand by the hold before its hatch is opened, that I bring all the cabin-loaded bags with me, that none of them is touched by any Cuban and that I keep every bag in sight. Our men in Havana are forbidden to meet me before Customs and Immigration; the cabin staff of the aeroplane are only interested in getting out as soon as possible and have no wish to help me. Although it is only 4 a.m. the temperature is in the high eighties and the humidity is almost 100 per cent.

I drape myself with bags and squeeze and shove past the line of seats, getting jammed several times as I go and 'tut-tutted' by several petulant little twerps who think it is their privilege to get off first. The door of the aeroplane will not open: various futile remarks are shouted from someone outside to our head steward. He fiddles about with a handle and nitters back. I am in a frightful stew because I presume the hold is being opened; also the weight of the bags which I have hung round me is giving me a neck-ache.

Finally the door opens. A humid wave of heat rolls in and envelopes me in a smothering blanket. I struggle down the mobile staircase. At the bottom there are several people in different uniforms who have one intention, to herd me back to the other passengers. I produce my passport and the waybill and after some shouting and arm-waving I am allowed to scuttle round the nose of the aeroplane and under the wing; sure enough, the hatch has been opened. But there is nobody there and I can see my two horrible bags by the entrance. So, no-one has pinched them. I wait in the stifling heat. Suddenly a mass of figures appear out of the gloom, swarm into the hold and start unloading.

I am standing with my bags around my feet. A friendly baggage handler has fetched my two private bags which a steward had carried down and left at the foot of the mobile stairs. A bus has run over the bag of apples, their pulped squashiness oozes juice through the burst-apart zips and seams. A truck draws up. After much argument, involving shouts, gesticulations and finally shrugs, I commandeer it for myself. I am boiling with the heat and exasperation and snatch off my hat to cool my head. I release a reservoir of sweat which cascades down my face; it is so salty that it stings my eyes and I blunder about, blinded. Whilst I do this squads of soldiers, policemen and baggage handlers dash about and in spite of my ineffectual bleats grab my bags and hurl them aboard. I should have been the only person to touch them. In spite of my flustered condition I am intrigued to see that some of the police are garbed in riding-britches and boots and they have the rudiments of spurs on their heels: generic throwbacks, like the prehistoric toes which one of Dominie's foals had on its fetlock.

My driver is taking me in the Land Rover from the Embassy to my hotel. We are travelling down the darkened roads of Havana. All looks deserted, rather like those sombre black and white films showing Berlin with trilby-hatted spies lurking in doorways. A figure in uniform skulks in a shadow, a chink of light appears and disappears in a window, a cat flickers round a corner. As we travel down the streets, lined with arcades, the rows of pillars resemble avenues of petrified tree trunks. On the sea wall of the Malecon Corniche road, courting couples are sitting in pairs. Each pair seems to be exactly the same distance apart. Interesting anthropologically, I think, and stop the driver to pace out the distance between two couples: one . . . two . . . three . . . four . . . five . . . six. They stop snogging and stare uneasily at me. The distance apart from the next couple is also six paces. I start on the third but the driver who has been following me in the car bleats some querulous remarks so I get in the car and now he is driving to the hotel, muttering to himself.

There is a trio of English here: two men and a woman, 30-year-olds with sharp eyes and unnecessary rucksacks. She wears a T-shirt upon which has been printed the portrait of Ché Guevara. Whether by fluke or artistry, each nipple is exactly behind Guevara's eyes, pushing them out so that they give him a startled expression. We sat opposite each other at breakfast. I examined the smaller man with fastidious dislike as he smeared his beard with fried eggs.

'What are you doing here?' he asked, catching my eye.

'I'm here on business, I'm a Queen's Messenger.'

He turned to his companions.

'Goodness gwacious,' he said in an annoying, whinnying voice, 'I say, rartha, jolly good, he's here as a Qween's Messengah.'

I was irked: 'Now I've taught you how to speak properly, perhaps I can show you how to eat.'

The female tittered, which rather warmed my heart to her.

The third Brit, a bland-looking man in spectacles, a peace-maker at heart, said: 'Perhaps you know this place well enough to advise us what to visit.'

'Well, your friend is obviously an admirer of Ché Guevara. He was one of the most brutal prisoner governors since Hitler's regime; there were four prisons when the communists took over this country, now there are 200, perhaps you can go on a tour of them.'

He smiled and nodded politely, which made me feel rather ill-mannered.

Having had breakfast, I have spent the last four hours walking round Havana. It is very pleasant although run down. There is the faded charm of a courtesan living on her memories. Like most communist states the streets are quiet with a lack of bustle and *joie de vivre* and little traffic. There have been a few Russian-made cars introduced during the reign of Castro, but not many other vehicles since 1958 and the dominant cars are of the USA, 1950s in style. That was the decade when American cars were at their most grotesque: huge fins at the rear, vast chromium-plated bosoms at the front; metallic grinning faces, bulging, overhanging bottoms. The rusting, cannibalised hulks sway and lurch through the streets as dinosaur relics of a previous era. In the old, debauched, flippant days there had been a law that every house had to be different and so the little doll's houses were designed with a great variety and combination of banisters, balustrades, columns, colonnades, sills, sashes, porticoes, porches; all these in plasterwork or carved from coral and embellished with scrolls and swatches. This variety was emphasised with different colours but little has seen a lick of paint since 1958. There was a shipment of cheap East European paint a couple of years ago and a few buildings have been daubed with it. The three basic colours are eye-wrenchingly garish: an acid green, an apoplectic pink, and the deep blue that boys with irredeemable acne were painted with at school. Now and then one can glimpse inside open front doors which reveal narrow, steep staircases with ornately carved wood, marble floors and cool courtyards with pillars, and long-dried pools and fountains, all festooned with lines of washing. A few buildings are still well maintained. The Spanish Embassy is a good example of this: with its pale wash and its plethora of ornamentation it looks like a wedding-cake decorated by a master of icing-sugar. Our Embassy, nearby, is a drear couple of floors on the top of a squalidly built twelve-storey block; its lift is a mobile pissoir but as it often is out of order one is able to plod up the flights of stairs, savouring the leprous plaster and scabby paint and the stink of too many people cooking and crapping together.

Christianity has been abolished, its fripperies and tokens removed as obnoxious evidence of religion: 'the opium of the people'. My Embassy driver, a Caribbean from St Lucia, said: 'They tore down a figure of the Madonna because they did not believe in her, yet they have left a statue of Venus – and she certainly was not Fidel Castro's mother.'

Most of the churches are boarded up and crumbling, but there is an attractive little church with open doors, by the docks. I enter. It is being used partly as an office and partly as a political show-room. The walls are bedecked with photographs of seedy men in rows, the ceiling draped with banners. A garish poster of Castro and his murdering accomplice Ché Guevara is pinned above the place where there once was an altar. There are four cheap desks behind which sit four bored people tapping on four rackety typewriters. In unison they look up at my entrance and greet me with one big scowl. I stare down at them, up at the banners, along to the poster and having glanced once more at the surly quartet I say 'disgusting blasphemers' and quit.

This place is making me rude and bad-tempered.

Poor old Cuba, the people are exceptionally gifted, whether in the arts or sport, but talent and innovation is being crushed under the iron press of socialism.

*11 **November.** Remembrance Sunday. There are only about five of the old village families left. This includes us, if one thinks of 110 years as 'old', which it isn't really. We think of the family headquarters as Gosfield, five miles away. Anyhow, when they* *read the names out from the war memorial, I am one of the few who know of most of them, and I try to concentrate and send my mental messages to each one: 'Thanks a lot, sorry you were killed, see, you haven't been forgotten.' At Sunday School, when I was a child, we had to learn them by heart, the good Essex names: Percy Wakeling, Ernest Wakeling, Bert Ridgewell, the Reynoldses, Coppinses, Dixeys and so on; lastly George Quartermain. Those were the eighteen villagers killed in the First World War. Only John Watson and Edward Scholefield were killed in the next one. I try specially hard for Scholefield. I was very fond of old Mrs Scholefield, with her beautiful throaty voice and charming gentle ways; fond also of her amusing, giggling attractive daughter Joanna, who was so adored by the American officers and who faded to death with cancer. Having lost her husband, then her daughter, Mrs Scholefield then lost her son. I try to zero in on him for her sake. The new parson cannot even pronounce his name correctly.*

14 November. I have two companions flying to Mexico with me, both women: one is a jolly Lancashire girl, a 'floater' to the Embassy, with a strange, high, fluting, quirkily attractive voice; the other, older, elegantly dressed and with short hair, is the wife of one of the Embassy staff. The Lancastrian has a guidebook from Grey Line Bus Tours, it mentions a day-long trip to 'places of Archaeological Interest'. I shall book myself into a tour for tomorrow.

I have been tramping the unattractive, quake-skewed streets of Mexico City. Earthquakes have destroyed much that would be old or interesting, and have skewed or humped up many pavements. Buildings have sunk into the spongy substrata and lean and lurch. The pollution is repulsive; I have been told that over 100 tons of human excrement goes up in dust per day. I have a sore throat, a runny nose and a headache. But in pleasant comparison I pass several stalls selling deliciously scented roast chickens, pancakes and tortillas. I like the mini-markets of stalls, though many of the wares seems limited to cheap watches or cassettes. There are many security guards: they are dressed in blue with flak jackets and carry light machine guns. Most are women: it is unpleasant seeing police with guns, it is obnoxious seeing the guns being toted by women, the bearers of life.

The Mexicans have an intense, macabre engrossment with death, and it is exaggerated at the moment, the Dia del Muertos (the Day of the Dead, their equivalent of Halloween) having recently been celebrated. Fly-papers stuck to walls depict skeletons rising from coffins. In a bookshop a child's book is open to reveal the picture of a jolly family of Mexican skeletons in their drawing-room: Mr Skeleton has a huge moustache above his grinning teeth; Mrs Skeleton's skull peers coyly from the ruffles of a poke bonnet; Master and Miss Skeleton play with bones on the carpet beside Dog Skeleton and Cat Skeleton who argue over a rib cage; Baby Skeleton is being carried in a shawl on the back of Nanny Skeleton. In the shop windows every type of material is used: an oculist's shop has a skull of polystyrene, looking cool and trendy wearing its sunglasses; another shop depicts a papier-mâché band, all skeletons, wearing sombreros and ponchos and playing guitars, grinning like anything in their creepy merriment; more sombre are the skeleton crew carved from wood, sailing a little boat across the shop window of a travel agency; paper cut-outs of dancing skeletons, several dressed becomingly in the frilled flounces of flamenco dresses, dangle from the ceiling of an interior decorator's; from sugar are the little skulls in the sweet shops; in cake mixture is a larger skull in the baker's, obviously feminine for the smooth dome of its crown is bedecked by Shirley Temple ringlets in cream piping. Even a Snoopy in a toy shop wears a black jacket with white bones printed on it to convert his cuddly plumpness into a skeleton.

Sombre also are the murals. Some are alfresco, painted on the sides of buildings, others are in churches and public buildings. What they lack in artistic talent and charm they gain in fervour and dramatic impact. They are huge, normally covering a whole wall. The dominant, overbearing colours are a deep, blood-red and a sooty black. They often depict clerics: upon crags, cardinals in carmine brood amid thunder clouds and scowl down upon the massed array of penitents at their feet; horses, made wobbly and unsubstantial by the artist's peculiar talent of portraying living things with flesh and muscle but no bone, stomp through teeming hordes of ineffective foes; the heroes astride their backs are magnificently apparelled either in Spanish armour or with sombrero and bandoleer. They all have fierce moustaches.

*

Cathedral Square is an impressive and attractive exception to the rest of the city: its flagged flooring and surrounds of imposing arcaded buildings are reminiscent of Paris. The cathedral has a large central dome and two bell-shaped belfries to the front. As I step inside I am enveloped in the familiar scent of incense. The building is pleasantly light and airy. There are several statues of saints with tortured 'peach-stone' grimaces and the craftsmen have thoroughly enjoyed depicting Christ's wounds: His flesh is bruised, His wounds gape and are encrusted with clotted blood; on one statue his knee-caps are split so that you can see the bone. They stress the human, animal side of Him, not the spiritual. The many side chapels are ablaze with gold and gilding, the main altar is encrusted with it in great gobbets. I liked best the side chapel of the altar de Nuestra Señora de Zapopan. The centre piece is a little doll: she has pink cheeks, a large wig of dark hair surmounted by a huge golden crown and she wears a large cape of white satin with gold embroidery. In the adjacent chapel the statue of St Antonio Abad has a very pink piglet at his feet. A rather nice prayer on a board in three languages begins: 'Father of Mercy and God of all Consolation . . .'

Churches always seem to contain lonely people. Their loneliness is emphasised by my dread misgiving that they are praying to No-one. A youth kneels at the feet of the Madonna. His eyes gaze up imploringly at her, his lips flutter in continuous prayer. His face is ashen, he is very ill. Poor young man: he ought to be outside in the sunshine, exultant with the girls, not alone here in the gloom, pleading for his life.

There is a church adjacent to the cathedral. This is lighter and brighter and smells very pleasantly of the vases of chrysanthemums which are on every altar. There is much evidence of the Madonna, in headwear of halo, crown, wimple or scarf.

I am in the Museum of Anthropology. It is one of the best in the world but to me it is full of loathsome things: ugliness, brutality, cruelty, beastliness, horror and hate; gaping fanged mouths, tortured bodies, monsters from hell; everyone is grinning, either in anguish or ferocity. Only beautiful are some flint knives: simple, stark, functional. They were used to gash open human rib cages so that sacrificial victims could have their still throbbing hearts ripped out of their bodies. 6000 people a year were thus slaughtered in Cholula (such a pretty name). Even simple objects lack charm, the Central and Southern Americans never invented the potter's wheel so the potentially graceful lines of bowl or jug have irritating wobbles or cants. Gold, the metal of the angels, manages to be ugly: the ornaments are clumsily wrought, fussily styled, often embossed with brutish faces. The 'noble face of the knight wearing a snake's head' is often said to be the most beautiful object of Aztec art. It is not repulsive merely because it is so weather-worn that one cannot fully distinguish its full beastliness. It reminds me of one of the most horrible things I have seen: a grass snake with a frog staring at me with mute horror from its gaping jaws.

The Spanish Conquistadors behaved repulsively. With brutality and bigotry they cruelly eliminated civilisations. They burnt the literature, melted the treasures, murdered the people – for example in one silver mine in Colombia 1,500,000 Amerindians were worked to death in less than two years. However, if civilisations had to be destroyed, and art vandalised, those of the Central American Indians were surely the best candidates.

15 November. After a quick breakfast of coffee and croissant I have boarded the tourist mini-bus. There are seven of us in it. The guide-cum-driver is called Manuel – I think, I can hardly hear his low sheepish mumble nor understand his strong accent. One of us is a Polish psychiatrist: he is affable but looks sinister, tall and thin with a short-cut black beard, dark glasses and tight black clothes over which he wears a scarlet anorak. There is a family of four Americans. Dale, the patriarch, is immensely fat, probably about 25 stone, but seems surprisingly light-footed. He is a geologist, his conversation is wide-ranging and interesting. Karen, his wife, is friendly and carries many things hanging on straps: bags, cameras, and little pouches and purses. They have a son and a daughter: Bogart is thirteen and wears a complicated set of metalware over his teeth; Honeydew is fifteen and wears an expression of the utmost boredom. She is always the last off the bus and the first on. When Manuel is pointing out something to us she stands aside, gazing into the distance with blank eyes, chewing the cud and periodically looking at her watch.

We stop at Tenayuca first. This is the 'Chichimeca Indian Ceremonial Centre, pre-dating the Aztecs, featuring the original stone serpents which have since been copied by the other tribes.' At last I know how to pronounce Quetzalcoatl, the Feathered Serpent, it is Ket-sal-kwatl. Tenayuca is basically a stepped and staired pyramid with lines of serpent's heads and human skulls along the walls. It is shut, because of some renewed archaeological excavations. Manuel has to stand on tiptoes to point out several obscure items over a wall.

We re-embus and drive the 40 miles to Tula.

There is still a considerable distance before we escape the influence of Mexico City. The continuity of the slum alongside the streets finally fragments into shanty villages alongside the road; between them the land is dusty and smothered with litter varying from burnt-out cars to huge heaps of trash, dumped at random in creek or on verge. Corn is being cultivated, people slowly ply hoes and mattocks in the fields, and a few tractors or pairs of oxen draw rollers or harrows. Most of the crop looks like maize.

The soil becomes even more dusty, shrubs and bushes give way to cactus and succulents including prickly pears and the spiny octopus of the maguey, from which tequila is distilled. Here and there are horse-breeding stations; the animals look fat and fit, better fed and bred than the people who tend them.

'What are you doing in this part of the world?' I ask the Pole.

'What indeed,' he replies sadly, shaking his head, 'what indeed?'

Like most Poles I have met he has great charm and is rather odd.

Tula was the capital of the Toltec empire. They were, if it is possible, even nastier and crueller than the other tribes, though there is no evidence that they enjoyed the Mayan pastime of pulling out fingernails or the Aztec habit of drowning small girls. When scanned closely their buildings are foul, covered with repulsive friezes: human hearts being borne off by eagles and jaguars, or human skeletons (Manuel's 'men weetout skins') being eaten feet-first by snakes. But from afar the conglomeration of courtyards, terraces, staircases, pyramids and walls produces a most attractive unity.

Manuel's attempt to explain all this is highly inept, I am writing this as he speaks:

'So he was keel-ed as sacrifice and thees woman went with thees child to thees place whose name was – er – um – I forget – so thees child he was teach in that religion and after years he decide to defeat to the contrary faction. After twenty years thees contrary faction then decide to keel heem so they gave heem the sour-ed drink and he has relations with a brisk woman. Thees ees not permitted. And so he goes once again to the peeramid of Chula and after twenty years I forget to tell you that he was a teecher of all thees culture, how to read and how to write and all that the nobles. But once again he has thees problem with the brisks of the temple of the God of the Smoking Mirror so he decide to die and he take a – um – er how you say? a, a, um, er – I dunno, what the word? – a sing on the water? a – I forget a no – a um – thees yea! CANOE! A CANOE! . . . but some say he fires hees quetzal feathers to rise in the sky as a beautiful bird and he change to the morning star. Now we see the ball-court. Take a look it ees like a capital I. Thees people throw the ball through stony cycles. See, at the end of thees court ees the reclining figure of a god holding a receptacle designed to receive the still beating heart of the capitain of the winning team.'

'Of the losing team, surely,' I say.

'No,' says Manuel. 'Eet ees a privilage reserved for the winning team.'

'The losing,' says Dean, the fatty, 'I read it in a book.'

Manuel goes into a sulk (he was right).

Grumpily he takes us up a flight of steps onto a wide platform, upon which eight huge stone-carved figures stand. Their size and shape are reminiscent of their cousins further north, of the totem poles of the Red Indians of Canada.

The ruined city of Teotihuacán. It is beautiful. From close up, the art and artefacts of the South American civilisations are likely to be ugly and often are horrible but on a larger scale their architecture and civil engineering are of great beauty and satisfying cohesion: as I look down the Road of the Dead, 40 paces wide and a mile and a half long, I see a parade of stone-built terraces, walls, flights of steps, courtyards, quadrangles and pyramids, a chaos of planes and angles and surfaces which merge to form one totally satisfactory unity. Much of this homogeneity is achieved by the use of the local stone as building material; also there is conformity with the angles of stair-flights and buttresses and walls. Above all, although everything seems so vast, it is designed for humanity and not machinery; one can imagine oneself strolling between the walls or calling to friends from the terraces.

I have rarely been to such an awe-inspiring place. More than a thousand years ago this city held a quarter of a million people and so the few tourists cannot intrude into the abandoned loneliness, the brooding stillness, the shadow of something once great and busy and powerful but now long gone, the sense of foreboding. Once, these courtyards were full of the bustle of trade and barter; these alleyways were full of perambulating families and squabbling neighbours and yelling, shoving children and pontificating politicians and priests; from the heights of those towering pyramids hearts were torn out of human sacrifices and the bodies hurled down the steps.

They're bloody steep, these stairs.

They must have had very long legs and tiny feet: the steps are about a foot high but only half a foot wide. There are 242 of them on this, the Pyramid of the Sun, if I've counted right. We are six or seven thousand feet above sea-level also, which does not help in one's stamina. I pass Bogart halfway up: 'I guess the view is as good here as it is from the top,' he says.

I am standing here, on the summit, when his surly and bored sister arrives. She is pink and sweaty and panting and I suddenly realise that she will be attractive in a year or so's time.

As she and I talk we hear a noise reminiscent of a Pacific Class steam engine hauling 50 waggon-loads of pig iron up a slope.

'Oh no! Pa!', exclaims Honeydew, worried, but proud.

Sure enough, a cotton-clad sun dawns over the crest of the pyramid. I am torn between admiration for Dean's determination and his leg muscles, and concern that he will throw a fit. He stands beside us. He says nothing, but with a noise like a donkey hee-hawing gulps in huge retchings of oxygen. I exchange a few terse pleasantries and then move away, lest I should have to give him the kiss of life.

'What is a daughter for?' I think with self-justification.

I tottered into the hotel at 6 p.m. Having not had a drink since breakfast, fearing that my bladder might summon my attention halfway round a temple or halfway up a pyramid, I made a bee-line for the bar. My two ex-escorts were already there, cosily ensconced in a couple of armchairs, their short skirts showing their good legs, pertly crossed, their fingernails painted, their hair cut and primped, their eyes aloof but not ignorant of the ogling of a row of fellows sitting by the bar. I collapsed beside them and gulped down a huge glass of iced water and a pint of beer, and then one of the girls bought me a tequila. This is the national drink of Mexico, and is made from the heart of the spiky maguey cactus. I did not like it, the taste was slightly that of stale tobacco, reminiscent of a railway carriage's fug early in the morning. We went off later and having wandered round the streets for a bit dined in a pleasant restaurant on mushrooms and saffron-flavoured paella washed down with a dry white wine.

17 November. Mr Gartland and his two sons came with the dining-room table they have made from our walnut and elm. The basic design is a removable top, four feet wide by eleven feet long, and six legs connected by stretchers. It is a beautiful job. I had asked them to make it simple, and the only ornamentation is a mitring of the legs and stretchers and the grain convolutions of the twelve planks of walnut which have been fitted together to make the top. I said I wanted no glue or screws: it must be jointed and pegged in the traditional fashion. Mr Gartland used a spokeshave instead of sandpapering the surface and one can see minute undulations on the table top like the faintest of wavelets on the surface of a pool. He has polished it with beeswax and it feels like silk under one's hands. Apart from the top, which needed four of us to carry into the dining-room, it came in prefabricated pieces, and the three craftsmen spent all morning putting it together, hammering away at the oak pegs and then smoothing off their butt ends.

Mr Gartland then took a photograph, presented me with a large bill and left.

Dominie and I keep going into the dining-room and practising sitting by the table. The whole room smells of honey from the beeswax. The old dining-room table, which was a 17th-century refectory table, and very beautiful but too narrow, has been put alongside a wall to serve as a side- and carving-board.

21 November, Pakistan. Today I fly from Islamabad to Karachi and back to Islamabad.

Sometimes there steals over a crowd of people a sudden hush: the bride has arrived at the church, a famous filmstar has come into the restaurant, the local wifebeater has turned up at the whist drive. I am sitting in the second row of seats in the Pakistan Airways aeroplane, about to fly to Karachi. All about me there is a murmuring conversation as people fiddle about with their hand luggage and settle into their seats. Suddenly, I am aware of an electric silence. I turn round. An absolutely stunning woman has entered the aeroplane. She is tall and willowy. Her face is serenely beautiful. Her eyes are large and intelligent and lustrous. Her nose is thin and fine. Her lips are voluptuous but not coarse. Her sari and headscarf – it is too elegantly draped to be called a chuddar – festoon in long draping folds about her. It is Benazir Bhutto. She rewards my uncouth gawping with a beaming smile and whisping past with a sigh of silk settles down in the seat diagonally opposite: a bird-of-paradise settling on its perch. Once settled, she produces a golden pen and proceeds to underline paragraphs in the *Pakistan Times*. Her hands are long and graceful, made even longer by scarlet, pointed fingernails. A couple of sinister little men and a governessy woman fuss about her. I suspect that she has chosen all three deliberately for their short, squat hairiness, to compare against her tall elegance. The head steward, all bobs and bows and grins, offers something to drink. 'She is off to visit her husband in prison,' he whispers in awe.

22 November. I started up the side of Mount Prospect/Happiness at 8 o'clock and reached the summit a couple of hours later. I saw only two other people on the way up: one fellow sitting meditating on a rock, looking at the view over the plain of Islamabad; another chap, herding Nubian-type goats, said 'good morning' at the same time as I said 'asalaam alaikum.' There were many small birds rustling about in the bushes; they usually turned out to be tufted or vented bulbuls, although one was a whistling thrush, a large, handsome, smart bird with long legs and blue-black, spotty plumage. It was amid one of the little groves of Bhutan pine, an attractive tree with needles up to a foot long and pendulous cones. I found no fossils but there were many quartz crystals in clusters. Some of these accretions had shattered as if hit by a hammer. I could see no cause for this. Is it a natural explosion or do some of the locals collect the crystals as jewellery or for some other reason?

I decided to return by a different, longer route; where it descends a gorge, the latter part alongside a stream, it is also steeper. There were more bushes, so I saw more birds: the largest was a tree pie, an attractive corvid with a tail even longer than a magpie's and elegantly plumaged in browns, greys and blacks; the prettiest was a black redstart, standing on a rock in the stream, his tail-coat a velvety black, his britches a scarlet that glowed deeply like a red-hot cinder. A lizard was less formal, being clad in a wrinkled leather suit of sooty grey-green with yellow speckles; an ugly brute about a foot long, he bobbed his head and gulped at me several times before scuttling up a cliff face. There was an extraordinary stick insect: although it was almost as long as a finger it was not much thicker than a hairpin; it was rose-coloured, and clasped its two front legs meticulously together in prayer. There was also an impressive igneumen fly, over an inch long and girt in armour of blue-black cast iron with copper legs.

After half an hour I came upon a large troop of monkeys playing amid the branches of a big banyan. They were long-tailed, about knee-high when squatting on their haunches, and of a rusty ginger colour. They panicked and rushed around shouting at each other and leaping from branch to branch and pushing and jostling and pointing and peering at me from under bushes and then scampering off with wheezing cries of alarm. I picked up a stone and they vanished in a trice (stupid of me, I thought later).

The stream was surprisingly unattractive. For a start, to deduce from its 'tidemarks', it was only a trickle in comparison to its normal flow. Secondly, the lime in the water had left a furry white deposit like the inside of our kettles at home, so everything looked slightly mildewed.

But the pools and sunken tanks beside them were enchanting, with waters so fresh and pellucid that I could almost dip my sweating head in them and inhale their cool clarity. There were a few nice little frogs or toads swimming in most of them, and many butterflies sipping water off the moss, some of them no bigger than my thumbnail. There were whirlygig beetles, but larger than ours at home and striped; they looked like demented sunflower seeds arabesqueing on the surface of the pools.

I reached the road at noon and then hobbled on for another hour – my right foot hurt quite badly – to reach my hotel at lunch-time.

4 December. Kerry and I put ten lambs into the pony trailer and take them to market. This is the first time I have ever sold any of my livestock this way – normally I just sell them to the knacker/butcher by the Pretty Lady Inn – and I have the feeling of apprehensive excitement I always get at an auction. We register ourselves and then I have time to roam around and inspect the goings-on. There are a few cattle for sale, and comparing their huge placidity with the small fretfulness of the sheep I can understand the amiable scorn the cowboy feels for the shepherd. There was a large mob of pigs. They were not happy: people who see a pig's bottom seem unable to resist thwacking it with a stick.

Before the sale, the 'conditioners' of the auctioneer assesses the beast for its suitability. All mine were rejected: 'Too small, give them another month.' I felt most crestfallen – sheepish, I should say.

A breezy, alert-looking cove came up. 'What did you hope to get for them?' he asked.

'£25 each,' I said.

'I'll take them off your hands, save you taking them home and feeding them, I'll give you £20.'

I should haggle and ask for £24, I thought but said, before I could stop myself: 'Done.'

We loaded them onto his sheep trailer and off we went our separate ways, me a bit sadder but wiser. I think I made the right decision: it would have probably cost me another fiver to fatten them and transport them, and prices are falling anyway. But Kerry and I have learned the importance of presenting them when they are in the right condition.

Robert came with me, having arrived here from his Island of Yell. One of his rams has just died and he is looking for a replacement so I introduced him to Wullie who knows someone up north who has a good Texel ram for sale. We stood in the slops of the cattle section and talked of virility and potency and breeding in general. A couple of years ago one of Wullie's rams escaped into a neighbour's field and began to screw the ewes.

'Don't worry,' his neighbour said after he had telephoned him, 'it's getting to night-fall, he'll only tup half a dozen during the night, we'll catch him tomorrow sunrise.'

The result of this night's activity were duly born and were easy to mark out, the neighbour's flock being entirely Suffolk Blackfaces and Wullie's ram being a Cheviot/Texel cross.

'Guess how many ewes that ram of mine tupped in that one night?' said Wullie.

We guessed: a dozen or so, perhaps?

'74,' said Wullie, grinning and chuckling and rubbing his hands, as proud as if it had been himself.

11 December. As my driver, the little, neat, Irish one, takes me to Heathrow in the morning I tell him about Wullie's ram and his 74-ewe one-night-stand.

'Tuh! My! I bet his winkle hurt in the morning!' he cries.

Turkey: I like the Turks. For a start, they quite like us. I suppose they haven't met too many of our football fans. The British soldier has always admired 'Johnny Turk' as a good and brave fighter, a worthy opponent, not like the civilian-killing scum of the IRA who have the impudence to call themselves 'soldiers'. He treats his animals well. I have never seen a horse or mule treated cruelly by a Turk, very unlike the Greeks who are our so-called 'cousins', but who, together with the Japanese, I consider to be the most beastly to their animals. The Turks often have a good sense of priority. I like the way that even the most important of the Ottoman rulers had to have a trade, Suleiman the Great passed his apprenticeship as a goldsmith. My father said that no job is really worthwhile unless it is in production: one might admire a barrister for his eloquence, or a don for his knowledge, or a jockey for his skill, or a sailor for his courage, but their work is parasitical compared with those of farmer, miller, miner, blacksmith or weaver. I sometimes feel that my present job is fairly unproductive but then compensate myself with the thought that also, every year, I produce over 2000 tons of food, enough willow to make several hundred cricket bats, and a quarter of a book; and that with my gun and my spade I help feed my family and guests for much of the year.

The long drive from the aerodrome to the city is pleasant, through undulating countryside, but one is always uneasy at the sight of the people standing at the verge: they seem to hover there, looking at us coming, leaning out as if poised in anticipation for a sudden dash across, like hens.

I like the sensibly phonetic way the Turks spell: taksi, polis, telefon, kahve, kokteyl; it helps to say the last with a Yorkshire accent.

12 December. I thought I'd walk to the Citadel. The pavements are abustle. There is some poverty about, but even the poorest Turks are not servile. There is dignity, whether it is that of the scribe – a shiny-suited man sitting in a corner with his ancient typewriter on a packing-case before him – or the seller of nothing more than your weight – a man who will not beg, but earns his living with the use of a battered set of bathroom scales. Others polish shoes: they make an art of it, their shoe-cleaning equipment is like a miniature mosque in wood and metal; some-where, on a chest gleaming with studs and minarets of brass and complicated with steps and blocks of mahogany, you place your foot to be ministrated to by an artisan who takes immense pride in his craft of polishing and buffing. I have a particular loathing of people kneeling at my feet, so walk about in dusty shoes followed by hectoring cries or mutters of disparagement.

The town is drab and modern in the lower part, badly and shoddily built in the Berlin style of the 1920s or 1930s, so that it is crumbling and flaking, but as one climbs up towards the Citadel the streets become more narrow and there is more bustle and activity. Even at this time of year the costers' stalls are full of fruit and nuts, there are many kinds of 'bees-milk', mostly dripping from combs. I bought some sheep bells from an ironmonger: I might put one on Basil, one on Matilda and one on the Stare-Eyed-Ewe-who-Leads-the-Greedy-Ones. I overpaid the shopkeeper; he returned most of my money, shaking his grey cropped head reprovingly.

The original Angora is an ancient walled town on the top of a hill. The walls are tall and impressive and still have fifteen of the twenty towers built by the Seljuk Turks, who constructed the walls upon Galatian and Roman foundations. Inside, it is packed with stone and timber houses in various stages of disintegration. There is a maze of little streets and alleyways, most of them too narrow for vehicles. All lintels are low, steps small, door latches close to the ground. I suddenly realise why it is so gnome-like (elf-like would be too ethereal), everything has been built for men about eight inches shorter than I am. There are many little old ladies: tiny, bent; clothed in baggy trousers, floppy slippers or sandals, frayed cardigans and with scarfs over their heads, chuddar-wise; they sit on doorsteps and gaze thoughtfully at you as you pass, or scrub stone staircases, or walk very very very slowly up the flagged streets to visit the old crones next door. Many of the old men have bow-legs and thick, grizzled moustaches and eyebrows. They potter about in pairs, smoking pipes. The children are polite and don't goggle and giggle, they play football in the little courtyards; chickens peck about, pigeons flutter from the roofs, there are many charming cats.

I walked back via the Museum of Anatolian Civilisations. I have been to this converted caravanserai before but returned to see the superb bronze standards in the shape of stags or bulls and the gold jewellery. I wondered what pretty girl wore the lovely diadem with the golden ribbons hanging at the back. She's been dead 3000 years.

I finally visited the Anitkabir, Ataturk's mausoleum. It is impressive, almost Mesopotamian with its ceremonial approach avenue of lions, its large, colonnaded courtyard and starkly simple rectangular pavilions and main building, which contains the solitary marble sarcophagus. There is a small museum full of the personal trivialities of Ataturk's private life: his favourite pen, his spectacles, his shoes. It reminded me of the museum of Napoleon in Fontainebleau – and, like Fontainebleau, it discloses that he was a tiny little man. However, when looking at Ataturk's diminutive clothes one does not have to marvel at what mischief such a little shrimp caused, or how the portraits of him and his family, for all the ostentation and finery, reveal that they were kith and almost kin of Al Capone and his bandit confederates.

25 December. The church full for Midnight Mass. Father Christmas came as usual and filled the stockings round the fireplace in the smoking-room. It was our turn to entertain Sam's crowd from Don Johns; we were eighteen for lunch, five of us being over 80 years old. Dominie produced shrimps and smoked salmon in white sauce on toast for the first course, turkey and stuffing and bacon and sausage and bread sauce and cranberry sauce and roast potatoes and roast parsnips and Brussels sprouts and gravy for the main course, and plum pudding and mince pies with brandy butter for the finish. Then we traipsed out of the dining-room for the drawing-room at 3 o'clock, to hear the Queen's speech on the television. When it was over and they played the National Anthem the oldies solemnly rose to their feet and stood at attention, we younger ones sheepishly following suit. Tea later, before the fires in the drawing-room and the front hall, unwrapping presents. Hart got mildly tiddly on cider and kept laughing and eyeing Nanny.

27 December. The fear of Iraqi terrorism is having a noticeable effect: at 7 o'clock this morning Heathrow looked almost deserted, my aeroplane to Copenhagen was only half full and the steward told me that only six people had booked the return flight to London.

I reached Stockholm in the afternoon, early for once, so I was able to tour the *Vasa*, the flagship of King Gustav which, like Henry VIII's *Mary Rose*, sank ignominiously during her maiden voyage. She was salvaged intact and now lies in a specially built hangar, looming in the half-light like the huge snouted skull of a colossal beast. She is over 200 feet long. Her profusely ornate sterncastle rears 100 feet above the keel: no wonder she turned turtle after the first puff of wind. She weighed 1200 tons when with her full complement of guns and smothered with over 70,000 carvings, mostly gilded.

The dining-room of the hotel restaurant was full of quietly prim diners when I entered but a pair of charming Swedes stood up, introduced themselves, solemnly shook my hand, and invited me to sit with them.

They were an oldish married couple: he tall and grave with a long, lined face; she small and grave with a long, grey pig-tail. They spoke slowly and meticulously with an attractive lilting to their accent. We disagreed on almost everything we discussed, but they were so interesting in what they said, and dissented with such polite good-humour, that it was a thoroughly pleasant evening.

They were republicans, socialists, vegetarians, anti-field sports; they disapproved of flower gardens, fast cars and carol singing; they approved of organic farms, bicycles and meditation.

They meditate for an hour, every morning, before breakfast.

'What do you think about?' I asked.

'We try to think of nothing. It makes our minds receptive.'

'Receptive of what?'

'Of Inspirations. Of Intuitions. Of Realisations.'

I said I thought it a waste of time. At Gordonstoun we had to meditate for ten minutes every morning, sitting meekly at our desks in silence; all I meditated about were schemes to get into the kitchen and seduce – or failing that, rape – the Little Cook, the one with plump, voluptuous lips and mesmerising, bobbling bosoms.

I said that I reckoned we've got all of Eternity to meditate, when we will have nothing else to do but lie in our coffins and rot.

They seemed to think that there is much more to Eternity than that; in fact, they were rather looking forward to it.

28 December. Having all the morning off I wander round Stockholm which I think one of the most beautiful of cities. It is built on many islands and these are connected by a multitude of graceful bridges. The skyscape is of domes, spires, steeples and the masts and spars of sailing ships; there are handsome palaces, theatres and churches. The predominant colours are pleasant and soothing: salmons, apricots and primrose, often with the ornamentation picked out in white, or in gold if on the leaden onion-domes and spires of church or palace. They have an excellent aptitude for leaving spaces plain, which emphasises the adjacent ornamentation. One of the most attractive is modern: the city hall, built in 1923 in pink brick with a copper roof and a tall tower surmounted by a graceful copper belfry; this, in its turn, is capped by a golden ornament depicting the three crowns of Sweden. The Gamla Stan district is the oldest part of the city and is charming with little cobbled streets and squares, but its cathedral is closed. So are two other churches I try to enter. One has a scruffy little notice saying it will be closed until the 2nd of May. How peculiar. Half the shops are shut too. Does this city close for winter? A vast, snow-muffled haven of hibernation? The sky is now overcast, great chunks of ice batter against the piers of the bridges. The few people about look weedy and pale, like sun-starved plants; how can these lanky, effete people be bred from the burly, rumbustious Vikings?

There is a small group of people standing on the verge of a pavement, by a traffic light. The light depicts a little red man, even an idiot can tell it is forbidding pedestrians to cross because it is the turn of the traffic to have the right of way. Even an idiot, also, can see that all along the half-mile stretch of road there is not a single moving vehicle in sight.

I accordingly set across the road.

'Uppehåll! Stanna! Åter-Komma!'

I stop in the middle of the road and look inquiringly back.

With no further remark a tall, wiry man, with runny, very pale blue eyes behind rimless spectacles points at the kerb at his feet with a finger which quivers with righteous indignation.

'Yes?' I say.

He does not condescend to answer, he just points on.

I know what his silent pointing means. It means 'come back abjectly to this pavement, you naughty disobedient person who has the arrogant conceit to walk across the street in contravention of bye-law 2,344,967 (c) which says you must submissively hang about until the glorious officious light yonder turns from red to green.'

'What is it?' I ask, still standing in the middle of the road.

He continues to speak with his finger only, so I reply with my shoulders, giving a shrug which insinuates: 'The poor ignorant ill-educated alien does not speak English.'

Then I continue my crossing.

'Stop! Return!' he hollers in God's own language.

I turn round, amazement etched upon my features. 'Why?' I ask.

'That small red man. Small, but not small enough that it cannot be noticed by every pedestrian. A pedestrian is a person who walks upon a pavement. Not someone who drives a mechanised vehicle upon a street. The small red man says you, the pedestrian, waits to let the mechanised vehicles past.'

'But there is no traffic in sight,' I object.

'That is of no concern. The little red man says "do not cross the street" so you do not cross the street until there is a little green walking man instead of the little red standing man.'

'I have no intention of taking futile and unnecessary orders from a machine,' I say in righteous wrath.

'Then perhaps it would have been best if you had stayed in your own country and not come to ours.'

The little red man is suddenly replaced by the little green man so we debate no further.

Disgruntled, I return to the hotel to pack and eat. In regard of the Festive Season I order Roast Reindeer for lunch.

1 January, 1991. State of the family as the New Year opens: Henrietta is being a full-time mother to Ranulf and Charlotte and wife to Jimmy, all of them in Kenya at present with Jimmy's parents; George happily married to Fiona and living in World's End Farmhouse, working for Euromoney on the new magazine he has founded; Charlie enjoying his work as producer of 'A Week in Politics', and still walking-out with Lucy; Candy, having finished her Prue Leith cookery course, is going round the world with Jane Sharpe and they too are spending Christmas with Jimmy's parents in Kenya; Kate, our ex-ward, is doing very well as the head of her department selling advertising space in the 'Director' magazine, she has a pleasant but middle-aged and oft-married boyfriend whom her grandmother, Mrs B, loathes; her brother Nicholas is still tapping away at his computer keyboards in Ipswich, Mrs B, Violet Rutland and Teddy all in their eighties but all seem remarkably well and active.

Poor Mrs Monk marooned in her house all day because of the qualtaig, the first footing: waiting for a dark-haired man to be first to enter. All of us are fair, except for Crisp who is in bed with 'flu.

6 January. Land in Nairobi at 8.30 a.m. and check in at the Mutheiga Club at 10. There is a letter from Candy there, saying 'hello' and sorry she has missed me. Jimmy meets me, he is wearing khaki shorts and bush jacket and looks thoroughly at home, which, of course, he is, having been born and bred here. He drives me to Lake Naivasha in his father's car.

We go along the crest of the Rift Valley. We pass the huge crater of Susua then the smaller crater of Longunot. I had flown over it less than three hours ago and had noticed it as a perfect bowl with a deep fumarole to one side. One could judge the viscosity of the lava flows which had once drooled down the mountainsides or puddled in huge gobbets on the plain below for they are mineral-rich and have trees growing on them which show up darker against the pastoral surroundings; and the fumarole has been solidified into the shape of a pockmark in boiling mud.

People are selling things by the road, attractive baskets of raffia with chocolate-coloured designs upon them, fleeces, bowls, vegetables and fruit, especially plums which are presented on easels, and are green or red.

Whenever we come upon a police check or traffic stop we are saluted and waved on with huge smiles. Not until we got out of the car to point our binoculars at an eagle did we discover why: there is a metal letter J on the bumper to signify that the owner of the car is a judge, its leather covering having blown off.

The last hour of driving is over tracks, inches deep in powdery dust which fills the car even though we have shut the windows.

We arrived at the house of Jimmy's aunt after about two and a half hours. Jimmy's aunt is called Mrs Icely. She is very small, with white hair, twinkling blue eyes and is wearing a blue bush suit; because of an arthritic hip she has to walk with a stick. She is accompanied by two small, dirty, argumentative terriers. She has had a busy and interesting life and loves Kenya, though she preferred it as it once was rather than the gone-to-seediness that it is now becoming. Her husband has been dead for several years, so she manages her estate which nowadays is mainly confined to pasture for cattle-grazing and a stud farm for thoroughbred horses.

Her house is built of local stone in an Italianesque style with balconies, arches and outside flights of steps linking walled terraces and flowerbedded platforms; the whole complex is shaded by trees and bound about with bougainvillaea and other creepers. It is built on a clifftop overlooking the lake, sometimes one can look down and see hippopotami disporting themselves like seals in the papyrus swamps which edge the waters, but there are none in sight today, though the surface of the lake is speckled with coot, cormorants, divers and duck which glide and paddle around the floating islands of water hyacinth.

Jimmy takes me around the estate. It is all very attractive. The basic conformation is of steep rocky knolls and ridges with shallow dales between them; the rocky areas are sometimes eroded into cliffs, or are covered with trees and scrub; as they sweep down to the valleys the single cover of woody growth becomes broken up into groves and glades which eventually merge into the pastures. The total effect is of English parkland: it needs a double look to see that the tall trees with flattened-out branches are not cedars but fever trees, that the swarth is dried up and dusty and of exotic grass, and that the thick green hedges are not hawthorn but massive and fearsome barricades of cactus. This is the sort of scenery in which primitive man was nurtured, it still is the instinct of most men to regard such landscape as the most idyllic: the original Garden of Eden, copied by Capability Brown and Repton. Contented Friesians and zebu graze, or lounge in the shade of the trees. The horses look magnificent because the heat causes their coats to be fine and glossy: Mrs Icely's stallion resembles a statue of burnished bronze.

As we proceed, many of the farm workers wave at Jimmy with shouts of 'Jambo! jambo!' and Jimmy and they then chatter to each other in Swahili. There is a particularly attractive dale, surrounded by trees and overlooking the lake. Jimmy looks wistful: 'That is where I would have built my house, if I had managed to get a work permit.'

The house is built round a pool-filled yard. There is a large drawing-room, almost bereft of furniture; what little there is consists mainly of comfortable but venerable armchairs and sofas semi-circling a large fireplace. Mrs Icely sits on the most ragged and worn end of the sofa, beside a little table which bears a lamp, some country magazines, a small, incompetent, portable wireless and a large ashtray. The two Jack Russells sit beside, occasionally starting up and vigorously gnawing at their fleas which seem mainly to have congregated on the smalls of their backs. As we talk Mrs Icely chain-smokes through a cigarette holder and drinks large quantities of vodka. Jimmy has told me she likes her tipple at lunch-time, but drinks no alcohol in the evening.

After lunch and a siesta Jimmy takes me to the lakeside. There are many interesting birds, amongst them Jimmy identifies a purple grenadier, a pygmy falcon, a jacana, a white-headed barbet, mousebirds, orioles, drongos, grebes, pochard, a green wood hoopoe (whose dark body and thin, red curved beak make it look more like a chough than a hoopoe) and two charming, fat little parrots sitting side by side on a branch, green, with hooked red noses and yellow scarves – yellow-collared love-birds. Most beautiful of all is the most common bird: the superb starling, with its plumage of green and blue iridescence set off with a white necklace and rufous waistcoat.

Jimmy drives me through scrubland to 'the crater'. We look down to the circular lake, far below, dark green and poisonous. The steep walls of the caldera are clothed in trees. All is quiet, there is no wind, but sometimes the clear notes of bell-birds ring out to break the silence. Suddenly the peace is shattered by a racketing of grunts, rumbles and yells which echo from the cliffs opposite: it is a company of baboon discussing our presence, or perhaps that of the leopard who lives somewhere in the rocks below.

On the drive back we see Thompson's gazelle, with its noticeable side stripe, chocolate-coloured on its tawny flanks, and impala whose horns are perhaps the most beautiful of all, a double upward sweep into the outlines of a lyre.

We have Hottentot teal for dinner. Afterwards a servant lights the fire and we try to listen to the BBC World News on the useless little wireless. The aerial is pointed around in various directions but to no avail.

Mrs Icely says she is sorry to see Margaret Thatcher sacked as Prime

Minister. I say I am too, but perhaps it is a healthy sign that the British will not tolerate a dictator. You could see that she was getting above herself when she took the victory parade after the Falklands War; usurping the Queen's place. She had become overbearing, which is why her replacement is a man with absolutely nil personality: if he resembles anything, it is, with his metallic voice and complete lack of charisma, a Dalek. Maggie has done four important things. Firstly, she taught Gorbachev the tenets of Capitalism: he may not agree with them, but in her hours-long discussions with him he must have learned much of the Capitalist points of view; I think history might credit Maggie with accelerating the disintegration of Communism in East Europe. Another thing she may have done is to teach that charity should not be delegated, that the State is not the sole distributor of time or money to those in need, but it is also the responsibility of the individual: as my father taught me, at least 10% of one's income or one's time should be spent on other people. Thirdly, having had to live and work under the intolerable power of the trade-union leaders, the bumptious barons of mob rule like Frank Cousins and Jack Jones and Ray Buckden and Red Robbo, I consider that the breaking of trade-union tyranny has been a great achievement. Finally, of course, her drive and inspiration during the Falklands War. Whatever the past, we all agree it will be sickening for her if there is a war with Iraq, as seems likely, for she will chafe at not being our Boadicea again.

8 January. A most pleasant awakening: the warm African light streaming through the four windows of my bedroom, the chattering of birds in the branches of the huge fig tree just outside, the cosy quacks of the duck in the lake below, the sound of a servant polishing my shoes outside my door and finally the arrival of a tray bearing a large pot of tea.

After a good English breakfast of eggs and bacon and toast, Jimmy and I say goodbye to Mrs Icely and drive off to Nairobi. After about a mile we come upon a group of six giraffe. Two are sitting and look ludicrously prim with their lanky legs tucked beneath them, their elegant necks swaying like tulip stems and their way of peering down their long noses.

There is a smashed and buckled sign beside the road. I can just read what it says:

DRIVE WITH CARE.

We have arrived at the Couldreys'. Henrietta is thinner but looks very pretty and happy. Ranulf has lost his Christopher Robin look by having a hair-cut: he is wreathed in smiles and tells me he has seen a 'nelephant' and has fed a giraffe by putting nuts on its long black tongue. Charlotte has doubled in size. She is going to have bright golden hair.

The garden is abrim with exotic plants, particularly attractive is a creeper with yellow flowers shaped like Sherlock Holmes's pipe (*Thumbergia mysorensis*), and a huge jacaranda tree smothered in pale blue flowers.

We are served a delicious dinner of yellow-necked spur-fowl, roast, with mashed potatoes, followed by a mango mousse. Betty was fascinating about the Kikuyu language: apparently it has not only genders (male, female and neuter), tenses (past, present and future), voices (active and passive) and cases, but also esoteric conditions such as dead, alive, unfortunate. 'Unfortunate' includes 'taboo', 'ill', 'mad', 'crippled' and 'rich'.

10 January. Arrive late in Lusaka, no time to ramble about. I enter the Intercontinental Hotel before nightfall. About ten years ago I tried to get an order here for fully furnishing this hotel on a 'turn-key' basis. I did not get the order. But I see that they pinched our designs and specifications.

I have passed some of the evening reading a collection of local newspapers: the headlines in African papers often seem to be more eye-catching than ours, I particularly like:

CITY MARKET MAN NARROWLY ESCAPES CIRCUMCISION
KNIFE
ALLEGED SODOMIST SAID HE WANTED FISHING HOOKS
BREAD KNIFE CASTRATION "BIZARRE" SAYS JUDGE

MORE LUNATICS TO THRONG STREETS
RESURRECTION STARTLES NURSE
CROCKS UNLEASHED INTO LAKE
WEIRD GOAT PULLS CROWDS
NURSE PROBED

13 January. *Arrive in London 16 hours late. Monk comes out of his cottage to greet me as I arrive. He says that Dominie is at her mother's house, sorting out chattels with her brothers, Candy has arrived back from Kenya and is still in bed, and they have planted the avenue.*

I am very pleased with the avenue. It is about 160 paces long and 16 paces wide at the near end, narrowing to 12 paces at the far end to give an extra impression of length. The trees are the giant, double flowering cherry (Prunus avium plena). They are standards, about 6 to 7 feet high, and have been posted and tubed. They lead the eye to the far gap through Park Field Wood, which makes a dark frame for the view of the village and the church, about a mile away and 50 feet lower. The urn that Dominie's brothers gave is well placed in the centre of the gap, eye-catching, but not intrusive. My next job there will be to clear the wood of fallen timber, fell the trees which are spindly or distorted or crowding better neighbours, and brash the lower branches so I will be able to walk easily amongst the trees.

After my normal breakfast of a cup of coffee I walk over to Buntings Green Cottage. Henrietta, Jimmy and the grandchildren are all at home, brown and cheerful.

Candy is very blonde and tanned and smiley after her tour round the world. When she finally gets out of bed (at noon) I take her round the garden she has not seen for seven months. I show her where I had buried Bertie and we both get a bit misty-eyed.

In the afternoon I prune the trees my father had planted on the verges of Cangle Lane. I met old Andrews the swineherd bicycling down here once. We had a natter and he said to me: 'When I die and if I go to heaven – which I shouldn't – I will be walking down a lane as pretty as this with a blonde on either arm and a fat, happy pig at my heels.'

30 January. I had hoped I would go to Tel Aviv by RAF: if not by Tornado at least in a Beverly. Instead, I had to catch the routine El Al 315 flight from Heathrow. The aeroplane was packed with a bizarre crowd, moustached (even the women), furtive, shifty, dressed in semi-battle dress. I presumed they were terrorists, spies and members of the SAS but apparently most of them were journalists and television camera crews.

A very old, cynically amusing Leeds Jewess was next to me.

'Why are you going to Israel?' I asked.

'For a holiday,' she replied.

'Surely this is the *worst* time possible for a holiday?'

'This is the *only* time possible. What other reason is there to go to such a ghastly place as Tel Aviv, except to show one's support during a war? Also the rooms in the Hilton are only $20 a night.'

Andy Stewart and Harry, the tall, wry Australian/Jewish driver met me. They had pink hands and faces but their necks and wrists and clothes were begrimed and filthy. 'It's these bloody noddy suits,' said Andy. 'We had three air-raid alarms last night, each time we had to put on the suits and the charcoal which they're impregnated with comes off at the slightest touch. We are short of water and it's difficult to wash.' He said that in general morale was high. Harry said the thing which annoyed him most was hearing the Arabs next door standing on the roof of their house and cheering the Scud missiles as they flew over: 'Most unneighbourly,' he grumbled.

Everyone looked as if they were going ferreting, walking about with large rectangular boxes on their backs. 'And where is *your* gas-mask?' Andy asked.

'I was told you would issue me with one.'

'I was told you would arrive with one.'

So I was about the only person in Israel liable to be gassed.

Later on, in the Embassy, I met a security officer who had just come from Kuwait. He had brought a memento, a brass shell casing taken from the inside of a burnt-out Iraqi tank. The casing, once a couple of feet long, had buckled and shrunk into a fist-sized blob. 'You should polish it,' I said, 'it's covered in smuts.'

He looked dismayed: 'Certainly not,' he exclaimed, 'those smuts are the crew!'

*

I thought things would be grim as I stood by the open hatch of the return-flying aeroplane, waiting for my bags to go on last, and counted scores of baby push-chairs being loaded. Sure enough, when I boarded, the air was being rent by the howls of babies and the shrieks of children: it was a true Exodus.

The return flight was boringly uneventful: no fighters escorted us out of Israeli airspace.

8 February. There has been more snow and ice during the night. The snow is about half a foot deep. The garden looks enchanting when I release the dogs into it for their early morning walkies. There are still a few hips and haws and holly and cotoneaster berries left, they glow scarlet amid the snow-smothered hedges and bushes. The birches are so burdened down by the weight that they look like huge ostrich feathers. Birds roost motionless upon the twigs of the trees in the Wild Garden, their feathers fluffed out, and I can make out the tracks of pheasants and rabbits. Bodger and Humphrey love the snow. Bodger rubs his muzzle along the ground, wiping his shaggy mongrel whiskers clean; Humphrey has to bound up and down as he runs through it. Nigel quite likes it but because of his ineffective front legs cannot get through it; Murphey and Foxy loathe it as it is taller than them and freezes their stomachs and Claude is too stupid to realise that it has snowed. The Land Rover is the only vehicle able to get through it; Dominie and I take Henrietta, Fiona, Violet, Teddy and the Monks to shop in Halstead, and then deliver them back to their respective homes. Most of the rest of the morning is spent dealing with the livestock. Dominie is busy ferrying kettles of hot water from the kitchen to the drinking troughs in the barns and stables, thawing out the plumbing; and I am tottering across the fields lugging bales of hay on my back to fill the fodder racks. I hate tight clothes, particularly gloves — they give my fingers claustrophobia — and so the binder twine bites into my hands and makes them raw and red; the cold slaps my cheeks and stings my eyes; my ankles wobble as I walk over the unevenness of the frozen hoof prints which pockmark the pastures; ice clatters as I tramp through puddled plough ruts; bits of hay fall between my nape and shirt collar. I feel I am doing a proper job.

Dinner at Buntings Green Cottage with Henrietta and Jimmy. Jimmy had shot some pigeons in New Wood, and Henrietta has made a delicious sort of casserole of pigeons, honey and figs. Retire to bed, tired, aching and well content.

I heard owls lamenting with cold and hunger during the night.

*

13 March, Berlin. Today I visited one of the world's most fabulous and beautiful women. I knew she was in Berlin but it was only yesterday that I found that it was here in the erstwhile West part of the city, not in the East where she had had her home before the war. She was all alone when I met her. She is old now – I first heard of her when I was twelve – nevertheless I was surprised to see that she had cauliflower ears and was missing an eye. But she is still beautiful: her swan-necked silhouette is of classic and perfect elegance, from the front she stared past me with that famous, enigmatic half-smile. Then a gang of people entered her room and so I left Nefertiti to her other admirers.

I take the underground railway to the Tiergarten then walk to the Brandenburg Gate. All that is left of the Wall, which was about six feet thick here, is a grey, rough-surfaced scar on the ground, evidence of a frightful old wound.

I am rather proud of my blue passport, my 'civilian' one. It is actually three books bound together; this was done because some of the visas in the two expired passports are 'Indefinitely' registered. The first of the trio was issued on 16 July 1970 when I am described as:

> textile manufacturer
> height – 6 foot
> eyes – green
> hair – fair
> no distinguishing marks.

Many of the visa or frontier stamps bring back nostalgic memories: Bhutan, Nigeria, the USA, Corsica, Majorca, Zambia, Madeira, India; the time I took all the family to Venice; when Dominie and I holidayed in Egypt, and Greece, and Turkey; the failed expedition to Hungary and the trekking in Nepal; the business trips to Arabia and Africa. So I take my blue passport with me to the Berlin East/West border not only because it attracts less attention than my red one, but mainly because I want a frontier stamp as a memento.

I suddenly realise that I am over the border, my passport unstamped. There are no frontier guards any more. It is a strange feeling, an anticlimax. To my right there is much of the wall still standing, thin and long and grey like the tombstone of a mass grave. There is little graffiti, you got shot if you approached too near it this side. One of the many people hacking away at its surface is a Scotsman in a kilt. He is attracting more attention than the wall. He knows it.

I walk up a broad street, I suddenly see its name: it is Unter den Linden, once one of the most famous and exotic streets in the world, now a drab parade of standard communist shoeboxes. The shops are dull, but the Japanese have already moved in, there are Jap motor bicycles behind a new plate-glass window. I can see the great water tower dominating the sky. It is graceful, a ball pierced by a needle; it was built by the East to overawe the West but when the sun shines on it the reflection blazes back as a fiery cross: hence its nickname – the Pope's Revenge.

Arrived home in time for a late dinner. Dominie is back from sorting out the chattels at Brewhurst. She said that she suddenly knew that it was all over when she and Hamish were sitting in the almost empty drawing-room, in the evening, and she realised that, for the first time ever, she could not hear any crickets singing in the hearth. The house had died.

13 March. As I drove through the parish I thought how the recent changes typify country life in general:
- *the old rectory is now inhabited by commuters, we no longer have a parson living in the village, we have a quarter of one, shared with Earls Colne, Wakes Colne and White Colne (The last parson to live in the Old Rectory was Mr Sykes. He tried to tutor me in Latin and nearly exploded with the effort of not cuffing me. One day he was in the Five Bells, watching the television. His son was on it, playing rugger. He scored a magnificent try. Mr Sykes leapt to his feet, shouted 'Well done, my son!' and fell down as dead as a mutton. The old man deserved to go that way, we all reckoned.);*
- *my barn by Boozey's Green has gone, burned down by vandals;*
- *pass Pudney's builders yard, they were here for 200 years, the firm has folded, their yard is now a new housing-estate;*
- *the village green has a sign on it with the village coat-of-arms, those of Matilda de Burgate Engayne (the village was named 'Little Matilda' for a few hundred years);*

- *there is litter all over the green;*
- *the Five Bells has a new pub sign, advertising some brewery;*
- *there used to be a magnificent chestnut beside the pub, it has been felled and in grotesque parody there is a huge plastic tree in its place, holes are in it for children to crawl in and out;*
- *over the valley, on the site of the little railway station of Earls Colne, the hideous bulk of the new flour mill looms (but the grove of cricket-bat willow I planted this side of the river is beginning to hide it);*
- *below Earls Colne, all along the long sloping bank of the River Colne, where once there were over one hundred acres of agricultural land, divided up by hedges of may and blackthorn, and studded with venerable oaks and elms, there is a single expanse of lawn, pockmarked with sandy pits – a golf course;*
- *there is litter on the lane to Overshot Mill, and some sod has left a mattress in a field entrance;*
- *where once water sluiced over the road in a ford, the Peb has been boringly piped under the lane;*
- *the old oaks which grew on the green triangle at the Countess Cross road junction are gone, all felled by the Great Tempest;*
- *between us and Colchester a rank of skeleton ogres stride along the skyline; electric pylons.*

18 March. Touch down at Islamabad aerodrome in the early morning.

It is amusing as we (my escort, driver and myself) force our way through the crowds towards the Land Rover, pushing our trollies laden with diplomatic bags: everyone tries to be helpful, and they all boss each other about with officious proddings and shoutings: 'Make way for these gentlemen', 'Look, you are standing in the way', 'Out, out, do not obstruct', 'Back, every persons, back', 'Remove your baggage and valuables from the path of these VIPs', 'See what you are doing, obstructing, obstructing . . .'. Then when we have loaded up the car and are driving out of the Diplomatic Car Park, with immense dignity and formality and well-drilled arm-movements the policeman at the entrance holds up the (non-existent) traffic to let us out.

We drive past some troupers with a performing monkey and a couple of dancing bears. The bears have magnificently ornate collars but are otherwise drab and ill-kempt. They shuffle about disconsolately to the tweetling of an archaic type of bagpipe. I'm told that they teach them to dance by putting them on red-hot plates.

As we go down Islamabad Main Street I see a squadron of Lancers. They look very fine. They are led by a couple of officers whose huge upturned moustaches resemble buffalo horns. Each trooper sits bolt upright on his horse, every uniform and accoutrement is pressed, polished or brushed, according to specification. The whole affair looks very British.

There is much here which reminds me of Britain. Many people speak English. They play cricket, even up the meanest alleyway or on the most threadbare patch of grass. People ride solemnly bolt-upright on heavy black bicycles. The taxis are fat round bustling little Morris Oxfords and many of them, and other cars, have GB plates and Union Jacks. The policemen, however hot the weather, are enveloped in heavy thick woollen jerseys. Everyone else wears woollies; cardigans, which in England are now only seen in repeats of Agatha Christie mysteries, are worn over the long-tailed shirt and pyjama trousers, the ordinary jersey is knitted in grey or beige yarns with the traditional designs of my schooldays – the lozenge or the wavy stripe. Soldiers wear huge black boots, from which, no doubt, they removed the bobbles with red-hot spoons; belts and gaiters are of blancoed webbing; they tote the old familiar Lee Enfield .303, they march to the bagpipes and they whitewash stones lined up outside their barrack gates.

19 March. This afternoon I went bird watching with John Birch from the High Commission. We sought, particularly, the steppe eagle which is migrating through at this time of the year. We found none whilst pottering around the foothills of the Margalla Hills and the agricultural land of the plain; finally we discovered a dozen steppe eagles in Islamabad City's Municipal rubbish dump. The dump seems to be mainly of shreds of plastic and millions of eggshells which are piled up into stinking heaps upon which the eagles, kites and hooded crows wander, quarrel, pick and peck. In some areas the land-starved peasants have even ploughed the rubbish in and grow bearded wheat and oats upon the foully contaminated soil.

Having inspected the eagles, we went to a grove of wild mango trees in which roosted a colony of flying foxes. Enveloped in their membranous wings they hung from the branches like dirty plastic bags: a few awoke, as twilight was on its way, and they opened their shawls to disclose sharp little faces, beady eyes and russet fur. Once awake, each beast set about a terrific scratching, either they were beset with fleas or were undertaking thorough ablutions.

Why don't birds hang upside down like bats? Why is it only flying mammals which do? How did they start? They could not have developed the ability by slow degrees, starting at a horizontal position and gradually, through the generations, drooping more and more upside downwards. Perhaps a bird hanging upside down would have to grow its feathers back to front to let the rain off, then, for streamlining, they would have to learn to fly backwards.

The Mongolians have a legend that the bat hangs upside down so that he can keep watch on the heavens lest they should fall upon him.

20 March. My driver dropped me at the foot of the Margalla Hills at noon and I rambled about for the next six hours. Most of that time was spent climbing Mount Prospect.

Civilisation had arrived at the first vantage point, the knoll which is reached after about half an hour's walk: the concrete seat put there previously had been smashed, there was a profusion of litter, two ugly tables in iron and cement had been erected near the seat, graffiti in black paint had been squirted over them – one said 'Thrash Point', another 'eat shit'. The municipality had removed the prayer flags from the little tree but had self-importantly nailed a label upon it saying 'Acacia Catechu'; the whole area stank of human ordure.

Although it is spring there were not many flowers out, but I found a pleasant sprinkling of violets, of a pale lilac colour. There was an abundance of a nice little moth: when its wings were folded it looked as if it was wearing a dark overcoat ornamented with large tawny spots, but when flying it lifted its coat-tails to reveal brilliant scarlet petticoats.

The peak of Mount Prospect-cum-Happiness was still and peaceful and I could sit and meditate over the plains hazing far into the distance, and Islamabad stretched beneath me, moaning gently to itself, whilst the Bhutan pines sighed in dolorous sympathy above my head. The whole continent of India crept towards me, at three inches per century. The sun marked an hour on the dial of the sky: I slept.

On my way back I found a large crystal of quartz, of a clouded amber: I got bored with carrying it after a time so put it on top of a little pile of stones in an ingle in a cliff wall which looked as if it might be someone's shrine.

I was returning by a different route. Last time I had veered left, down a gulley, this time I turned right. The path was pleasant at first, though slippery with pine needles, but after a while I became uneasy that it was merely a livestock trail, cow pats and hoof marks being the only sign of use and a strong smell of cattle urine and goat BO hanging about in warm air-pockets; the path became so narrow that much of it became obscured by overhanging bushes. However after 20 minutes I saw a few prints of a bare human foot and a short while later I found a discarded cigarette packet – brand K2.

I saw some goats, possibly wild, on the crags on the other side of the canyon, they were russet and had lop ears in the Nubian style.

Eventually the path crossed the canyon. I had to ford a torrent. This crossing-point was shaded by some big banyan trees. The limestone in the water had congealed into cream-coloured pools and pans of still pure water, in the small waterfalls between them the lime had formed into sheets and curtains. Beneath the trees there were two wide plat-forms of beaten earth and carpets had been laid upon them, whilst green banners fluttered in the warm wind. Four white-whiskered patri-archs squatted on the carpets. I waved politely at them and they waved back, their manner was amiable but I circumnavigated them and crossed the torrent by jumping from stone to stone, for to continue along the path meant walking over the carpets and I did not know if to do so would be an insult. Might I have to take my shoes off? If I did so, would the old boys think I was an idiot or being sarcastic, or would they expect a gift? All I had was a pencil, a piece of paper and two rupees.

The path eventually levelled out and I came upon a village. Its one-floor dwellings of honey-coloured stone or brick merged attractively with the surroundings but the romance of the scene was spoiled by the outskirts of the place being the community rubbish tip, a sour-stinking eyesore: most conspicuous in the heap of trash was the sinister shape of a human leg in dirty plaster-of-Paris. The main lane was a meandering, litter-filled gulley into which seeped trickles of sewerage. A few people picked their way slowly through the puddles of bits of rubbish, but mostly they relaxed, leaning against walls or squatting upon terraces. They all seemed friendly enough: several children called out 'hello' and 'good morning'; an old man creaked to his feet and with an enormous grin flashed a smart military salute; a bunch of youths sitting on a wall said that they were Hindus, that their village was called Said Pur and that the village industry was potting. I passed a most interesting building of several storeys, built of stone and with ornate windows and balconies, it could have been a Hindu temple or perhaps a merchant's mansion; it looked dusty and unused. Towards the centre of the village large pots had been put out to dry on the terrace walls. Chickens and kites competed for scraps of food – the chickens keeping well away from the talons of their competitors. On the outskirts of the village some children were playing cricket. There were a few tents with fruit and vegetables displayed for sale outside. Flocks wandered about, mostly goats; the few sheep looked strangely sinister, having a black triangular face patch like the death's head mask of Venice.

I passed a brook. A man had driven his Morris 1000 into the middle and was busy splashing and scrubbing its round flanks with the affectionate attention that his grandfather may have had in the same way in the same place on his elephant. Some water-buffalo lounged past. They do not have the magnificent crescent horns of those in Burma, they have ugly, curly, tubular little attachments which look like blood puddings. The beasts are hairless and resemble huge, black, perambulating leather bags. Perhaps they will evolve into some sort of aquatic mammal like a dugong.

25 March. *Harry [Lord] Tennyson occasionally writes to me from his self-imposed exile in Cape Town. Recently he wrote about Madge Holroyd. He had met her in the* *early days of SOE, in the beginning of the war, when he was a new recruit and she was my father's secretary. (Previously, she had been his secretary in Courtaulds Ltd and, like many of the other 'home staff', drivers, secretaries, filing clerks and such-like, my father transferred them en-bloc from St Martins-le-Grand to Baker Street.)*

Harry wrote that 'after working for your father she was moved to "The Hythe" which was SOE's Station IX, devoted to experimental work of all kinds, ranging from automatic weapons with silencers to X-craft midget submarines! She was then sent to the East and had to escape out of Burma on foot – a long and painful journey – and finally married the Harbour Master, a Commander RN, in Hong Kong. She now has a large family and a beautiful grand-daughter. She is a dear person and is now, of course, an old lady of 81. When I knew her in those faraway days, she was an attractive young lady. We still keep in touch, I sent her a copy of your book and she has asked to meet you. Can you arrange this?'

Having contacted Mrs Holroyd I discovered that she was not a member of the Special Forces Club, so suggested that we meet there for lunch. I then wrote to the chairman of the Committee giving her background, saying I was lunching her at the club on the 25th of March, and suggesting that there may be a few of the older members who remembered her and would like to see her again: if so, I would stand them drinks at the bar before lunch, perhaps if there were two or three I could even feed them.

There were fourteen of them waiting at the bar when I arrived, all as thirsty as camels. Madge arrived about twenty minutes later: she looked exactly as a Madge Holroyd should look like, a sweet little dumpling of a person, with curly white hair and a benevolent smile. There was a roar of welcome at her arrival, and more drinks were drunk and reminiscences exchanged and the odd tear shed and it was nearly 2 o'clock before I could winnow out a chosen few and sit them all round the lunch table. I forget their names now: they included a woman who had been in cyphers and decod-ing, a venerable man with silver hair who had been in charge of sabotage (in Denmark, I think), a quiet old man with a pipe and scarred hands, a man who could speak Serbian, a vivacious woman with much make-up and a French accent and a man who said almost nothing but smiled and smiled at Madge.

The conversation was almost unbelievable; I would have thought they were putting it on for my benefit, if I had not heard of some of it before: sabotage, espionage, escape, terror, laughter, torture, despair, exaltation, self-sacrifice and the sheer joi-de-vivre of being young and doing something exciting; 'I know that there were terri-ble things going on, and that I lost many friends to horrible deaths, but those were amongst the happiest days of my life,' Madge said. 'Funny, it was the shortage of nylons that got me most, in the spring of '40 I got so desperate that I had to go to Paris to buy some.'

'Surely, Paris was occupied then,' I said.

'Oh yes. But I asked your father to put me on one of the flights when they were dropping a couple of our agents near the city. We were met by some partisans, and one of them, such a nice girl, took me to Paris and I stocked up on nylons and wine and took a night runner MTB from near Caen to Portsmouth. It only took four days.'

She spoke of it as if it had been a quick trip to Frinton.

Eventually she kissed us all goodbye, and tottered off, and I paid the bill, not as large as I feared, others had secretly contributed, and I took the train home marvelling that the older generation had so much more to them than our own effete, pampered, unadventurous selves.

But then I thought: I started a diary exactly two years ago. During that time I have achieved half a million miles, another grandchild, one daughter-in-law, about 17,000 more trees and 4000 tons of farm produce; I have seen angels flying over the Gobi desert and have gone out to hear the Whisper of the Stars; I have met a Green-Eyed girl on a desert isle, a Dignified Man with a dream and four holy men on a carpet.

Perhaps all that I scribbled down about it is worth making neat and tidy and turning into a book.

INDEX